HELL SHIP

Also by Michael Veitch

Turning Point
Barney Greatrex
44 Days
Heroes of the Skies
Southern Surveyor
The Forgotten Islands
Fly
Flak

HELL SHIP

The true story of the plague ship
Ticonderoga, one of the most calamitous
voyages in Australian history

MICHAEL VEITCH

ALLEN&UNWIN
SYDNEY•MELBOURNE•AUCKLAND•LONDON

Allen & Unwin
83 Alexander Street
Crows Nest NSW 2065
Australia
Phone: (61 2) 8425 0100
Email: info@allenandunwin.com
Web: www.allenandunwin.com

A catalogue record for this
book is available from the
National Library of Australia

ISBN 978 1 76087 746 0

Internal design by Midland Typesetters, Australia
Set in Sabon by Midland Typesetters, Australia
Printed in Australia by McPherson's Printing Group

10 9 8 7 6 5 4 3 2 1

The paper in this book is FSC® certified.
FSC® promotes environmentally responsible,
socially beneficial and economically viable
management of the world's forests.

To the boat people from every land and every era.

Contents

Prologue

There is only one known image of my great-great-grandfather, Dr James William Henry Veitch. It is a classic Victorian-era portrait, taken in a Melbourne photographic studio sometime—we believe—in the late 1880s. A large man, he stands confidently in front of a canvas backdrop painted to resemble the fashionable drawing room of a home of the well-to-do. His left elbow rests against the back of a turned wooden chair, which one suspects is a little too low for comfort. Beside him, seated on a chaise longue and affecting a similar air of repose, is his wife of many years, my great-great-grandmother, Annie. She, by contrast, is small and delicate—almost bird-like.

The two had met over 30 years earlier on the ship that had brought them to Australia from England at the height of the gold rush. Annie Morrison, travelling as a single, educated assisted female emigrant, had expectations of obtaining a position such as a governess with a prosperous colonial family; James, descending from a long line of naval surgeons, and having recently secured his first contract as assistant surgeon on board a government-commissioned emigrant vessel, anticipated the beginning of a long and prestigious career at sea. Instead, what awaited them on the voyage would change and haunt them for the rest of their lives.

On an uncharacteristically sultry Liverpool day in August 1852, both of them—still in their twenties and as yet unknown to each other—had made their way up the steep timber gangway of the great black-sided ship before turning for a final glimpse of the home they were leaving behind. Only one of them, however, knew it was forever.

* * * *

Like the fragile and feverish ghosts of those who perished within the wooden tomb of the ship, their story has lingered in my family for generations. Only in his later decades could my own father bring himself to utter that strange-sounding name in anything more than a whisper: *Ticonderoga*. It was as if what had been seen all those years ago by the grand old man—the revered doctor, the hero ancestor, the first and most noble of our clan to bring our old Scots name to this part of the world—was too terrible to be contained within a single individual, or even a single generation.

I study Annie's face in the photograph. In it, I see those familiar, fine-boned, pleasant features that have graced many of the women in my family. I imagine her voice soft with the burr of her native Argyllshire—she came from Tobermory on the Isle of Mull in the Western Isles of Scotland. Her dark-eyed gaze, like her husband's, is fixed on a point a little to their right, where the man behind the camera has directed them to concentrate their attention—quite immobile—until the exposure is complete. Well over a century later, I am immensely grateful for that unknown photographer's diligence, as there is something rather magnificent about his portrait of Dr James William Henry and Annie Veitch.

They are both dressed in their finest clothes: Annie in the formal black of a respectable Victorian lady, James wearing his woollen country gentleman's garments with ease, his right hand thrust jauntily into a front trouser pocket. His small pair of steel-rimmed spectacles appear dwarfed by his large face, which is itself framed by a ring of white whiskers, despite his head being quite bald. His cheeks and chin are shaved smooth, revealing a fine and clear complexion (the Veitch men have always been blessed with good skin). His frame is solid but not fat, the mouth set straight and outwardly expressionless, but as I look I cannot help but detect the slightest hint of a smile.

It is his eyes, however, that intrigue me most. His gaze is strong and deliberate, but also welcoming. I am convinced—family bias aside—that I can see in that steady face a man upon whom countless others had long come to rely. Years earlier, in their desperate and dying hours, many of the wretched passengers on board his ship may well have arrived at the same conclusion about the kind and tireless Dr Veitch, and the devotion he showed to them during the single, calamitous voyage to Australia of the vessel they dubbed the 'floating charnel house', the 'plague ship', the 'Hell Ship': the *Ticonderoga*.

She was a clipper—said to be one of the most magnificent afloat. While still in port in Birkenhead, crowds from nearby Liverpool would flock across the Mersey to gaze at this four-masted beauty with her exotic name: American built, fine-lined like a thoroughbred and over a thousand tons. Her twin decks, they were told, would accommodate nearly 800 souls. Imagine that!

They would be mainly Scots, cleared ruthlessly from their ancestral homes in the Highlands, then subjected to famine and in terrible straits: many were crofters, exiled to the edges of their landlords' estates, struggling to feed their families from tiny, unsustainable patches of soil, desperate for a better life on the other side of the world. Many of them spoke no English, others from the small villages in the glens had not so much as laid eyes upon the ocean in their entire lives. They stood by the dock, gaping at its vast expanse in wonder.

As a child, I had been told the story by my father, who in turn had been told by his, who would have heard it from Henry Veitch, the youngest son of James William Henry himself. Looking back, I seem to have come to it slowly, in fragments, and I suspect my father was disappointed in my response to this, our family's single truly dramatic chapter.

In fact, the story of the *Ticonderoga* affected me deeply. One image in particular lodged itself early in my brain and has remained with me all these years. It is that of the ship's lower deck—or rather the entrance to it. As a child, I would envisage that black hatchway plunging away from the sunlight into the dark and polluted chamber of death below. Here, in their hundreds, the passengers—men, women, infants—lay writhing in the agony and delirium of the typhus epidemic that had exploded in the dank and overcrowded bowels of the vessel, tearing through their ranks, killing over a hundred in just a few weeks and pitching many more into an illness so desperate that they would never fully recover from it. At first the dead had been buried with proper decorum at sea; however, as their numbers doubled and then trebled, they were simply hurled overboard—like 'stiff-legged rag dolls' as one passenger would remember it—as horrified family members looked on in shock.

As awful as this was for me, as a child, to contemplate, there was one particular detail of the passengers' suffering I was mercifully spared: the stench. Typhus, I learned later, is a particularly grim disease. Besides the racking flu-like cough and agonising muscle spasms, the scarlet rash, the delirium and the deadly burning fever, it also savages its victims with a stink—supposedly resembling rotting flesh—so rancid that the smell of a single typhus patient can be overwhelming, even today behind the closed door of a hospital ward.

I saw (indeed, I can still see) that yawning black hole—the closest thing my young imagination could conceive to a vision of hell—opening wide to grab me, to engulf me, to suck me down into its unspeakable horror.

When, after 90 days at sea, the *Ticonderoga* limped to her destination and entered the heads of Port Phillip Bay, it is little wonder that those who observed her uttered the words 'ghost ship'. Upon inspection by the authorities, her condition caused deep shock even in those hard colonial men, long inured to the dismal standards of nineteenth-century medicine. It was a fact of life at sea that people died—particularly on the long journey from Britain to Australia—but nobody had ever seen anything like what had occurred on board the *Ticonderoga*.

When news of her arrival spread, she was forbidden to travel up the bay to Melbourne, and instead ordered to disgorge her wasted human cargo onto an isolated beach. The site became a makeshift quarantine station that then evolved into an institution lasting more than a century.

On this lonely shore, Dr Veitch shouldered a double burden since the ship's senior surgeon, Dr Sanger, had himself succumbed to the disease. For more than six weeks, Dr Veitch continued to oversee those in quarantine, assisted now by a handful of the passengers, particularly a quiet, striking Highland woman to whom fatigue meant nothing, and who had been one of the first to respond, without question, to his urgent pleas for help. Even here, on the beach, many would continue to die.

After the last of the funerals, and the inquiry that sought to ensure nothing like this disaster would ever occur again, Veitch took his dark-eyed Annie far from the sea, settling with her in central Victoria, where he lived his years as a quiet country doctor and local councillor, never setting foot on a ship again.

Although I never gave my father any indication of just how strongly I was affected by the tale, the time has come for me to take up the mantle of my family's saga, and recount the doomed journey of the *Ticonderoga* and the poor souls she carried. It is, of course, more than the story of just one man, or just one family. Hundreds survived the voyage and went on to establish themselves as the first in long lines of Australian families that prosper to this day. On this island continent, we are all of us, save for those who walked here millennia ago, boat people. This is the story of how some of us arrived, aboard the doomed *Ticonderoga*.

My father died more than a decade ago. Were he still alive, though, I would ask him—along with many other things—whether he felt his connection to the *Ticonderoga* saga was a privilege or a burden. I suspect he would answer, 'Both'. I am yet to form my own conclusion.

I

A lonely beach

Brothers-in-law William Cannon and Patrick Sullivan squinted to the sun, not quite yet at its midday peak, resting for a moment on their shovels. Their trade of lime-burning was hot work, made more so by this warm November morning. In front of them, across a few hundred yards of coarse, white sand dunes, stretched a narrow ribbon of beach. Beyond that lay the sparkling expanse of Port Phillip Bay. If both men were to have strolled the short distance to the beach, then set off in opposite directions, one of them would have had only a short journey to the west before reaching the mouth of the bay at Point Nepean, where the narrow gap—known simply as the Heads—opens to the treacherous and unpredictable waters of Bass Strait. The other man, heading east and following the great sweep of the bay's shoreline as it turned north, would have faced a trek of several arduous days through eucalypt and ti-tree scrub to the top of the bay before reaching the bustling settlement of Port Phillip and the town of Melbourne, now in the grip of gold fever. He could then, if he chose, have continued along the shoreline to the south-west, passing the smaller port settlement of William's Town—as it was then known—before eventually arriving, not quite full circle, at Point Lonsdale, the opposite jaw of the mouth of this large and almost landlocked bay.

The lime-burning and fishing leases that Sullivan and Cannon, along with a number of other pioneering families, had acquired for their lonely stretch of beach made for a sparse, though not unprofitable, life. The expanding city hungrily devoured every ounce of the quicklime their kilns could produce from the piles of aeons-old sea creatures around them, providing the mortar for the bricks, streets and lanes of Melbourne. Sullivan had even put down some roots, constructing a tidy whitewashed three-bedroom cottage using local stone and wattle and daub walls. Outside, a small well had been sunk, providing passably fresh water struck just a few feet beneath the sandy surface. Large expanses of gnarled ancient ti-trees provided the dense, heavy fuel required to heat the lime kilns as well as the men's winter hearths. In the several years these two men and others had worked their leases, not much had changed along their peaceful stretch of beach, and this November morning they had no reason to suspect that their idyllic little world would soon to be consumed by catastrophe.

In the middle of their regular mid-morning break, the men lit a pipe and spoke quietly about the afternoon's work. Suddenly, Sullivan's face darkened as something across the water drew his gaze. 'Look there,' he said, his voice low and ominous. His companion looked up, and both men fell into silence as they observed a magnificent black sailing ship apparently heading straight for them.

For Sullivan and Cannon, the sight of passing ships further out on the bay was nothing new. In July 1851, Victoria had finally been carved out of New South Wales and proclaimed a partially self-governing Crown colony, with a promise that it would become a full colony in its own right in five years' time. Then, barely a month later, the electrifying announcement came: gold—apparently in unbelievable quantities—had been found at Clunes near the inland settlement of Ballarat. From that moment, it seemed to Sullivan and Cannon, the steady trickle of ships became a torrent.

In March 1851, for example, the records show just a handful of major ships dropping anchor in Melbourne: the *Dockenhuden*, *Harriette Nathan*, *Ranchi* and *Favourite*—schooners and barques bringing a few hundred passengers, mainly from other Australian ports. A year later, after the shockwave of gold had begun to reverberate, Port Phillip recorded no less than 43 arrivals, almost all of them emigrant vessels of all sizes and from all parts of the world. There was the 450-ton *Celia* from Gothenburg, the barque *Wilhelmine* from Batavia, the 851-ton *Lady Elgin* from Plymouth, and the 257-ton *George* from Singapore. Everyone, it seemed, suddenly wanted to come to Victoria.

The previous September, they had even watched the arrival of the gigantic clipper *Marco Polo*, which astonished the world by powering past the Heads a mere 68 days after departing Liverpool, with her master, the famous Captain James Nicol 'Bully' Forbes, proudly standing on the forecastle, brandishing a copy of an English newspaper kept in pristine condition from the morning of his departure, 4 July 1852. Across the route known as the 'Great Circle', through the fiercest of Southern Ocean storms, Forbes had ridden his ship like a wild beast, close to the edge of Antarctica as well as his terrified passengers' wits. At the height of one such gale, his vessel tearing along at a demented speed, one passenger braved the pitching deck to approach Forbes as he stood beside the wheel, apparently mesmerised by the demonic elements swirling around him. For the sake of his own and the other passengers' comfort, he begged the Captain to consider reefing some sail and slowing down a little. The captain's reply, 'Sir, I'm afraid it is a case of Hell or Melbourne'[1] passed quickly into maritime folklore. Averaging a daily total of 336 nautical miles, 'Bully' Forbes' record would stand for years.

As impressive as the *Marco Polo* and many other vessels had been, though, neither Sullivan nor Cannon had seen anything quite like the great, black, deathly quiet ship that was now approaching from the far side of the bay and preparing to hove-to just a few hundred yards off their peaceful beach. She was, they could tell, an emigrant vessel—and a big one. Not quite as large as the *Marco Polo*, but with finer lines; her darkly painted hull still fresh despite a long sea voyage; four masts, and the distinctive steep-raked, slicing bow of the American-built clippers. A beautiful ship indeed, noted her two lonely observers, but something about her was not right. Where on earth were her passengers? Particularly on such a fine day as this, the exhaustion and anxiety of months spent crammed into a few square feet of dank space below deck alongside hundreds of others would normally finally give way to joyous relief and celebration. Only now, gliding up this calm and generous bay, having survived the endless uncertainties and warded off the haunting visions of rocks splitting open wooden walls with seas rushing in to rip loved ones from outstretched arms, could a future at last be contemplated. Those who had trunks had them brought up from the lower holds to the upper deck, where they would select their finest outfit for their arrival. The ladies in particular would look splendid, adorning the ship like exotic birds with their red and green satins to mark their arrival at the dawn of a new life. But this ship, as the men remarked, was 'like a ghost ship': silent.

The dark vessel came to a halt. Only then could some movement be detected on the deck—just a few figures, moving listlessly, without pace or conviction. Then from the cathead, the clack-clacking of the capstan could be heard as the anchor chain was released. The rigging, they saw, looked untidy—even haphazard. The entire vessel in fact, belying the quality of its construction, had a certain neglected appearance. Then, with a gasp, Sullivan pointed to the top of the mainmast, where a small square of yellow just caught a murmur of breeze. In a moment of horror, they recognised the dreaded 'Yellow Jack', the signal for other ships to stay well clear. This ship was carrying disease.

2

Birkenhead

On a summer's morning in late July, exactly three months before the *Ticonderoga* dropped anchor off the little beach to the south of Melbourne, Mrs Smith stood by a small dock on the Mersey River and turned to check Mr Smith's dress and bearing with the fastidious eye of a woman conscious of her husband's place in the world. She needn't have worried—William was as well turned out as ever, and as keen as any man upon whom fortune had smiled to make a good impression. Having just a few months previously been suddenly elevated from his position among the humble ranks of J.S. De Wolf & Company's shipping clerks to become Superintendent of the Colonial Land and Emigration Commission's most recent embarkation depot at Birkenhead, he was well aware of the opportunity he and his wife had been handed. For her own part, Ann had been appointed depot matron, and was as determined as her husband to fill her role to the letter.

Even as they stood gazing expectantly across the river, they could make out the ferry now steaming slowly towards them from the sprawl of Liverpool a kilometre or so away on the far bank. On board they knew there was a full load of men, women and even entire families—all of whom, in a few days, would undertake the most momentous and perilous journey of their lives, from which they would be unlikely ever to return. It was also by far the largest contingent of passengers they had been called upon to accommodate during their brief time running the depot, and important eyes would be observing their efforts. Besides, the brief few days these people were about to spend in their care would be the last impressions they would ever have of the Smith's homeland.

This ferry load was not the first to arrive. Over the past few days, other emigrants had checked in from all parts of Britain. Some 140 Englishmen and women from Somerset and Cornwall had arrived by train and were already well settled, and several boatloads of Irish had also turned up, having made a rough crossing over the Irish Sea to Holyhead in open-decked packet steamers, then travelled by train to Liverpool. This ferry was rather special, though, carrying as it did the first of the 643 individuals who would comprise by far the largest single group of passengers for the voyage. These people were making the longest and saddest journey of all—from the remote and mysterious Scottish Highlands.

The depot itself was an impressive facility, comprising two main buildings, one recently converted to accommodate up to 400 emigrants, the other as a storage area for their luggage. Living and dining quarters, washing facilities, a cook house, a sick room and several offices had been installed, as had a small Church of England chapel. Anyone standing inside would have been impressed by its sweeping sense of space and grand 21-foot ceilings. Twin rows of cast-iron pillars supported a second floor, which itself boasted further 14-foot ceilings and a timbered roof. Everywhere was well illuminated, with two rows of generous skylights. Large rows of dining tables and benches had been assembled in orderly rows, each grouped according to the areas from which the various passengers had come. The lower walls were three feet thick and whitewashed.

Outside the front door was a large forecourt, which led to the dock, and close by could be found a railway turntable and track spur connected to the main line, from which every part of Britain could be reached by train. To the amazement of some, gas heating had been installed, and there was even hot and cold running water. It was undoubtedly the largest and most impressive building most of the travellers had ever seen.

Birkenhead was the fourth, last and most important of the Colonial Land and Emigration Commission's embarkation depots, established for those leaving Britain by government-assisted passage. Others had been set up at the ports of Plymouth, Southampton and Deptford near London, but these had largely been adapted from private boarding houses and were relatively small in nature. Birkenhead was the first properly planned and truly dedicated facility.[1]

Birkenhead had, however, been built for another purpose entirely: it was originally meant to be a series of warehouses, but the buildings were never used for that purpose. Like much of the recent infrastructure along the Birkenhead side of the Mersey River, they had been constructed as part of the town's push to carve out for itself a piece of the massive shipping trade currently passing through Liverpool—then the busiest port in Britain. The Birkenhead Dock Commissioners' ambitions were indeed lofty. Having declared that they were ready to take on their Goliath neighbour across the water, they began, in the 1840s, to lobby heavily for dock construction rights, planned a grand renovation of the city centre and even commenced a large-scale expansion of Birkenhead's local Wallasey Pool, a stretch of tidal water into which the local Wallasey Creek ran before emptying into the Mersey River. This modest backwater, it was proposed, was to be engineered into a large complex of inland harbours with the somewhat grandiose title 'The Great Float', and would be the keystone in Birkenhead's revival.

However, it all came to nought. The hard men of Liverpool's docking and shipping trade were never going to tolerate a rival—however nascent—directly across the river, and proceeded to throw every conceivable obstruction in the way of the ambitious men of

Birkenhead—who admittedly, for their part, were doing a fine job of muddling it all up on their own. A litany of engineering failures and financial mismanagement threw the town firmly into reverse, as confirmed in the 1851 census, which revealed that Birkenhead's population had gone backwards from around 40,000 in 1846–47 to just over 24,000 in 1851. The grand designs for the revival of the town centre were quietly shelved.

Having failed to take on the shipping trade, Birkenhead was thrown a lifeline in the form of emigration. By the late 1840s, one of Britain's chief exports—besides textiles, machinery and the many other innovations of the Industrial Revolution—was people, and Birkenhead was set to take advantage of a human exodus.

From the mid-1840s, Britain was farewelling more than 200,000 people each year for North America[2] in what has been described as an unregulated 'free enterprise free-for-all', with the bulk of those leaving from Liverpool.[3] In this sprawling, labyrinthine port town, desperate and unworldly travellers faced an array of villains well-honed in exploiting their vulnerability. Ship brokers, or 'recruiters', who speculated in berths and received a commission for every one they filled, hired runners (known also in Dickensian fashion as 'crimps', 'touts' and even 'man-catchers') who literally man-handled arriving passengers from railway stations or the harbour side. Quickly hustled into makeshift offices, they were often cajoled or threatened into handing over their precious funds to secure a berth, sight unseen. When eventually on board the ship, they would often find that the vessel and its conditions in no way matched the brokers' promises. If there was a delay of days or weeks before their departure, other runners would force people into one of the city's many hundreds of dubious lodging houses, around which an entire industry had sprouted. People were forced physically: 'They pull them by the collar, take their arms and, generally speaking, the runners who were successful enough to lay hold of the boxes are pretty sure of carrying the passenger with them'.[4] Thus isolated, they became prey to unscrupulous landlords charging exorbitant fees for tiny, sub-standard rooms, often already over-booked by other unsuspecting families. Stories of poor but innocent country folk being abused in this way led to strident articles in the press, and growing government embarrassment.

As the numbers of people passing through Liverpool to their respective vessels increased, so did the city's reputation as a sinkhole of disease and crime. To the government, this huge port city was becoming a liability, a victim of its own success. Added to this was the port authority's rigid insistence that no lights or fires be lit on board a ship while in port—for reasons of fire risk—under any circumstances. This prevented emigrants from boarding their designated vessel in an early and orderly fashion, instead being forced into a mad rush on the day of their departure when hundreds of passengers and their luggage bolted to settle into their ship during daylight hours, with not even a warm meal or cup of tea to welcome them.

Eventually, two respected Liverpool shipping companies, J.S. De Wolf & Company and Barton & Brown, wishing to expand into the emigrant trade, became fed up with Liverpool's intransigence on the shipboard fire rule and began to ask the government about the possibility of embarking government-assisted passengers from the Birkenhead side of the Mersey. Birkenhead jumped at the overture. Yes, its spokesmen declared, the lighting of fires and lights on board docked or harboured vessels would present no problem, and they could also boast a number of new buildings ably suited for conversion to a safe and well-run emigrant depot. They also threw in free use of a warehouse behind the depot in Cathcart Street, as well as very attractive terms for the moving of cargo.

The timing was perfect. Liverpool had become a headache for the government, so Birkenhead was given the go-ahead to convert its warehouses and begin operating as the Colonial Land and Emigration Commission's brand new Birkenhead depot for government-assisted emigrants. Staff were sourced, with J.S. De Wolf & Company recommending one of its clerks and his wife, William and Ann Smith, to run it. Liverpool was furious, but its protestations were ignored and, with the paint barely dry, Birkenhead's first intake of migrants arrived in January 1852.

3

Wakefield and 'the Board'

I herewith transmit to you a Commission, under the Royal Sign
Manual, constituting you to be Commissioners for the sale of the
waste lands of the Crown throughout the British Colonies and for
applying the proceeds of such sales towards the removal thither of
emigrants from this country.

With these words on 14 January 1840, Her Majesty's Colonial
Secretary, Lord John Russell, signed a series of documents bringing
into life one of the world's earliest official institutions dedicated
specifically to social relief, the Colonial Land and Emigration
Commission—more simply known via a hang-on to one of its
earlier incarnations as simply 'the Board'. Whatever the nomen-
clature, the need for such a body had long seemed evident to a
series of progressive thinkers both inside and outside the British
Parliament. One of these was the dynamic, though bizarre, figure
of Edward Gibbon Wakefield. As a former diplomat and government official, Wakefield had married well, but when his recently
deceased wife's funds proved insufficient to fuel his considerable ambitions, he staged an extraordinary abduction of one

Ellen Turner, a fifteen-year-old heiress he had never met, from her
school by means of a forged note to the effect that her parents
were ill and required her immediate presence. He then spirited
her to Gretna Green; there, under duress, the girl agreed to marry
him under the no-questions-asked Scottish marriage laws of the
day. Her outraged family eventually annulled the marriage and
dragged Wakefield to court, where he was sentenced to three years
in Newgate Prison. It was here, imbuing himself in the writings
of classical theorists and economists such as Adam Smith, that he
underwent something of a transformation, renounced his roguish
behaviour and found his true calling.

Wakefield's observations of his fellow prisoners, as well the
reasons for their incarceration, led him to believe that the induced
but benevolent removal of Britain's poor to her territories would
be to the considerable benefit of both parties. The theory became
a cause for which he was to advocate vociferously for the rest of
his life. Economic development, believed Wakefield, relied on a
balance between land, capital and labour. In both Britain and the
colonies, for opposite reasons, this balance was out of kilter. Britain
suffered from an excess of labourers—some of whom he had himself
encountered in prison—and Australia from such a shortage that her
businesses and industries were unable to be properly developed.
If some of those now living in poverty in Britain could be given a
new chance at life in Australia, many would be kept out of prison,
and the situation of both countries improved.

His colourful past notwithstanding, the notoriously persuasive
Wakefield managed to excite several more respectable figures about
his theories, who became known as the Colonial Reformers or
even 'Wakefieldians'. He managed to reinvent himself as an expert
on all matters pertaining to the colonies, and in the mid-1830s
attached himself to the Earl of Durham, the Governor-General of
Canada, to whom he became an unofficial adviser. Meanwhile,
the British establishment—and particularly the prime minister
of the day, Lord Melbourne—continued to detest Wakefield, and

successfully prevented him from realising his dream of entering parliament.

The power of his personality nonetheless remained undiminished, and Wakefield became a master manipulator from behind the scenes of British and colonial political life. Almost everyone who met him commented on the power of his charisma, and in later life a political foe was to declare that 'the only security against Wakefield was to hate him intensely'.[1]

Undeterred, Wakefield presented his scheme to various Australian colonial governments, convincing them to cease their practice of giving away grants of unused Crown land to new settlers, and to instead sell them at auction to the highest bidder. The funds thus raised, he proposed, would provide the monetary engine to assist scores of impoverished but otherwise respectable British emigrants to make a one-way journey to Australia, where they were sorely needed. Such a complex and global operation needed to be run by a single organisation, and Wakefield and others lobbied hard for the Colonial Land and Emigration Commission to be established. He also managed to negotiate the reduction of the cost of an assisted passage to Australia from £30 to £18, and the British government advanced the figure of £10,000 against future land sales in the Australian colonies to assist some of its desperate population to get there.

From a large and chaotic office—in fact, a rented private house at 8 Park Street Westminster—the Board recruited several former Royal Navy officers as agents situated across the country and in Ireland, and went to work directing the funds generated from the respective colonies to bringing people to their particular part of the Empire. This naval influence would permeate much of the Board's practices, particularly in the running of its emigrant embarkation depots, which were organised along similar lines to ships at sea.

The notion of the Board's assisted, or in some instances such as with the Highland Scots, free passage out of poverty appealed to a great many destitute or near-destitute Britons, and by 1848 a staff of 30 was processing 46,000 letters a year. According to a contemporary account, the Board's office was always a flurry of human activity, with hundreds of people every day showing up at its doors for a chance at a new beginning:

> It is of no use pretending not to know where Park Street Westminster is . . . Follow the stream of fustian jackets, corduroy trousers and smock-frocks, keep in the rear of the chattering excited parties of half-shaven mechanics, slatternly females and slip-shod children. They are all moving in one direction which, if we can but get at it through the crowd, is the much-sought office of the Commissioner of Land and Emigration.[2]

Although catering to the needs of many parts of the British Empire, the Board's primary interest focused on Australia. During the 1840s, it advertised widely across Britain for agricultural labourers to travel to New South Wales and Victoria, primarily to service the ever-expanding Australian wool clip. Initially, the demand was sluggish, with Canada and the colonies of South Africa proving more popular destinations—not to mention America, which—as it was no longer part of the British Empire—did not interest the Board.

Australia's reputation as an emigrant destination took a further hit when a speculative land bubble burst spectacularly in the 1840s, leading to a severe economic depression that hit land and wool prices hard, forcing some squatters unable to either feed or sell their sheep to boil them down for tallow-making. By the late 1840s, assisted passage to Australia was suspended altogether and the Board's future looked bleak. All this would turn around, however, with the discovery of gold.

Wakefield continued his life in tumultuous fashion, eventually playing a leading role in the founding of the convict-free colony of South Australia (a port town and a main street of Adelaide still today bear his name), and finally New Zealand, where he ended his days—a difficult and controversial figure to the last. While playing no direct role in the running of the Board itself, it was undoubtedly a product of Wakefield's determination and vision. For 37 years, it pursued its stated aim of 'assist[ing] in the removal thither of emigrants from this country',[3] winding down only in 1877 when the various colonial governments began to develop emigration schemes of their own.

Whatever people may have thought of Wakefield personally, it was difficult to dispute his passionate observations that, approaching the halfway point of the nineteenth century, not all Britain's subjects were enjoying the fruits of her imperial prosperity, particularly those classes not empowered by either wealth or title.

* * * *

In London in the summer of 1851, the Great Exhibition attracted an average daily audience of just over 42,000 people, all gasping in awe as they gazed up to the soaring glass roof of Joseph Paxton's Crystal Palace. Just over half a kilometre long, this engineering wonder was built entirely of glass and cast iron to nominally display the industrial products of 44 countries around the world, but was in fact primarily a propaganda exercise to show off the might of imperial Britain. Indeed, the past several decades of the nineteenth century had seen extraordinary developments in British society. Avoiding the expenditure in manpower and material of a major war, this small island was on its way to acquiring the largest and most wide-reaching political and economic empire in history.

In recent years, the railway system and public omnibuses had opened up the country to people hitherto confined to the boundaries of their local parish, often presenting them with their first glimpse of the sea. The telegraph and the penny post allowed affordable communication from any part of the country to another, and cheap, mass-produced items adorned the mantelpieces of the affluent homes of the new merchant and industrial classes.[4]

As hordes of ordinary Britons filed into the Crystal Palace—in all, a full third of the country's entire population would visit the

Great Exhibition over its six months' duration—they could, for perhaps the only time in their lives, rub shoulders with the rich and powerful. Here, under the glass, all stood equally enthralled by the tens of thousands of items—large and small—heralding the triumph of the Industrial Revolution. People could inspect machines that made envelopes, and others that automatically compiled votes. They could observe a demonstration of cotton being produced from the bud to the final product, and gaze at the largest diamond of that, or any other, age: the legendary Koh-i-noor. They could marvel at the first forays of photography in Mathew Brady's newly invented daguerreotypes and inspect exquisite gold, silver and enamel artefacts from the Empire's undisputed jewel, India.

The dazzling technologies of the Great Exhibition ushered in improvements barely dreamed of a decade earlier: for the first time, glass became available for household windows;[5] soap—previously a hand-made luxury—was now turned out in factories, although it was heavily taxed. Washable cotton underwear became cheap and went some way towards lifting standards of hygiene, as did the instigation of flushing toilets—another wonder of the modern age debuted in the Great Exhibition. But change was slow, and long before such benefits of industrialisation could begin to filter down to the masses, life for Britain's poor—particularly her agricultural poor—would become drastically worse.

Swelled to beyond their capacity by agrarian workers whose traditional ways of life had been obliterated by the factory and the machine age, Britain's cities were devolving into the nightmares of Charles Dickens' descriptions: filthy, diseased, crime-ridden cesspits of despair, fuelled by an ever-increasing ocean of the unemployed.

Despite the myriad innovations of the age, such basics as reliable clean water remained out of reach for millions. In London, the only source was the Thames, already used as an open sewer, but likewise in towns and villages across the country, the nation's poor were compelled to queue at their local pump and haul water of uncertain quality over long distances and often up flights of rickety stairs.[6]

Although average life expectancy was slowly and gradually increasing, in mid-century it was still hovering somewhere around the mid-forties, a statistic swelled by high levels of infant mortality, which had actually increased in the 1850s to a staggering 41 per cent of children not surviving their first five years. Churchyards, the traditional place of burials, began to run out of space, forcing the government to pass the *Burial Act* in 1852 giving local authorities the power to establish and run public cemeteries for the first time.

Should they survive infancy, life for children was particularly grim. If not carried off by one of the regular epidemics of cholera or diphtheria, the youngest poor could expect to meet their end in a variety of horrendous and exploitative industries. Children as young as eight were employed as 'piecers', standing next to the textile machines repairing breaks in the thread, or as 'scavengers', crawling underneath the moving mechanisms to clear obstructions. The cities employed thousands who had not yet reached their tenth birthday as chimney sweeps, but perhaps nothing was more unspeakable than what was found in the hundreds of coal pits mushrooming across the country. An inquiry into mining in Britain in the 1840s revealed that 1189 women and 1152 girls under the age of eighteen were toiling in wretched conditions in eastern Scottish mines alone. Accidents were commonplace, and caused barely a ripple outside the victims' immediate families. In 1838, a sudden downpour flooded a coal mine in Barnsley, Yorkshire, killing 26 boy and girl child miners, only one of them over the age of thirteen.[7]

In addition, crop failures, economic depressions, and rural enclosures—particularly in the Scottish Highlands, which endured its own unique human catastrophe—led to a dramatic increase in the numbers of those left to sink to the bottom of the Empire's ocean of prosperity, or be swallowed up by the shadows of Blake's 'dark satanic mills'.

Fifty years earlier, convict transportation was seen as effective social engineering—the means of surgically removing an entire underclass to the Australian colonies on the other side of the world, a place so removed from Britain that they would be of no bother to society ever again. By the 1850s, however, the penal transportation system was falling out of favour, not least among the colonials themselves, who had quite early come to the conclusion that their country had far greater potential than its role merely as a dumping ground for felons would allow. Now it was seen as necessary to induce—even assist—large numbers of selected persons to leave voluntarily. In any case, Australia needed them—and badly.

4

Australia 1851:
Gold versus wool

Throughout the 1830s and 1840s, Australia's growth in wool was hemmed in by an acute shortage of labour. Squatters and landholders became desperate. In 1840, a shepherd in Australia could earn up to £45 a year, three times what his counterpart back in England could bring home, with the deal usually sweetened further by free board and lodging and a generous weekly food allowance that included mutton, flour, sugar and tea.[1]

The depression flattened off the demand in the mid-1840s, but with the discovery of gold and the rush of the early 1850s, thousands of men walked off jobs in towns and cities alike to flock to the goldfields in search of instant—and usually elusive—wealth. The rural labour problem suddenly became a crisis. The question of who exactly would service the wool industry became an obsession with Australian growers and politicians, particularly as the gigantic clip of 1852 loomed. Luckily, however, Edward Gibbon Wakefield and his Colonial Reformers had a plan.

While the Great Exhibition was holding Britain enthralled, 1851 was also a tumultuous year for Victoria. In July of that year, under a large eucalypt near the southern bank of Melbourne's Yarra River in what is now that city's Botanic Gardens, the long-cherished dream of the city's patrons was realised when the *Australian Colonies Government Act 1850* came into effect. The Act transformed Victoria from the Port Phillip District of New South Wales to a Crown colony in its own right, with full independence to arrive by 1855. The erudite French and Swiss-educated poet and painter Charles La Trobe was to be Victoria's first Lieutenant-Governor. That year, Victorian sheep farmers produced 18 million pounds of wool from 6 million sheep; the whole clip was baled up and sent to fuel the voracious mills of Yorkshire and Lancashire. Nothing, however, was as dramatic as the announcement that gold had been discovered.

In fact, gold had already been found at various places around Victoria and elsewhere, going back to 1839 when the explorer Paul de Strzelecki stumbled across it in the Victorian Alps. Various sheep farmers had uncovered it too, but rightly fearing a flood of crazed and undesirable diggers, they had kept it to themselves. Having listened in dread to the descriptions of chaos that had followed the Californian gold rush of a couple of years earlier, the authorities were likewise loath to let the secret out. Only when the goldfield discoveries in New South Wales threatened Victoria's economy did La Trobe relent and attempt to face the matter front-on by offering a reward of £300 for anyone who could find gold within 200 miles of Melbourne. The announcement acted as the starting gun to a stampede that would last for years, transforming Victorian colonial society forever.

A complete mental madness appears to have seized almost every member of the community, and as a natural consequence, there has been a universal rush to the diggings. Any attempt to describe the numberless scenes—grave, gay and ludicrous—would require the graphic power of a Dickens . . . People of all trades, callings and pursuits, were quickly transformed into miners, and many a hand which had been trained to kid gloves, or accustomed to wield nothing heavier than the grey goose quill became nervous to clutch the pick and crow-bar or 'rock the cradle' at our infant mines.

So proclaimed the *Bathurst Free Press* in May 1851, which, like everyone else, was at a loss to process this sudden derangement that had turned society on its head overnight.

With the discovery that the area around the sleepy inland settlements of Castlemaine and Bendigo in fact sat atop one of the world's richest shallow alluvial goldfields, it seemed that the entire population of Melbourne, then Australia, immediately wanted to go there. In just two years, this antipodean El Dorado yielded around 4 million ounces, almost all of it found within 5 metres of the surface. In a few years, the largest nugget in the world was revealed: a 69-kilogram monster wryly dubbed the 'Welcome Stranger'; it was so enormous that it had to be broken on an anvil into three pieces in order to weigh it.

In the following ten years, Victoria produced more than one-third of the world's entire gold output, bewitching the imaginations of the public and press alike, particularly in London, where newspaper articles declared that 'their stores of gold surpassed the wealth which the stately galleons brought to Spain from South America in the days of Sir Francis Drake'. The arrival of a gold ship in the Port of London would often lead to scenes of mayhem on the Thames, as described by *The Times* in October 1852:

The ship *Medway* has arrived in the Thames from Melbourne, Port Phillip, with no less than 67,000 oz. golddust, valued at 270,000 pounds. Immediately on the vessel arriving at Limehouse she was surrounded by a complete fleet of small boats filled with crimps, lodging-house keepers, and other of the longshore fraternity, who made numerous ineffectual efforts to get on board to remove the seamen's effects under the impression, from the valuable nature of the ship's cargo, that the men must be equally well stored . . . The *Medway* brings one of the most valuable cargoes ever imported by a private vessel into the port of London. It amounts in the aggregate, with cargo and golddust in the hands of passengers, to nearly 600,000 pounds.

By early 1853, armed vessels were each week escorting into London ships from Melbourne carrying gold worth between £170,000 and £200,000.

The rush was not simply one of gold, but of people. From an office in Regent Street, positioned strategically close by that of the Board, crowds assembled daily to undertake the great voyage and visit the diggings—if only in their imaginations. They gazed in wonder at moving panoramas extolling the beauty of the Antipodes, painted by popular artists of the time. There were also seascapes and pictures of exotic Australian animals, as well as handsome scenes of Victoria's Yarra Valley, Goulbourn and Geelong, as well as the Parramatta River and Blue Mountains of New South Wales. The wonders of the voyage itself were extolled in colourful images of flying fish and porpoises, as well as the many stops along the way: Madeira, Rio de Janeiro and the Cape of Good Hope. The fact that these had now largely been by-passed by the Great Circle route seemed of little consequence to those displaying their images to the captivated spectators.

After starting its life as the ugly duckling of emigration, Victoria was suddenly the most popular destination on Earth. Numbers of new arrivals to Australia in general soon eclipsed the entire total of convicts who had been landed there during the previous 70 years. In the two years from 1851, Victoria's population increased sixfold from 77,000 to 540,000. Over the next two decades, Australia's population overall would treble from 430,000 to 1.7 million by 1871.[2]

But the rush had a terrible downside. The indigenous people of the Kulin nation, the alliance of tribes which had lived and hunted in central Victoria for millenia, already under seige, were catastrophically displaced. Entire forests and tracts of scrub vanished seemingly overnight. Like the frenzy in California, the consequences of such a sudden and uncontrolled injection of wealth into the economy were dangerous and unpredictable. Newly cashed-up miners went on spending sprees, warping the prices of basic items, which soon skyrocketed. Ironically, Melbourne itself became a ghost town, seemingly inhabited by no one but the very old or very young, as men followed their lust for quick wealth to the goldfields. Eighty per cent of the local police force quit, leaving the city to thugs, criminals and packs of marauding dogs. Ships lay idle in the port of Melbourne, unable to sail for lack of crew who had jumped ship as soon as the anchor was dropped. Reports of sea captains vainly trying to restrain their absconding sailors at gunpoint became legion.

It was even worse on the land. Shearers and farmhands, although traditionally well paid, simply walked off their stations to join the ant-like masses scratching over the clays of central Victoria with their new, over-priced picks and shovels.

Meanwhile, the wool still needed to be gathered, and the contracts had to be honoured. News of the rush began to filter back to England and a looming dread settled on the wealthy brows of mill owners. The notion that the annual avalanche of Australian wool could be interrupted, let alone stopped, and the wheels of British industry silenced for no more pedestrian a reason than a paucity of labour was unthinkable.

Anxious letters from Australia were received, then passed on— amplified with urgency—to the government in Westminster. The wool growers of Australia estimated themselves to be facing a 10,000-worker shortfall, and this number was growing. At this rate, the clip for 1852, which was due to be shorn and processed in the Australian spring and promised to be another big one, would remain on the sheep's back, and the spinning textile mills of England's industrial north would grind to a halt.

From both England and Australia, fingers were pointed in the direction of the Board, which was seen to simply not be doing its job. What was the good of money from the sale of colonial land being handed over, it was argued, if the Board could not even provide sufficient numbers of people to stave off economic catastrophe? It was decided that the Board's criteria for accepting emigrants would be overhauled significantly, particularly with regard to children.

Prior to 1851, families with more than three children under ten years of age and two children under seven were excluded from the Board's scheme.[3] Such a burden of offspring, it was argued, would inhibit their parents' capacity for productive work once they arrived in the colonies. The other factor was the vulnerability of small children to contract and spread disease in the confined incubator of a sailing ship. Small families, and single young men and women—particularly rural and agricultural workers—were the ideal emigrants, and it was to luring these that the Board had directed its attentions.

But in Victoria it was precisely such unencumbered young men who were now deserting towns and cities in droves and heading for the goldfields. The policy would now be turned on its head. Sheep growers and farmers argued that the anchor of a family was in fact the main factor—indeed the only factor—preventing men from deserting, so the Board up-ended its rules to allow families to travel with up to four children under twelve years of age.

Overnight, families who had previously failed to qualify for the golden ticket of assisted passage found themselves accepted, and the exodus was on. So hungry were some Victorian pastoralists for labour that many emigrants had been snapped up for employment even before they embarked. One of the McRae families, for example (there were several on board the *Ticonderoga*)—Thomas, 46, Margaret, 36, and their five children ranging from four to fourteen—had travelled from their remote village of Kintail deep in the Highlands to Glasgow. From here they caught the ferry to Liverpool and then Birkenhead, where they met hundreds of other families likewise making the journey, such as Alexander and Nora Cameron and their two young children from the Isle of Bute near Glasgow. Whatever trepidations these men may have had about their future, unemployment was not one of them, as the Board had already indentured both families to landowners prepared to pay well for experienced farm labourers. Thomas McRae was to work on a property at Buninyong near Ballarat, while Alexander Cameron, a forester by trade, would live and work at Werribee near Melbourne.

To have such numbers of young families travelling was a new innovation, and emigration vessels that previously had experienced children and infants only in limited numbers would now appear to be overrun by them.

* * * *

This, however, was the last thing on the minds of the superintendents of the embarkation depot, William and Ann Smith, on this sunny August morning, as they prepared to greet this ferry-load of new arrivals—all Scots—stepping onto the little jetty, full of hope and anticipation. For the moment, their primary concern was to make a good impression on the imposing gentleman standing beside them dressed impeccably in a naval officer's uniform, eyes fixed on the approaching ferry. No less a figure than Captain Charles George Edward Patey RN, an officer with an exemplary record, a veteran of the Mediterranean who had been made commander by age 27, captain by 33, and who would eventually retire a rear-admiral, had been the Board's choice to be its representative here at the new Birkenhead depot. His brief was simple: to organise the passengers along naval lines, and to make sure the Board's directives were being carried out to the letter. William and Ann Smith knew that every aspect of their performance would be observed closely.

For the next few days, until they boarded the ship that would take them to a new life across the seas, these people would be in the Smiths' care. They would be welcomed, fed, organised into groups or 'desks', briefed on the routines of ship life, quizzed and scrutinised by Captain Patey and his small staff to be of sound character, medically inspected and given at least some idea of what to expect on the long journey ahead. It would inevitably be a challenging and confusing time, but the Smiths were determined to do their utmost to make it as easy and as pleasant for the passengers as possible, as well as to give Captain Patey no reason to submit an unfavourable report to London. Just a few hundred yards away, tied up on a separate wharf just out of sight behind the main building of the depot, the great ship herself sat waiting.

'Hello, hello, welcome,' the Smiths cheerily assured the passengers making their way cautiously down the gangway of the ferry, children—and there were many of them—in tow. They gathered by the growing pile of trunks and luggage boxes being assembled on the jetty. Mrs Smith noticed the women first, in their finest bonnets and shawls but shy and skittish, still uncertain of this unfamiliar world. They nodded demurely towards the Smiths with dark, wary eyes, offering fleeting smiles. The men too were dressed in their finest clothes, although these were often patched and threadbare. They glanced, blank-faced, at their new surroundings, watching constantly over their wives and families. The children, noted the Smiths, were strangely silent. And every one of them was thin.

Then, slowly, a sound—a murmur—started to rise from the group of several dozen as they gathered their bearings and sorted their luggage, a soft, muted sing-song unlike anything Mr and Mrs Smith had ever heard, even in the melting pot of Liverpool. The matron gasped, alarmed yet intrigued by this strange, ancient sound. It was 'the Gaelic', the tongue of those proud, but now blighted inhabitants of the wild and faraway Highlands of Scotland. 'Welcome, you're all very welcome,' offered the Smiths more tentatively. But by the mute smiles they received, it soon became clear that large numbers of these people spoke not so much as a word of English.

The unique and tragic saga of the Highland Scots had begun decades earlier, and ended with the bleak acceptance that life as they had known it had become untenable, and that their only hope of staving off catastrophe for themselves and their children was to forgo their beloved homeland forever. Of all the peoples of Britain leaving their homes in the middle of the nineteenth century, however, it was the Highlanders who had the greatest reason, and yet the least desire, to do so.

5

The Scots

In faraway London, the British Home Secretary, Sir George Grey, had, like everyone else, heard stories of the dire plight of the Highlanders but, sceptical of rumours, requested that some person of eminence proceed there and report back first hand. The task fell to Sir John McNeill, Chairman of Scotland's Board of Supervision, a relief organisation charged with administering the country's rudimentary Poor Laws. McNeill, a well-connected surgeon and diplomat, toured a number of the most destitute parishes of the Highlands and islands and was appalled by what he saw. The resulting report was harsh and unsympathetic, blaming the Highlanders themselves for their predicament, accusing them of innate laziness, and harbouring an attitude 'of expecting relief as a right'.[1] Its conclusion was blunt, stating that only via emigration could the Highlanders' complete destitution be averted. With this in mind, in September 1851, a uniquely Scottish charity was established, the Skye Emigration Society. When it became obvious that such poverty as was observed on Skye was in fact endemic throughout the entire Highlands, it assumed the name by which it was to be widely known—the Highland and Island Emigration Society.

Its aim was simple: to induce large numbers of impoverished Highlanders to emigrate, primarily to Australia, and to raise the necessary capital in order for them to do so. However, not so much as a single penny, it was made clear at the outset, would be forthcoming from the government. Operating semi-autonomously under the aegis of the Board, the Highland and Island Emigration Society would concern itself solely with the plight of the Highlanders and be given authority to offer them conditions unavailable to other emigrating Britons. Its coffers, however, would be solely reliant on the generosity of private donors. In stark terms, its co-founder and chairman, the powerful Sir Charles Trevelyan, pointed out the reason for the Society's existence:

> The attention of the benevolent British Public has long been awakened to the lamentable destitution prevailing in the Island of Skye and other overpopulated Highland and Island districts. For five years past a great part of the people of these districts has been supported out of that portion of the munificent subscription raised in the winter of 1846–47, for the relief of the Famine in Ireland and Scotland . . . This Fund is now exhausted, and the condition of the people remains unimproved. They cannot support themselves in the land of their fathers; and the hardy and loyal Highlander is in danger of being converted into a professional mendicant. There is need of a complete and final remedy.[2]

Glib references to 'hardy and loyal' Highlanders aside, Trevelyan himself in fact had no love for the Scots, as he likewise had none for that other great Celtic race in crisis, the Irish. During the recent Great Famine, he had distinguished himself by his slow and recalcitrant delivery of government relief to the Irish population as 90 per cent of their staple food crop, the potato, failed and millions starved to death. A fanatical believer in the sanctity of the free market, he loathed the notion of government assistance of any kind to anyone under any circumstances, and in a letter to an Irish peer went so far as to label the famine 'an effective mechanism for reducing surplus population'.

Nevertheless, the need for the Society's services soon outstripped all initial expectations. Luckily, it evolved into something of a charity of fashion, with no less a figure than Prince Albert, husband of the reigning sovereign, Queen Victoria, becoming its patron, and a committee of management which included the Lord Mayor of London, the Governor of the Bank of England and such prominent social reformers as the Earl of Shaftesbury and Baron Lionel de Rothschild.

Highland landowners, no doubt relishing the opportunity to rid themselves of their impoverished tenants, contributed to the fund with uncharacteristic generosity, as did more humble members of the public. A Quartermaster Sergeant Hoban of the 13th Light Infantry contributed just over £4, and Highland soldiers abroad agreed to donate a day's pay.[3] Scots already settled in places like Canada and Australia raised hundreds of pounds for the cause, and the Queen herself contributed £300, with her husband Albert, a renowned kilt-wearer and fancier of all things Scottish, gave £100 to the fund.

It remained, however, a curious charity, offering neither relief nor shelter, food nor employment. The sole reason for the Society's existence was to deliver, in no uncertain terms, a blunt message to impoverished Highland Scots—'Go now or starve'[4]—and to expedite their removal to Australia as effectively as possible.

For those Scots now setting foot on Mr and Mrs Smith's Birkenhead jetty, their odyssey had begun with an information meeting at a local town or village, at which point the stark reality was laid before them that emigration was their best hope of avoiding destitution. Those charged to conduct such meetings were often shocked at the state of the people seated before them, as they later submitted in a report to the Society's chairman. As Mr Thomas Fraser, the Sheriff Substitute (a local judge) of the Isle of Skye and one of the architects of the Society, commented:

At our meeting yesterday, so many of the poor intending emigrants attended, all anxious for some information as to their prospects of getting away, that my court-room could not hold them, and we had to adjourn to the parish church. Many of these people are in a state bordering on starvation; and I have seldom had a more painful duty to perform than to address them without being able to give them any distinct information on the matter, which to them in their present circumstances is one of such frightful interest.[5]

The Reverend James McQueen observed:

The state of the people in general is most alarming. There never has been anything like the present distress. I can hardly describe my feelings, seeing and hearing their lamentable complaints, and seeing my fellow-creatures weeping before me, when I cannot help them. May God have mercy on them! I know not what will become of them.[6]

To the Scots, the Society offered a one-off, never-to-be-repeated opportunity of a heavily subsidised sea passage with terms far more generous than those proffered to the Irish or even the English in the care of the Board. There was still some cost involved, though, as well as a rigorous selection process, and by no means all who applied were successful. Applicants were required to possess rudimentary literacy (though often they did not), be relatively young, be unafraid of hard work and, importantly, display no yearning whatever to return to the mother country.

As an encouragement for this last point, they were required to sell everything they owned except the several sets of clothes they were told would be needed on the voyage. They also needed letters of reference from a minister of religion or a medical doctor attesting them to be of good character and—in an age before universal documentation—that they were in fact who they claimed to be.

The Society's preference was for able-bodied men, preferably with agricultural experience, and particularly with sheep. Single women of child-bearing age were also in demand in the female-scarce colonies. Hence shepherds, herdsmen and their wives, farm labourers and female domestic servants under the age of 45 were required to contribute just one solitary pound towards their full passage to Australia. This figure increased exponentially with age. Those between 45 and 60 were to pay £5, jumping to £11 for those between 50 and 60 years of age. The cost for children was 10 shillings each.

In reality, even these amounts were beyond many Scots, so for a large number of applicants who otherwise presented well, the full amount was loaned, to be reimbursed in instalments once they had settled in Australia—although this arrangement often fell by the wayside. The priority, it seems, was to see the dead weight of an underclass of 'mendicant' Highlanders removed from Britain, with the cost of doing so being a secondary consideration.

The Scots may well have been looked upon as fortunate by their fellow passengers, the English and Irish, travelling under the arrangement of the Board, as the price of emigration for them was considerably higher. As well as receiving a far less generous subsidy on their passage, they also needed to provide a non-refundable deposit with their application should they for any reason be unsuccessful or opt out of the process due to a change of mind.

All were required to supply at least two full sets of clothing, as the voyage would take them through extremes of climate none of them had experienced. For men, the list consisted of six shirts, six pairs of stockings, two pairs of shoes and two complete sets of outer garments, with a strong recommendation that several extra sets of not inexpensive woven woollen shirts also be included. Women were expected to provide six shifts, two flannel petticoats, six pairs of stockings, two pairs of shoes and two outer gowns.[7] Added to this were hats, shawls and bonnets and towels, but for reasons of hygiene, bringing along one's own bedding was prohibited. This was supplied by the Board, as was an issue of two pounds of soap per person—the first experience many had had of this highly taxed and unaffordable luxury.[8]

Whether they be English, Scots or Irish, wholly or partly assisted, the uprooting experience of emigration was universally life-changing, requiring almost incomprehensible stores of courage and strength. Until arriving at the embarkation depot, many had travelled no further than a few miles beyond the boundaries of their local village or parish in their entire lives.

The farewells of those departing were a long, drawn-out affair. For weeks and even months, extended rounds of visiting had commenced, each person in the village sensing the impending departure date as if it were they themselves who were leaving. Some implored them to stay, others expressed a desire—even a promise—to one day join them; all were anxious on their behalf.

On the day itself, trunks and boxes were packed and nailed shut before being loaded onto a hired carriage or wagon. Then, at the appointed hour, the emigrants would climb aboard and take a final look at those faces they had known all their lives, before surrendering to the tears and pulling away from their village forever.

If they were lucky, a short journey to a railway station or port ensued, from where a train or packet steamer would be boarded, headed—in the case of those bound for the Birkenhead depot—for Liverpool. For some of the Scots travelling from the Highlands or islands, a far longer trip lay ahead of them. In every case, a strict timetable had been provided that every emigrant was bound to follow. Lateness in presenting themselves at the depot, it was impressed upon them, was unacceptable, and could result in the forfeiting of the entire voyage.

* * * *

In the town of Tobermory, the largest settlement on the Inner Hebrides Isle of Mull, one such departure involved a woman who, like so many before her, was farewelling her little island home forever. With striking dark hair, fair complexion and high-cheeked features, she was still single in her late twenties, an age considered almost unmarriageable at the time.

To the Highland and Island Emigration Society, however, Annie Morrison was the perfect candidate: fit, educated, presentable and most importantly, of child-bearing age. There would, they assured her, be no shortage of excellent positions awaiting her in Victoria as a governess to a well-heeled family, not to mention a good many acceptable gentlemen suitors seeking a wife. Hence Annie—the sole representative of her beautiful but dying island of Mull—embraced her ageing father and stepped onto the steamer at Tobermory to begin her long journey to the other side of the world.

As with all Highlanders, the trauma of leaving was almost unbearable, but the truth, as agonising as it was, was that there was now nothing here for Annie Morrison, nor thousands like her. Over the course of her lifetime, Annie had seen Mull's population wane from 10,000 to just 3000 as people were cleared away in favour of sheep. This had left little more than the kelp industry, which, though dirty work, had sustained much of Mull's population.

The kelp was gathered from the sea, then burned with heather and hay in a trench covered with stones and turf. The residue white soda ash was shovelled into sacks and sent to the manufacturing centres for Britain where it was used in the making of soap, glass and gunpowder. In 1820, however, the tax on cheaper Spanish Barilla was reduced, then finally abolished altogether in 1845, at which point the local industry collapsed and the people of the islands began to dwindle away, first to the cities, then to the emigrant ships.

As the boat pulled away, Annie could barely bring herself to look back. Instead, she watched the outline of Kilchoan, the most westerly settlement on mainland Britain, and the pretty seaside village of Oban pass by as the little boat chuffed its way south. She had no expectations of what lay ahead, only a determined resolve that life would somehow be better.

* * * *

For her last few days in Britain, Annie, along with all the departing emigrants, would be well looked after under the care of Mr and

Mrs Smith at their Birkenhead depot. Built to accommodate and
feed up to several hundred at a time, the Board drew upon the regulations and practices of the Royal Navy not just for efficiency, but
to prepare the passengers for the regimented and curtailed life they
would soon be experiencing at sea. As passengers would be divided
up into groups when on the ship, so too were they at the depot.
Three large and separate dormitories housed the single men and the
single women, and the married couples and their children. The noise
of the latter in particular can only be imagined as up to 70 different
families could be all sharing the same large, open quarters. The beds
were arranged to replicate the layout of the berths of the ship and
must have resembled a vast human shelving system. Four feet off
the ground, running the entire length of the upstairs room, timber
shelves were installed then divided by a board every few feet, creating
a cavity into which mattresses of stuffed straw were installed. Each
person in their respective pigeonhole slept only a few inches from
their neighbour, separated by a low, thin piece of board. As it would
be on the long voyage, privacy was eroded to nothing.

Immediately on the emigrants' arrival, the shipboard routine was
introduced. Every passenger was to be up by 7 a.m., with breakfast
between 8 and 9 a.m., but not before beds were rolled up and the
bedding area swept out. Dinner would be at 1, supper at 6 and lights
out would be at 10.

The dining arrangements too were regimented, but at least the
food was plentiful, with the Board insisting that three good meals
a day be provided, often of a higher quality than many were accustomed to at home. To ease the potential for friction, people were
divided along national and religious lines, sitting with others of a
similar ilk in groups of tables marked as 'Scots Presbyterian', 'Irish
Roman Catholic' and so on. Roughly fourteen adults sat to a table,
or 'mess', to which a 'mess captain' was appointed by vote on a
regularly rotating basis. Bearing a chit to the kitchen, the 'captain'
would carry a large earthenware bowl filled with roasted mutton or
beef back to their respective mess. Tea, sugar, bread and butter, and

salt—luxuries for some—were also provided.[9] It was explained that on board ship much of the cooking would need to be done by the passengers themselves, and skills and experience in the art of preparing food were established and noted.

After meals, floors, tables and surfaces would be cleaned and swept according to a strict roster. The superintendents of all the depots were anxious to prevent any hint of disease being traceable back to their institutions, so medical inspections were carried out with particular emphasis on the eradication of lice, fleas and other visible parasites. Clothing was washed and dried, but as depots themselves were thinly staffed, chores and maintenance—such as the continual whitewashing of walls and surfaces—were carried out by the passengers. It would be similar on board ship, when every person would be assigned sets of jobs and obligations, which they were expected to carry out to the best of their abilities.

Friendships and acquaintances were forged, and those unused to the close proximity of strangers quickly learned to abandon such qualms. All the while, the talk of the voyage consumed every conversation. What would the ship be like? Who was the captain and what was his experience? What of the standard of food on board, and would there be sufficient quantities to last the journey? What would life be like in that far-off colony of Victoria? These and other questions filled the depot with a constant murmur of anticipation. As for exactly how long their journey would last, their inquiries were met with only vague answers as this could not be determined. They were told to expect up to four months at sea, as provisions would be carried for 120 days, plying a route that would take them to not a single stop along the way. Once they stepped on board, they would not be disembarking until they reached Victoria.

In their hours of free time at the depot, some passengers could not resist boarding one of the regular shuttle ferries across the Mersey to catch a glimpse of the seemingly enormous metropolis of Liverpool, with all her inherent dangers and diseases. Others stood at the adjacent wharf where their ship was tied up, being busily prepared for sail by her small army of crew. Carpenters could be heard banging and sawing away in her interior, making final adjustments to the extensive refit she had recently undergone. While not permitted to come too close, many stood in awe, taking in the sight of this magnificent vessel, as sturdy and impregnable as a castle, and by far the largest object fashioned by the hand of man most of them had ever seen. Surely this leviathan would bear them in safety across the world's oceans? On her stern, smartly painted in white lettering that stood out clearly against the black of her hull, was her curious name. They read it over to each other, then looked up once again at the words, '*Ticonderoga*—New York'.

6

The age of the clippers

On a freezing December morning in 1850, 15,000 people gathered expectantly around the edge of Boston harbour, eyes fixed on the enormous yard of renowned ship designer, now shipbuilder, Donald McKay. Men stamped their feet and women, as much as they dared, lifted their skirts out of the frozen mud and slush. In front of them, the masts of the great ship pointed like gigantic fingers towards a low and ominous sky. Her sleek black hull—for the moment secure in its cradle—seemed to resemble a powerful animal about to be unleashed from its tether.

In this seafaring age, interest in the launch of any new ship was always high, but with this, the first vessel both wholly designed and built by the enigmatic, Canadian-born McKay, the anticipation among the gathered Bostonians—as well as the wider maritime world—was intense. McKay's vessels were a new breed of ship. In the past few years, he had designed the 'extreme clippers' *Reindeer* and *Moses Wheeler*, of 800 and 900 tons respectively; these ships contained nothing less than a revolution within their sleek, futuristic lines. Now, for the first time, McKay had both designed and built his own ship, and the public was desperate to see it.

Those near the front, craning for a better view, could just make out the hollow curve of her graceful bow, designed to scythe through rather than straddle the water, and the almost feminine lines of her hull, widening gradually towards mid-ship, offering a concave shape to the waterline, all designed along complex principles of minimum weight and maximum strength.

To add to the theatrical setting that chilly Boston morning, clouds of steam rose and swirled from the vats of boiling whale oil being applied to melt the frozen tallow that covered the slipway that ran down to the icy water's edge. Suddenly, the excitement of the crowd rose as the sounds of mallets could be heard knocking away timber stays. 'Your name is . . . *Stag Hound!*' shouted a stentorian voice as a bottle of brandy was smashed against the ship's side. Then, slowly at first, the Goliath began to move. A tremendous roar rose up all around. The sound of the great hull sliding, thundering and finally streaking down the slipway towards the water was drowned out only by the sudden eruption of every bell in the city pealing out in celebration of the birth of the mighty vessel. From somewhere, a cannon boomed then a band struck up and the cheering continued. The *Stag Hound*, perhaps the greatest extreme clipper ever to have set sail, was launched.

The reign of the American 'Yankee clipper' ships was brief but spectacular, ushering in a revolution in speed and travel that broke open the world, transfixing populations across continents, who could now reach each other in times unimaginable a generation earlier. They would dominate the grand climax of the Age of Sail up until the beginning of the American Civil War, after which British shipbuilders would adopt and perfect the design, using harder, drier woods that lasted much longer than the American ships.

The initial spur for the clippers was trade. Towards the middle of the nineteenth century, after nearly two centuries, Britain at last began to dismantle her *Navigation Acts*, first installed by Oliver Cromwell's Commonwealth in 1651 as a protectionist bulwark against Dutch maritime traders. These laws stated that no trade in any English colony could be conducted by anyone other than English vessels manned by English sailors. As the British Empire grew, America in particular became increasingly infuriated at being thus shut out of the avenues of imperial commerce, such as the lucrative and expanding tea trade from places such as Hong Kong. The slight eventually became a contributing factor in the coming of the American Revolution.

For Britain, however, the *Navigation Acts* were a two-edged sword, and eventually her mollycoddled shipping industry began to fall behind, particularly in such areas as shipbuilding. In slow, round-bowed tubs, the design of which had not changed in a century, British merchantmen would ply their trade leisurely along the Empire's shipping lanes, stopping at several ports along the way and generally taking their time, showing little interest in those newer, faster American vessels they would sometimes encounter racing past them on the high seas, or in some foreign port a long way from home.

In 1849, Prime Minister Lord John Russell decided to move with the times and, despite howling protests from virtually every member of the House of Lords—not to mention the entire British shipbuilding industry—he pledged to embrace the gods of free trade and release his seafarers from two centuries of protection, just as his predecessor Robert Peel had done with the Corn Laws in 1846. The shock, when it came, was palpable. Suddenly, in 1850, the first tea of the season was brought to London by the American clipper the *Orient*, which tied up to London's East India Dock in 1850 to be greeted by a stunned crowd of locals who had never seen any vessel quite like it.

For 30 years from the mid-1840s until the advent of steam, the clippers rode the oceans as the true thoroughbreds of the Age of Sail. They were long, sleek and streamlined, riding low in the water and with their extra masts throwing up acres of sail to harness the wind. Some of the larger ships carried more than 30 individual sails with exotic names like moonrakers, royals and skysails. In conditions where other ships would shorten sail, the clippers would put on more and still more, heeling over until their booms and lee rails skimmed the surface of the water as it raced by at 10, 15 and even 20 knots or more. Their forecastles and other deck structures were trimmed down and configured to the centre of the ship to achieve the utmost balance.

Unlike their predecessors, which crashed their way doggedly through the waves like a battering ram, the clippers' elongated bows sliced an effortless passage, leaving barely a wake behind them, the water seeming to part willingly before the progress of these graceful queens of the oceans.

Their genesis was in the small, fast raiders of the primarily maritime War of 1812 between Britain and the United States. Speedy little brigs, brigantines, fore-and-aft and topsail schooners, none bigger than 200 tons, would swarm out of Baltimore and other Atlantic harbours to harry the plodding vessels of the Royal Navy—which, in their exasperation, declared that the American sailors must have some 'unlawful dealings with the great enemy of mankind for the malignant pleasure of annoying the English'.[1] They were made for speed and, unlike the traditional European vessels with their barge-like 'upside-down bell-shaped' bows and 'cod head and mackerel-tail' hull, they traded their space for the ability to transport a smaller cargo across the world in record times. Initially, that cargo was tea.

In 1843, a brilliant naval architect and ship design theorist named John Willis Griffiths was given a chance to put his academic ideas into practice by a New York-to-China trading firm, Howland & Aspinwall, which took the gamble of commissioning his 750-ton *Rainbow*, a ship so revolutionary that the maritime establishment declared it unsafe to sail, that her construction was 'contrary to the laws of nature'[2] and that she would never return from her maiden voyage. Instead, the *Rainbow* achieved remarkable average speeds of 14 knots and set a new record for the return trip from New York to Canton of three months, bringing back the first of the new season's tea chests for the highly competitive American market to the delight of the wealthy society ladies of New York and Washington.

In 1846, Griffiths built the even more remarkable *Sea Witch*, which stunned the world when, under the command of another of the great characters of the Age of Sail, 'Bully Bob' Waterman, she arrived from Hong Kong after just 77 days at sea, her holds bursting with the new season's tea. At this time, a conventional cargo vessel could be expected to complete the same trip in no less than 160 days.[3] Two years later, in March 1849, 'Bully Bob', who had in fact worked with Griffiths on the sail design of the ship, achieved another feat by appearing unscheduled as a fast-moving speck on the horizon approaching New York harbour. When curious telescopes revealed that it was *Sea Witch* under full sail, just 74 days out of Hong Kong, the city went into raptures. Bully Bob had beaten his own record of two years earlier by three whole days. It is a feat that still stands today—unbeaten by any ship under sail more than a century and a half later.

For three decades, the clippers ruled the world's oceans, and as the demand for speed grew, shipyards up and down the east coast of America became alive to their construction—as described romantically in one of the classic accounts of the sailing age, *Clipper Ships of America and Great Britain*:

> The hammer notes of ten thousand men rang from the shipyards sprawled along New York's East River, and up and down the north Atlantic coast town after town hummed and boomed with industry. Man seemed to rival Nature in a perfect orgy of inspired invention and turned out sleek thoroughbred after sleek thoroughbred, whose long white arms stretched outward to embrace the breeze and draw into themselves the very essence of moving, pulsing life. Captains, hanging up new records, were mobbed and feted and idolized.[4]

The word 'clipper' derived from the antiquated 'clip', meaning to move quickly, the most salient response from those first bearing witness to the speed of these new ships. They were given suitably romantic names such as *Flying Cloud, Ariel, Lightning, Sovereign of the Seas* and, one of the greatest of all, the 1534-ton Donald McKay-designed *Stag Hound*, which on one voyage, despite being partly dis-masted in a storm, still managed to break the record for the run from New York to San Francisco around Cape Horn, then one of the longest in the world. Initially tasked with whisking tea and other cargoes around the globe, it was the discovery of gold that ushered in the true heyday of the clippers, first in California then, in the early 1850s, Australia. Now the ships' most lucrative cargo would be people, both well-heeled passengers paying their own way to seek fortune and adventure and those more desperate souls being assisted by their government to start a new life in a new land. One group of those less advantaged people would make the journey in the *Ticonderoga*.

7

The *Ticonderoga*

She was built in New York in 1849 by Perrine, Patterson & Stack, at their yard at the bottom of North Second Street, Williamsburg, just across the East River from Manhattan.[1] The company had been established a few years previously by a former sea captain, William Perrine, his partner Ariel Patterson and a Canadian from Quebec, Thomas Stack. Although the company would be broken up by 1853, it built six ships in total, the *Ticonderoga* being one of their larger vessels, although the *John Stuart,* built in 1851, hit the water at a whopping 1654 tons.[2] Her initial owners were three New York brothers, Henry, William and John Harbeck, who began as a small company of merchants then store owners, stockbrokers and eventually successful shipowners. In all, they commissioned and owned three clippers, the *Ticonderoga* being named after the fort in Essex County, New York State, situated on a strategic spit of land between Lake George and Lake Champlain where a great battle had taken place in July 1758 during the Seven Years War between the British and French. According to sources, the word itself is Iroquois, meaning either the sound of flowing water, the meeting of two waters, or even the land between two waters. By whichever definition one chooses, the word, when spoken gently, seems to capture the gentle essence of a tumbling stream. There was nothing gentle, however, about the Battle of Ticonderoga, one of the darkest moments of the famous Scots regiment the Black Watch, which was almost wiped out attempting to take a fort from the resilient French.

Strangely, no image exists of the *Ticonderoga*—not a painting, photograph or even a sketch has survived to give us a picture of how she would have appeared. This is unusual, as many paintings—even photographs—exist of earlier vessels, and particularly considering that the *Ticonderoga* was said to be a most beautiful ship, attracting much interest among ship-savvy populations wherever she went.

Her fame spread even to London and, despite never once visiting the capitol, the popular *Illustrated London News* published an article on her, featuring a detailed cut-away diagram of her internal decks and layout but no actual image of the *Ticonderoga* herself. The story appeared shortly before she sailed and also described in great detail the work and function of the Birkenhead depot, providing several graphic illustrations of the buildings and the placement of the passengers therein. As for the ship herself, we are left only with educated assumptions as to her appearance. The British-built *Alnwick Castle*, at an almost identical tonnage and similar dimensions, is believed to have borne a striking similarity to the *Ticonderoga*.

This is not the only area of mystery surrounding the *Ticonderoga* and her infamous Australian voyage. Her exact tonnage is vague, as is the number of masts she carried, with as many sources citing three masts as four. Exactly how many passengers she carried to Melbourne is also a matter of contention, as well as her precise arrival date in Victoria, and even the numbers who died on board the voyage and later in quarantine. This vagueness somehow contributes to the everlasting notion of the 'ghost ship', as witnessed by the two local lime-burners as she entered Port Phillip Bay at the end of her disastrous run in November 1852.

Defining the *Ticonderoga*'s tonnage is in fact far from academic, as it was this that determined the number of passengers she was permitted to accommodate on her two very crowded decks on her trip south to Victoria. The number varies not only from source to source, but across the often bewildering definitions that varied between countries, particularly between the United States and Britain. The tonnage of the *Ticonderoga* would initially have been determined by the ancient Builder's Old Measurement, expressed in 'tons burden', a calculation based on a ship's length and maximum beam. This system was applied inconsistently, and was in any case considered unreliable, particularly as the ships of the mid-nineteenth century began to increase significantly in size. It was not until 1854 that Britain's Board of Trade introduced a single method for the measuring of ship's tonnage, the Moorsom System, based on dividing the ship's internal volume by 100 cubic feet (2.8 cubic metres) then subtracting internal machinery and structure to arrive at a more workable figure. Even so, the tonnage of the *Ticonderoga* fluctuates across 'registered', 'registered gross', 'net registered' and so on to between 1089, 1280 and even up to 1514 tons.

There are, however, many facts about the *Ticonderoga* that are not in dispute. At 169 feet long, she was by no means the biggest of the Yankee clippers, with some sources even referring to her as a 'semi-clipper'. By way of comparison, the *Marco Polo*, which made the same journey shortly before the *Ticonderoga* with Bully Forbes in command, was 14 feet longer at 183 feet and the great *Stag Hound*, at 226 feet, was larger again. But by all accounts, the *Ticonderoga* was a particularly fine-looking vessel with graceful, even delicate lines. She was built of copper-sheathed oak and her hull was painted jet black, with a fine white stripe running its length, framing the even row of wooden scuttles that ran from bow to stern. She was 37 feet wide, had a draught of 18 feet and her stowage capacity was enhanced by a feature not obvious upon initial observation: an extra deck. Many clippers were single-deck ships with an open, cavernous storage area, whereas the *Ticonderoga*'s extra lower level made her suitable for a variety of uses, such as the transport of emigrants. Word of her fine lines and construction went around the already ship-obsessed population of Liverpool, who are said to have come down in their droves to see for themselves the beautiful American clipper with the long and unusual name, and offer their opinion on her pedigree.

Little is known about the *Ticonderoga*'s early life. It appears she went to work immediately upon her launch in 1849, running back and forth across the Atlantic, her holds bursting with bales of cotton from America's southern states, destined for the mills of the English midlands. To enhance profit on their return journey westward to America, her crew would install bunks and mess tables (known as desks) and take on a load of privately paying passengers—many of them Irish—searching for a new life in a country that was not part of the loathed British Empire. In 1852, the year she sailed to Melbourne, she had already completed two Atlantic crossings, arriving in New York on 22 April with 300 passengers, then executing a quick turn-around with a load of cotton to arrive back in Liverpool by late May. A considerable quantity of stores were left over from one of these Atlantic runs, which were then utilised on the trip to Australia.

Her captain and part-owner was 30-year-old Irish-born Thomas Boyle, who installed his brother William as third mate and purser. A third Boyle, J.H. Boyle, appears to have been employed as the officer in charge of overseeing the provisions of the ship for her voyage to Australia, but his relationship to Thomas and William, if any, is unknown. One of several misconceptions regarding the *Ticonderoga* is the notion that she had previously served as a cattle transport. Her extra deck would appear to have been suited to the task of accommodating several hundred live beasts in hastily erected stalls, and some have even pointed to this as the source of the disease that later ravaged her. Several former passengers later mentioned this supposed episode in the ship's history in letters and recollections, but researchers have discounted it as a rumour, its origins now forgotten in time. Perhaps cattle spreading disease was an easier notion to accept than it having been brought on board by the passengers themselves.

8

Emigrants and numbers

From a crisis to find enough able bodies to rescue the 1852 Australian wool clip, the British and colonial governments now found that there were not enough ships to carry the deluge of those who suddenly wanted to go. Everyone, it now seemed, was determined to participate in this 'great race' south to Victoria to make their fortune before—as they had seen happen in California—the gold started to peter out. The statistics speak for themselves. In 1850, just over 16,000 emigrants, both assisted and private, made their way to Australia from the United Kingdom. In 1851, that figure jumped to 21,532. However, 1852 saw an extraordinary increase to 87,881 people leaving for Australia, making it the highest in the 50-year period between 1830 and 1880.[1]

The Board, for years having done its best to spruik the benefits of Australia with limited success, now found that it was swamped with applicants, and the ships it had previously relied on to transport its assisted emigrants were no longer available. These had long departed, scattered across the world's oceans, having filled their berths with the far more prosperous class of private passengers willing to pay their own way and delivering the shipowners a much larger profit per head.

The Board now scrambled to find new ships. In 1850, to increase passenger numbers, the relative luxury of a private cabin—for those few passengers able to afford it—was abolished, with everyone now corralled into the single class of steerage. They soon found, however, that few shipowners were interested in applying for the assisted emigrant trade when better-paying private passengers were willing to fill their berths. In Liverpool alone, shipping lines were struggling with a waiting list of over 7000 unassisted emigrants, having already shipped 6000 over the previous twelve months. Pressure came from the other side of the world too, as the Board's agent in Melbourne now recommended that vessels of no less than 800 tons be hired to bring over much larger numbers of the kinds of people who were not likely to head straight to the goldfields as soon they set foot on the wharf. The Board therefore had little choice but to look to a class of ships previously uncontemplated: those big, fast, twin-deck 'extreme clippers' of America.

Poring over their dimensions and sailing records, the Board discovered, to its considerable relief, that not only did these big new ships conform to British statutory regulations regarding the movement of assisted passengers, but that the mortality rate on board was in fact slightly lower than on smaller vessels. In addition, the Americans themselves—having experienced the boom time of emigration with the California gold fever—were now keen to revisit their success in this new rush to Australia, and were preparing to expand their reach with several large and new clippers. The economics added up as well. Whereas a smaller vessel that could offer more comfortable accommodation needed a higher number of privately paying passengers to make a profit, the larger ships' economies of scale could still make a tidy sum crowding a greater number into one large class.

When the Board's assessors did the figures, it was realised that some of these ships were capable of carrying close to a thousand people at time. Here, however, they had reason to pause. They were experienced in transporting numbers in the hundreds, sometimes up to 500 in a single vessel, but given the ever-present hoodoo of disease at sea, how feasible would it be to transport up to double those numbers at once? Plying back and forth across the Atlantic on voyages of a couple of weeks' duration was one thing; two or three months or more at sea travelling to the opposite side of the globe was a far more daunting prospect.

Whatever reservations the Board may have had about commissioning such large vessels, no fewer than four were nevertheless invited to tender, and all four were quickly accepted and the leases drawn up. They were the 1300-ton *Wanata*, virtually new from her builder's yard in New Brunswick; the 1495-ton German-owned *Borneuf*; the enormous 1625-ton *Marco Polo*—in fact, a triple-decked ship—and, the smallest as well the last to tender, the *Ticonderoga*. In 1852, each of these ships would make their way, heavily laden with passengers, to Victoria.

Anticipating the rush in demand to emigrate, the imperial government passed *An Act to Amend and Consolidate the Laws Relating to the Carriage of Passengers by Sea 1852*, known otherwise as simply the *Passengers Act*, setting out specific standards of accommodation, victualling and accountability with which British passenger ships were bound to comply. The new regulations stated, among other things, that every passenger be issued three quarts of water daily; sleeping berths should be not less than 6 feet in length and 18 inches in width, and that a complete and detailed list, the Master's List, be made of each embarking passenger.

Once the owners of the *Ticonderoga* signed the contract, her master, Captain Boyle, informed the Board that she would indeed be capable of accepting the maximum number of 630 'statue adults' legally permitted for her tonnage, at a cost to the Board of £17 each, undercutting the next nearest quote of £18, 17s and 6d. What constituted a 'statue adult', however, is—like tonnage—somewhat complicated. It was defined by the *Passengers Act* as being any passenger over fourteen years of age, or any two under fourteen. Infants less than one year old—and on the *Ticonderoga* there were many of those—did not count at all. This partially accounts for the uncertainty surrounding the exact number of individuals who boarded the *Ticonderoga* at Birkenhead. Official statistics differ. According to the Victorian Health Officer's report written after the voyage, there were 811, whereas the British Parliamentary Papers state 797. The *Ticonderoga*'s own passenger records state a total of 814. Whatever the exact figure, it represented a sound profit for her owners who would receive half the per head fee on embarkation, the other half on arrival.

Deep within the bowels of the British Public Record Office in Kew, just outside London, a list of ships chartered by the Board still exists. Despite the passing of more than a century and a half, the *Ticonderoga*'s contract remains in excellent condition, its terms laid out in the superb steel-nib copperplate handwriting of the day:

'Ticonderoga': Tonnage 1280: Colony—Melbourne:
Contract Price—£17:0:0
Date to be ready—26 July (1852) Birkenhead
Date of Departure—4 August (1852), Birkenhead
Brokers—Lindsay
Surgeons—J.C. Sanger, J.W.H. Veitch[2]

It goes on to break down the embarking emigrants into categories: 160 married men and an equal number of married women; 106 single females but only 68 single males; 126 boys under fourteen; 147 girls under fourteen. The manifest also mentions nationality: 140 English, 643 Scots, but only a handful of Irish—just fourteen. The quoted tonnage (which as stated varies in other sources) of 1280 conforms roughly to the permitted amount of statue adults, entered in the contract as '630½'. Underneath this figure, however, is a small but neat pencil mark reading '598', undated, and with no other reference or explanation. Perhaps an official in the Board sensed, presciently, that at 630—a figure that in fact translated to several hundred more actual living souls—the *Ticonderoga* would be seriously over-crowded.

9

Departure

By the third day at the Birkenhead emigration depot, the anticipation brewing among the hundreds of emigrants soon due to depart on the *Ticonderoga* was palpable. For people used to the quiet routine of rural village life, the past few days had been a whirlwind.

However, after three days of meals delivered and eaten around their individual 'mess' table with fourteen or so complete strangers, then being required to scour and clean their own utensils; of every morning having to roll up their bedding and sweep out their berths; of being interviewed by the imposing Captain Patey and found to be of 'good character'; of being medically examined and found fit to travel, they were—ready or not—about to face the great journey of many weeks at sea. The average age of the emigrants was somewhere around the mid-twenties, and at this stage the impending voyage still had the qualities of a great adventure: breathlessly anticipated, but utterly unknowable.

The depot only had space for around 400 at a time, but the *Ticonderoga* would be carrying twice that number, so a complicated loading timetable was drawn up lasting several days as groups of passengers underwent their processing. At this stage, the democracy of the depot began to come into question. The first to be loaded were the English, all 140 of them, mainly from Somerset and Gloucestershire, who by virtue of their birth right were given the best bunks towards the relatively stable stern of the ship. Next were loaded the Scots, then finally the Irish, who crowded into the poorer quarters in the bow.

Captain Thomas Boyle was proud of his ship, as he was of his contract to carry emigrants to Australia, and the responsibility that entailed. To prepare the *Ticonderoga* for the longest voyage it had undertaken as well as the largest number of people it had carried, he expended considerable effort and no small expense employing a small army of ship's carpenters to reconfigure her interior, with a view to achieving the highest possible standards of comfort and hygiene for his passengers. To this end, a number of features had been included. First, no less than twenty newly designed flushing water-closets—toilets—for both male and female passengers were installed at strategic positions on the upper deck. At a time when such innovations were only just beginning to appear in the newest London houses, this was indeed a significant advance on the traditional ship's 'heads', in which people had to position themselves over a hole in a wooden board jutting out from the side of the ship suspended precariously above the water. Instead, the *Ticonderoga*'s modern devices used gravity-fed seawater tanks to flush away waste, which had to be manually pumped full every day. It was undoubtedly the first time anyone on board had seen anything like them. Another was the inclusion of four lead-lined bath tubs, each measuring a generous 6 feet by 2 feet. Admittedly, they could only be filled with salt water (stores of freshwater would be strictly used only for drinking and cooking), and would be used exclusively by the ship's male population, but they were an advancement nonetheless.

Under the forecastle, Boyle had sealed off the main deck towards the bow with a solid bulkhead, beyond which were his crew's quarters. The remainder of the previously open deck was now divided into three sections: a men's ablution area, a central married quarters and, aft, the area for single women. This also now incorporated two new 'hospitals' or sick bays, the women's situated at the rear of the single women's quarters and the men's adjacent to their ablution area near the bow. At equidistant points, narrow gangways led down to the lower deck. This too had been similarly renovated with another single men's area in the bow and a larger married quarters taking up midship and the stern. The gangways linked the ship's two main areas for married people and their families, as well as the lower men's area with the male ablution section. There was also a new 'teacher's room' for group reading and lessons, and a 'matron's room' where the young women could be given their own lessons, though these were of a somewhat different nature to the men's.

With the prevailing belief, before the advent of modern medicine, that sickness and disease were largely airborne, great care had been taken by Boyle to ensure the flow of fresh, 'clean' air throughout his ship. Lattice wooden bulkheads had therefore been installed rather than solid wood, as well as another innovation, wind sails.[1] This basic air-conditioning system was similar to those found in mines, whereby vents on the open upper deck scooped up fresh air and distributed it throughout the ship's large and complicated interior. In rough or stormy weather, however, when the passengers arguably needed fresh air the most, they would be disengaged.

As well as the gangways, which themselves aided ventilation, extra openings had also been fitted between the decks. One of them, opening the single women's area to one of the married quarters below it, had steel bars bolted across it at 6-inch intervals to prevent any interaction between the two. Such was the morality of the times. Although believed to be imperative to good health at the time, this deliberate opening up of the ship's internal passages would, later in the voyage, allow the free circulation of something far more sinister than simply fresh air.

To bring at least some light into the lower deck, Boyle had 10-inch diameter windows or scuttles cut through to illuminate the stern area, with more situated 12 feet apart right around the deck. To enhance what light there was, the ship's entire interior had been covered in several coats of whitewash. By far the largest task undertaken by Boyle's carpenters, however, was the fitting of the *Ticonderoga*'s system of wooden bunks, which needed to be constructed and installed in their hundreds. Like some vast, two-tiered filing system, they were hammered, bolted and dowelled, piece by piece, around the ship's solid centre, whence they emanated like rows of wooden petals. New straw-stuffed mattresses were provided for each, as were new blankets. For hygiene, passengers were forbidden from bringing on board bedding of their own. These bunks, however, were small and narrow, and separated by just 3 feet from the next. This, in fact, was more space than the mere 2 feet of space between bunks as stipulated by the *Passengers Act*. A flimsy wooden wall protected modesty to some extent, and a thin curtain could be drawn across the foot of each bunk, but privacy on board the ship barely existed.

The *Ticonderoga* also exceeded the prescribed headspace between decks, as laid out in the Act that in 1852 had been amended by parliament but that had not come into effect by the time she sailed. A mere 6 feet of headspace between decks of emigrant ships due to sail through the tropics was all that was required by law, but the *Ticonderoga* exceeded this with a clearance of 7 feet, 10 inches in her main deck, and 6 feet, 11 inches in the lower.[2]

She was, however, still awfully dark. Despite Boyle's renovations, it was simply not possible for light to penetrate the ship's interior. Even on bright days, the lower deck in particular was a place of perpetual gloom, the strong but thick glass of the scuttles allowing for little more than a hazy, green-tinted illumination. In particular, those passengers allotted the lower bunk on the lower deck were destined to spend a large part of the voyage in a perpetual night. This is one of the reasons, it has been suggested, that no passenger diaries have survived from the *Ticonderoga*'s journey. Even among those literate enough, there was little light by which to write them.

Deeper into the ship, underneath her second deck, were the *Ticonderoga*'s holds, inside which her crew of 48 had been toiling for many days, loading the tremendous amount of stores that would be required to keep nearly 800 people alive for the next three months and more. This being virtually the longest voyage that any ship of the time was capable of undertaking—close to the farthest distance from one point on the globe to another, and with no scheduled stops along the way—provisions were chosen more for their qualities of long-term preservation than their nutrition. Although the *Ticonderoga*'s journey was expected to last between 80 and 90 days, provisions to last 120 days were taken on board; hence her holds needed to be big. Among the larger items she would carry would be:

- 520 barrels (being the equivalent of 48,711 pounds) of navy bread—a type of hard, simple biscuit
- fifteen tierces of 'India mess' or preserved beef ('tierce' being an antiquated unit of measurement amounting to 42 imperial gallons), plus 47 tierces of India pork
- 50 barrels of split peas
- 53 barrels of 'finest raw sugar' amounting to 10,496 pounds
- 27 barrels of rice
- 120 boxes of raisins
- eight casks (580 gallons) of mustard
- five 'puncheons' (7418 pounds) of treacle
- nineteen casks of pickles.

Added to this list were considerable stores of tinned foods (still a relatively new and not entirely trusted innovation), such as soup and bouilli (stewed or boiled meat), raw coffee, preserved potatoes, beef suet, pepper and salt.[3]

On private vessels on which passengers paid their own way, the luxury of live animals could be included for fresh meat on the voyage. This was not so for the assisted emigrants of the *Ticonderoga*. Fresh water was also an essential item, and one notoriously difficult both to transport and preserve. The *Passengers Act* allowed for just over three and a half litres to be provided per passenger per day, and

on the upper deck of the *Ticonderoga*, Captain Boyle had installed
several large wooden water casks, into which he had pumped nearly
353,000 litres from the Mersey River, which he aimed to keep fresh
with the addition of charcoal. Nevertheless, it would struggle to
remain so on the long journey to Australia.

The diets of the Scots and Irish differed slightly but significantly
from those of the English, in that potatoes and oatmeal were considered staples. Potatoes, however, were not easy to keep, even in their
'preserved' form, which basically amounted to placing them in jars
filled with earth or ash and storing them in the coolest place possible
on the ship. With regard to the Scots and their diet, the *Passengers
Act* ruled that three and a half pounds of oatmeal be provided to
every passenger embarking from a Scottish or Irish port. Though
leaving from England, Captain Boyle insisted that such provisions of
oatmeal were provided for all his Gaelic passengers.

Apart from the food and provisions, the *Ticonderoga* also had
to take on board utensils and galley supplies for around 800 people
who would be dining in 126 'messes', around the large wooden
tables installed along the two covered decks adjacent to their bunks,
and in fine weather, even on the open upper deck. In their hundreds,
serving plates, bread baskets, butter dishes, water beakers and some
more curiously listed items such as 246 'tin pots with hooks' and
126 'potato nets' were all included.

The list had been worked out meticulously, checked and inspected
by Captain Patey who, to the relief of Mr and Mrs Smith, was
pleased with what he saw. He needed to be meticulous. There would
be no chances at replenishment of anything along the way. The
Ticonderoga's route, following the so-called Great Circle around the
bottom of the world, would make not a single stop along the way.
The next land her passengers would touch after departing the shores
of Britain would be Australia. Anything that was not taken aboard
at Birkenhead, the passengers and crew would have to do without.

In the late July heat, crew men had worked with the longshore-
men on the wharf, assembling the mass of provisions and carefully

arranging them like a gigantic three-dimensional jigsaw puzzle inside the gloomy hold and, using the ancient art of the stevedore, spreading the load so as not to upset the clipper's delicate trim.

On the first day of the new month of August, the long process of embarkation began. No matter how long this moment had been contemplated, and despite the months—even years—of anguish, the agonising decision making, the advice taken, the information absorbed, the long procession of farewells and last-minute regrets, nothing could prepare the *Ticonderoga*'s passengers for the totally alien environment they were now to enter. As they prepared to take leave of the Birkenhead depot, harried staff shouted names from lists as anxious parents formed lines and wrangled their excited children. In small groups, divided into nationalities, then into their respective messes, the passengers were marshalled in a great shuffling line towards the waiting ship.

Queues stretched back from the wharf to the depot as families tried to keep themselves and their luggage together, snaking towards the great black wall of the *Ticonderoga*'s hull 'like Noah and his Family going into the Ark', as one departing passenger observed.[4] Several brass bands had been hired for the occasion and stood on the wharf belting out favourites like 'Home Sweet Home', 'The Girl I Left Behind Me' and, of course, 'Rule Britannia'.[5]

With deck space on board at a premium, each person had been issued with two canvas bags into which they were told to pack only the clothing they would need for the voyage; the remainder was to stay in their boxes and trunks, which the crew had already stowed into the holds. After a month at sea, one box clearly marked 'wanted on the voyage' would be brought up to the upper deck for another month's clothing to be taken out and exchanged, with the dirty clothes being packed away. Almost nothing except food would be provided once on board, so every essential item, from children's nappies to cooking utensils, had to be carried by the passengers and stowed in the lockers under the already less than spacious bunks.

The ship's deck was alive with the crew, who seemed to crawl over every inch of her. Heads craned up to the top of the main and mizzen masts, where men could be observed high up in the spars and top masts checking and rechecking lines, shrouds and braces. Even tied up and beside the wharf, it seemed a dangerous place for anyone to be. What it must be like up there at sea and in rough weather was beyond imagining. Not that it appeared to concern them, as the crew's singing—both their work songs and traditional tunes of departure—rang out jauntily over the bulwarks.

More names were checked off more lists as passengers emerged onto the rickety gangplank, which felt more than unsteady under their feet. Then, setting foot for the first time on the upper deck, the line snaked down one of the hatches, which opened like a dark, gaping maw. Helped by one or more of the *Ticonderoga*'s crew, it was at this moment that her passengers were introduced to the crowded and claustrophobic underworld that would be their home for the next three months.

Some gasped as they ducked their heads at the entrance to the main deck, adjusting their eyes to the sudden darkness. Some gagged at the already strange mixture of smells of cut timber, white-wash and hot tar, as well as a strange, earthy smell left from the thousands of cotton bales that had been crammed into her from her previous incarnation as a cargo vessel. Some felt instant claustrophobia clawing at their chests. Embarkation staff and members of the crew, harried and impatient, saw them as quickly as possible to their assigned bunks then left them to stow their possessions in the small lockers as they attended to the next passenger. Panic about the tiny space in which they were expected to live over the coming months was experienced by many. Others were directed to proceed even further into the ship, down yet another gaping gangway to the *Ticonderoga*'s lower deck, feeling as if they were descending into a mine. The same thought crossed each of their minds as they lowered themselves and their families down into the hold: how could we ever get out of here in a hurry?

Another hour or so of settling in, and 795 passengers plus several dozen crew, including officers, able and ordinary seamen, several cooks and carpenters,[6] settled themselves into the spaces and crannies of the great ship. The noise of dozens of families and children and the shouted orders of the crew reverberated around the confined spaces in a cacophony of tongues and accents. The mood of the passengers varied, from the quiet anxiety of the mothers with children to the enthusiasm of the young, single men who—like young, single men everywhere—looked forward to what they saw as a great adventure on the way to wealth and good fortune in the far-off colonies. Already, they had begun to think of themselves as expert seamen.

Two men had already established themselves on board the *Ticonderoga* who were neither passengers nor crew, but who occupied a unique position somewhere between. It could be argued that theirs was one of the most important positions on the entire ship. It was upon the shoulders of these two men that the health and happiness of the passengers on the long voyage would rest. Already they had begun making the rounds of the decks, reacquainting themselves with passengers they had met during the medical inspections at the depot a day or two earlier. Together, they presented an unshakeable front of authority and good cheer as they patted the heads of some of the children, uttered reassuring words about the strength of the ship and the capable hands and experience of Captain Thomas Boyle and generally set a tone of calm. Of all the ship's officers, it was these two men with whom, over the weeks to come, the *Ticonderoga*'s passengers would become most familiar—for better and for worse. Over time, their roles would evolve from offering comfort and advice, and attending to minor health concerns and daily grievances, to those of warriors in a life-or-death struggle. They were the *Ticonderoga*'s two official surgeons, duly appointed by the Colonial Land and Emigration Commission, the seasoned and respected Dr Joseph Charles Sanger, 48, and his assistant, a younger man with a broad and steady face, Dr James William Henry Veitch, 27.

Finally, early in the afternoon of Wednesday, 4 August 1852, the ship's bell was struck to alert all those not travelling to depart the ship and groups of friends and well-wishers made their way towards the gangway, tears springing to their eyes, as well as those of the people about to depart. Then, as if announcing the arrival of an emperor, the bell tolled again to signal that the *Ticonderoga*'s master, Thomas Boyle, was coming aboard.

The captain would usually leave the final preparations to his first mate while he attended to paperwork and final discussions with the owners and emigration officials on shore about the route to be taken, and also what to expect about Port Phillip and its approaches—particularly the entrance to Port Phillip Bay, well known as a particularly difficult stretch of water to navigate. To this effect, he would also receive his Notes to Mariners, officially prepared for sea captains and containing the latest information and nautical advice about the sea lanes and ports they were to visit. There was also a last private briefing with Captain Patey, an experienced seaman himself. Once more, the route would be discussed, along with the foreseeable dangers, the crew and of course the welfare of the passengers. It was once again impressed upon Captain Boyle that he was carrying a large, virtually unprecedented number of people on a very long voyage, and that their welfare was paramount.

Boyle's arrival on board sent a charge of authority coursing through the *Ticonderoga*'s timbers, and the settling passengers could sense a new energy and confidence in the crew. Departure was now imminent and unstoppable. Captain Patey followed Boyle aboard, accompanied by Liverpool's Assistant Emigration Officer, Mr Kenneth Sutherland, who made one last round of the lower decks. The three held a brief final conference, exchanged paperwork officially handing the ship over to the captain and shook hands. All were pleased with what they saw of the *Ticonderoga*'s preparations.[7] Having given Boyle the all-clear to depart, Patey and Sutherland proceeded down the gangway. At the bottom waited one final figure to whom Sutherland uttered the words 'The ship is yours, Mr Pilot' as he passed. The man bowed slightly, then confidently strode up onto the vessel, the last person to come aboard. Greeting Captain Boyle, both men headed for the forecastle, positioning themselves just behind the helmsman, who clutched the *Ticonderoga*'s big wheel and prepared to hand it into the capable hands of the pilot, who would guide the big ship out through the mouth of the river into Liverpool Bay.

It was an uncharacteristically warm, muggy day with high cloud. Every one of the *Ticonderoga*'s nearly 800 passengers crowded onto the ship's upper deck. Suddenly, shouted commands to 'Cast off starboard! Cast off port!' were heard, then relayed down the length of the ship as ropes were dropped and slack taken up. Then the sound of a steam whistle and the churning of water could be heard as two steam-driven tugs began to pull the *Ticonderoga* away from the wharf. At once, a passenger gave a shout, 'Three cheers for Mr and Mrs Smith!' and three throaty 'hurrahs' rose in chorus. The two figures on the wharf acknowledged the gesture, Mr Smith removing his hat and bowing to those people whose last days in England he and his wife had done their best to make as easy as possible. Beside them, Captain Patey also accepted some of the praise with a salute. All three knew, however, that no matter what awaited their passengers on the journey, the days ahead would be a great deal harder than they could even imagine. Each offered up a silent prayer.

As the great ship moved slowly out into the wide Mersey River, people gathered along the river's banks to see her off. Small craft of all descriptions—skiffs, ferries and fishing boats, dwarfed by the great clipper ship—darted about her like excited minnows. Then there was a sudden booming, which echoed in a ripple across the river, and the *Ticonderoga* was enveloped in smoke, causing many of her passengers to let out a startled cry and wails to arise from the children. In a grand gesture of farewell, all eight of the ship's cannons—kept on all ships of size at the time—had been loaded blank and fired.[8] Those watching her on shore were heartily impressed and echoed the gunfire with a roar of approval of their own. Under partial sail and still accompanied by her tugs, the *Ticonderoga* emerged majestically from her self-created shroud of blue-grey smoke and headed down the Mersey as handkerchiefs were waved and eyes, swollen with tears, watched the shapes of loved ones and friends recede.

Once out into the river, the cry went out from the first mate, 'All ready forward?' and 'Mainsail, haul!' Then there was a rush of men heading aft, pulling on the braces to turn the gigantic spars towards the breeze. 'Steady your helm! Keep her full!' continued the cries as the *Ticonderoga* put on sail. Sometimes large ships would be caught in the doldrums, occasionally for weeks, pathetically close to their departure point, waiting for the winds to pick up and their journey to begin. The *Ticonderoga* was lucky this early August day, however, and a decent breeze was standing by to fill her sheets as she passed through the wide mouth of the Mersey. The small craft that had come to see her off gradually dropped away. The passengers looked up to the rigging in amazement, still unused to the sight of men clambering across it like monkeys, apparently oblivious to the deadly drop to the deck below. Then, with the brief sound of a steam whistle, the tugs pulled away.

Once past the mouth of the Mersey, the *Ticonderoga* shortened sail briefly to allow a pilot vessel to come alongside. The pilot wished the captain the best for the long journey and handed the big oak wheel over to the helmsman. A call went around for any last messages to be taken ashore and a few notes were hastily scribbled. Some passengers watched in silence as he descended the ship's ladder, taking with him their last connection to the old world. Now they were finally and entirely on their own. If all went to plan, nothing would be heard of the *Ticonderoga* or the souls on board until they reached the shores of Australia.

Suddenly, they were out into Liverpool Bay heading due west along the coast of Wales. Had they kept going, they would have sailed across the Irish Sea almost directly into Dublin Bay; instead, many hours later, they rounded the island of Holyhead, passed the famous South Stack Lighthouse then proceeded through St George's

Channel, running between Ireland and Wales, before turning onto the heading that would barely alter for two months: due south. Way over on the port side, some took a last glimpse at the home they knew they would never see again, and the last sight of land ebbed quietly over the horizon.

10

Clearances and famine: The tragedy of the Highlands

When the Scots emigrants walked up the gangway from the Birkenhead depot onto the *Ticonderoga*'s deck for the first time, more than a century had passed since the day in 1746 when, on a bleak moor near Inverness, the old dream of a Scottish king returning to the British throne was buried once and for all in blasts of musket and grapeshot. Yet, 106 years later, the Duke of Cumberland's guns still reverberated in echoes of despair throughout the Highlands.

Even in their forefathers' time, only a fraction of the clans[1] had supported the delusions of the so-called Young Pretender, Charles Edward Stuart. His wild-eyed followers hurled flowers into his path, dubbed him their 'Bonnie Prince', their dark-eyed Roman Catholic darling, their saviour—all this despite him having placed not so much as a foot on Scottish soil until the age of 25, and the fact that his title 'Prince' existed in name only. Most other Highlanders watched in dread and foreboding as this Great Jacobite Rebellion, this fancy of the Catholics and those mad, unpredictable Episcopalians, gathered its brief head of steam before shattering in disaster as a rag-tag army of half-starved clansmen withered in front of the Duke of Cumberland's Regiments of Foot, two of which happened to be Scottish themselves. But despite many not supporting the uprising, all would be made to suffer its defeat.

In the end, the grandson of a deposed and long-dead king would prove no match for the warrior son of a reigning monarch. Earning his sobriquet 'the Butcher', Cumberland carried out the orders given by his father, King George III, and saw to it that no clansman was left alive on the battlefield of Culloden. Dead and wounded were thrown together into pits and buried, dead or alive.

Thus began the pacification of the Highlands. In an indication of the depth of the shock felt by the Hanoverians at the Jacobin uprising, Cumberland embarked on a sustained and cold-blooded campaign, hunting down clansmen like dogs and eradicating Highland culture root and branch. The tartan was outlawed; the pipes forbidden. Roads were now policed and those caught speaking Gaelic were punished by imprisonment or death. With the passing of the *Heritable Jurisdictions (Scotland) Act*, the Highland chiefs were stripped of their powers, and eventually the entire clan system, which had evolved over a thousand years and formed the bedrock of Highland society, was smashed forever.

Worse even than this treatment at the hands of the old enemy, the English, however, was the betrayal by their own. Warlords no longer, the estate-owning lairds of southern Scotland—upon whose largesse and sufferance tens of thousands of tenant farmers had relied for centuries to eke out some kind of living on their tiny plots of fertile land, decided to cash in their centuries-old traditions and become rich.

Since as long as anyone could remember, in a system that had evolved little since feudal times, the land-owning gentry had sub-let their vast estates to tacksmen, who in turn leased 'tacks' or strips of fertile land collectively to the farming families of a village or town. The system, known as run rig, had served Highlanders for generations. The rent gathered from those at the bottom of the pyramid was, however, small, sometimes pitifully so. And while in previous times, the landowners had been happy to count their assets in numbers of loyal clansmen willing to wield a broadsword in their name, their desires from the mid-1700s became decidedly more worldly.

The landowning Scots quickly began to dissociate from the rough ways of the Highlanders. They married pretty English wives who preferred a townhouse in Belgravia to an estate in the glens, and who chose to venture no further north than a ball at a wealthy home on the outskirts of Edinburgh. They affected English manners, courted English friends and agreed with them that the Gaelic, after all, had always been a barbarous tongue for a barbarous people.

For it was now, towards the end of the eighteenth century, that the demand for meat, followed by the demand for wool, would transform the Highlands, draining the land of its ancient people forever. It was called 'the Clearances', and it would spell the death of Highland culture. The weapon deployed in this long and deliberate campaign of human catastrophe was the humble sheep.

There had, of course, always been sheep in the Highlands: small things kept in modest flocks, producing milk, small amounts of fine wool and, occasionally, tough mutton. They were thin and delicate creatures, unable to survive the harsh Highland winters, at the beginning of which they were brought down from their grazing places on the slopes to the lower, more protected climates. Often, they would over-winter with the tenant farmers themselves, man and beast under the same roof, in a way that later revolted outsiders.

Then, in the last years of the 1700s, came the time of the Cheviot, the Great Sheep. Named after the bitter hills running along the border of England and Scotland among which it was bred, the Cheviot was a man-made super sheep, producing one-third more wool and meat than the common blackface or Linton. It was also relatively disease free and could survive the harsh Highland winters that, insisted the locals initially, not even the strongest stag could bear.

Suddenly, land that had quietly supported a few hundred Highland families in a manner that remained unchanged for centuries was worth a fortune. Attention was directed towards the Highlands and its inhabitants as never before. The fear and loathing felt by a previous generation now gave way to pity and contempt for their squalid way of life, their dismal huts of sod and stone, their wooden ploughs, their paltry crops of oats and potato, their rough stills and bitter beer, their refusal to modernise, their stubborn beliefs in witches, faeries and other superstitions.

On their chestnut geldings, English and southern gentlemen—the industrious as well as the curious—made forays into the Highlands, notebook in hand, cursing the lack of roads and the absence of a decent inn. They rode up the river banks and into the villages, marking down every fertile valley and verdant hillside they could find along the way, tut-tutting as to how these people could be so immune to the wondrous progress of modern Britain. For their own sake, it was decided, they must—by force if necessary—be brought into the modern world, if only to liberate them from their own backwardness. Improvement became the moral imperative, and it was a subject not open for debate.

Driven from the south in massive flocks before southern Scots and English shepherds, the Cheviot came up the old cattle roads and crags to feed on the cotton grass and the alpine plants. They poured into glens and towns and villages like a bleating white river. To the landowners, armies of agents now offered previously unheard of rents. The only thing standing in the way of this tide of modernisation was the people.

The Napoleonic Wars, coinciding with the advent of the factory system and the new English industries of the early nineteenth century, brought the demand for wool to a crescendo. Public land was enclosed, fences appearing where none had existed before.

Unlike in some European countries, such as Switzerland, the rights of peasant tenants in the Highlands were not guaranteed. Even in England, the agricultural labouring classes had some hold on their tenure. Not so in Scotland. Families that had lived and died on the same plots were now handed eviction notices and ordered to leave. Many still spoke only the Gaelic and as they gathered as a village to listen to what these strangers from the south—the agents, the factors and the sheriffs—read to them, they could not understand a word of it. When they finally did, they could not believe what they were hearing.

Peacefully at first, the bewildered Highlanders accepted their lot with resignation. They were given the chance to dismantle their ancient wooden homes piece by piece and transport them to one of the new plots promised to them in a different part of their lord's estate. These were usually on the wild coast or in the Western Isles, where they would now be forced to learn new ways of life as herring fishers or kelp harvesters—trades about which they knew absolutely nothing. Better still, they were told, a berth was always ready for them on one of the emigrant ships waiting in Greenock to take them to far-away America, Canada or, later, Australia. Many of the landowners were so keen to be rid of their people that they paid their fares, up front, no questions asked.

As surely as the native inhabitants of Australia and America were dispossessed in the name of progress and industry, so too were the Highlanders of Scotland, forced out by the sheep farmer colonists, and their so-called four-footed clansman of the Highlands: the Cheviot.

In the first decades of the nineteenth century, as landowners began to taste the riches that ridding their lands of people and converting them to sheep pastures could bring, the Clearances accelerated both in scope and bitterness. Land that had been worth pennies per acre to the gentry now yielded shillings and pounds. Yet the people were not leaving fast enough.

Perhaps the most brutal episodes of the Clearances took place across the vast shire of Sutherland, owned almost in its entirety by the phenomenally wealthy George Granville Leveson-Gower, Marquess of Stafford and later first Duke of Sutherland. Said to be one of the richest men of nineteenth-century Britain—exceeding in wealth the fortune of even Baron Rothschild—he dubbed himself the 'Great Improver', although almost all he owned came through his wife, Elizabeth Leveson-Gower, nineteenth Countess of Sutherland. Not that his thousands of tenants would have recognised him. It was said that in twenty years, he had visited his vast northern estates just once. His agents, sheriffs and factors, on the other hand, would soon become extremely familiar.

In the valleys of Strathnaver, entire towns and villages were cleared away like worn-out furniture. Any delay, any resistance to the evictions—even verbal protest—was taken as defiance and dealt with ruthlessly by Stafford's men, particularly the infamous Factor for the Sutherland Estates, Patrick Sellar. His name, even today, induces a shudder of loathing to people in Scotland's north.

Sellar employed teams of men to move people on with increasing brutality. Those slow to respond to the writs of removal had their houses torn down, with teams of horses being used to rip out beams and walls. Gone were the days when they were at least permitted to take their timbers with them—wood being a rare commodity in the Highlands. Then fire became the preferred tool. Entire villages of Strathnaver were set ablaze, houses lit at both ends at once, often with their inhabitants still inside. No pity was shown for age. Old women and children were ordered out or pushed into the elements, their furniture—often their only worldly possessions—smashed to pieces or going up in flames with the houses. In one such eviction, an old woman perished inside a house Sellar had set alight. It took two years for him to come to trial, only to be acquitted in minutes by a jury of fellow landowners and agents, along with a grovelling apology from the presiding magistrate.

Local ministers of God, not even remaining silent throughout their ordeal, sided almost exclusively with the landowning gentry, who promised them new manses and carriage roads leading up to their front doors. Thus bought, they turned on their own flock, threatening the more stubborn evictees with hellfire and eternal damnation for the slightest disobedience. Bleating waves of Cheviot sheep broke over the hills even before some tenants had had time to obey the eviction orders.

The evicted Highlanders were given no real compensation, offered no halfway houses, and no emergency or interim accommodation, no transport and no assistance to reconstruct their lives in whatever place it was they had been sent to. They were simply ordered to pack up, leave their crops to rot in the ground, take their few cattle and go.

The alternative coastal allotments generously provided by the Duke and Duchess to their ejected and homeless tenants were so miserable and so inadequate that, in many instances, it was all but impossible to eke out an existence. Rocky stretches of worthless moor and bog, whipped endlessly by the winds and waves rolling in from the Arctic. Unused to seas and tides, many were drowned or swept out to sea attempting to learn such alien activities as salt-making. The soil was, for the most part, thin and unproductive. Crops were attempted, but seeds that were not blown away on the wind sprouted weak green shoots that were killed by salt and mildew. People who had, over generations, established sustainable patterns of harvest on their modest plots now simply had to rely on what was provided by the merciless sea. In a sense, it did not matter where they had been sent:

> Once expelled from the glen they had occupied for generations, it was of small consequence to them whether they travelled ten miles or four thousand. The loss was the same, the pain as great.[2]

One Highlander remembering his home before the time of the Clearances described being able to see the next village not more than three-quarters of a mile away from his own, with the next one the same distance beyond that. Now, four shepherds, their dogs and 3000 sheep occupied land that had once supported five townships.[3]

There were indeed improvements in the Highlands, but as one local observer, and one of the few local and articulate critics of the

Clearances, Donald MacLeod, observed in a series of letters written to Edinburgh newspapers:

> Roads, bridges, inns and manses to be sure, for the accommodation of the new gentlemen, tenantry and clergy, but those who spoke the Gaelic tongue were a proscribed race, and everything was done to get rid of them, by driving them into the forlorn hope of deriving subsistence from the sea while squatting on their miserable allotments where, in their wretched hovels, they lingered out an almost hopeless existence.[4]

There was some mobbing and deforcing of sheriff officers, and riots occasionally erupted at places like Strath Oykel and Gruids, but such resistance was quickly and ruthlessly put down in the courts. Soon, it petered out into resignation and despair:

> The old weaknesses of the Highlanders had ended it—their lack of leadership, their childish faith in the laird, who must surely now change his mind, and, most insidious of all, their melancholy belief that they had been a doomed race since Culloden. Their comfort came in the stirring sadness of their own destruction.[5]

In the midst of the various waves of cruelty, there were one or two who resisted the tide. The Chisholm Clan, who had held the green and dark valleys of the Upper Valley of the River Beauly near Loch Ness for generations, were well used to standing by their beliefs before the fury of authority. Remaining defiantly Roman Catholic since the Scottish Reformation of 1560, they continued to hide Catholic priests on their estate, even allowing them to preach the old faith to their wary congregations in secret locations.

In the face of pressure to turn his rich lands over to sheep at the expense of his people, Alexander Chisholm, the ageing twenty-third chief, resisted. Folklore has it that his only daughter, Mary, burst into the room where an all-night meeting was taking place between her father and a delegation of pleading sheep farmers, hurling abuse at them. She was ordered out of the room, but instead tipped off the servants who alerted the surrounding villagers. When morning came, it is said that a thousand people had gathered outside Alexander's door, begging him to protect them, telling him that these sheep men were worse than any enemy who had ever come to Strathglass with a broadsword in their hand. The southerners read the wind and made their escape up the glen. Looking back, they reported the old man being carried on the shoulders of his people as their saviour.

When Alexander died, his widow Elizabeth and daughter Mary continued their resistance to the Clearances, fiercely holding onto their tenants until William, the twenty-fourth Chisholm, and half-brother of Alexander, began the total dispersal of the clan. Now a married woman in London, Mary could do nothing and, broken-hearted, turned her back on the cause forever.

As if compensating in cruelty for his half-brother's mercy, William Chisholm began one of the most thorough Clearances of all. In the case of Strathglass, not even an alternative plot on the coast was offered to the exiled tenants, who were burned out of their homes. Their only alternative was an emigrant ship to Canada. By 1812, 10,000 Chisholm clansmen and women had been exiled to the New World, with but a single solitary tenant, an ageing farmer, remaining on the once populous estate.

Although it is impossible to be exact, it is estimated that between half and two-thirds of the population of the Scottish Highlands was dispersed by the Clearances in the first 30 years of the nineteenth century. Now half a million sheep grazed the otherwise empty glens, wandering across the ruins of myriad houses, nibbling at the occasional potato shoot that still managed to appear in what had been a garden patch that had once sustained several families, wandering through the ruins of kitchens, climbing over the broken stone walls and hearths of former homes.

With awful irony, the Highlands now became something of a tourist playground. English visitors began to arrive, invigorated by the area's magnificent walks and clean country air, now accessible with excellent new roads, bridges and inns. Deer and grouse shooting parties—which hunted for amusement the same game upon which others had relied for sustenance—began to pour into the area, happy to fork out the handsome fees the estate owners charged for the privilege. Highland culture even underwent something of a revival. The tartan and the Tam O'Shanter began to be sported by the young and fashionable of Edinburgh and London. The works of Sir Walter Scott and Robert Burns began a romanticisation of the Highlander that persists to this day. Of the Highlanders themselves, however, there was no sign whatsoever—save for a few wandering vagrants—and only piles of scorched stones to indicate they had ever been there at all.

Clinging to their thin allotments along the coast and the islands, many dispersed Highlanders scratched out a bleak existence, but the herring fishers found that the fish were unreliable—sometimes disappearing for a year or so before inexplicably returning—and storms along the wild west coast smashed boats and split apart nets. Many worked in the kelp industry, but when the Napoleonic Wars brought an end to tariffs on cheaper Spanish kelp, the Highland market collapsed.

Then, to pile further woe on misery, in the summer of 1846, clouds of white spores began to be carried across the Highlands by wind, man and beast after a tumultuous year of severe drought followed by savage storms and floods. This fine white powder settled on everything that grew. Almost overnight, the potato plants began to blacken, their leaves turning to slime. When opened, the tubers in the earth were found to be black and rotten, and smelt of death. The blight had arrived.

Although never as severe or as prolonged as the Great Famine that had broken the previous year and continued to rage across Ireland, the Highland famine put 200,000 people at risk of starvation. The potato had only been introduced to the Highlands and islands a century before, but, particularly after the Clearances, it was found to be one of the few crops that could be relied upon in the doubtful soils along the coast. By the 1840s, one half of the entire Scottish population lived on the potato for nine months of the year, while in the Highlands, it was estimated to be two-thirds.

The blight wreaked its havoc with astonishing speed. Entire fields which were healthy on a Friday were black and rotten by Sunday. By the summer, it was evident that the entire Highland potato crop had failed.

While the death rate across the Highlands increased threefold—primarily from malnutrition and associated illnesses—the massive level of mortality seen in Ireland was avoided. As had happened there, however, the sanctity of commerce remained inviolable, and even in the face of starvation, ships departed Scottish ports weighed down to the waterline with Scottish foodstuffs such as oatmeal to honour contracts signed in England and further abroad. Soon, vessels in harbours required naval protection from rioters on the docks.

A government relief fund of sorts was established whereby recipients were required to work hard on government projects—such as road building—in order to receive any support at all. The terms were harsh. If only one member of a family of any size was deemed to be working, the rest were ineligible for any relief whatever. By 1850, however, the relief had all but run out, while the blight in some areas persisted. It was the final straw for the Highlanders. For thousands, there was now no alternative but to emigrate.

With the blight eradicating any hope that the Scottish islands might become self-sufficient, the Skye Emigration Society was formed in 1851 to deal with the humanitarian crisis unfolding there. It soon evolved to include the entire Highlands as the Highland and Island Emigration Society, with its aims being

to procure help for those who wish to emigrate but have not the means of doing so, to afford information, encouragement and assistance to all whom emigration would be a relief from want and misery.[6]

And so began the mass exodus of the Highland Scots to all parts of the world, particularly Canada and Australia, answering the calls from the labour-starved colonies. There, they were assured, they were both wanted and needed. For many Scots travelling to Australia, the irony was not lost on them: sheep had forced them out of their old homes, and it was sheep that were now luring them to the new. Since 1845, in Ross and in the Isles, the Great Cheviot Sheep had been making sure that its cousins in Australia would not want for drovers.[7]

Over the next decade, an estimated 16,000 Highlanders finally decided that, after exile and famine, their best and only hope lay on the far side of the world.

II

Life at sea

The humid conditions on board the *Ticonderoga* continued during the first few days of sailing, during which the passengers had their first experience of weather at sea—and it was not pleasant. Soon after departing, a sudden squall had burst overhead in a thick summer downpour. Torrents of rain lashed the ship and the sea stirred in white-capped fury. Confined below for the first time, the passengers heard the main hatches leading up to the open deck being noisily battened down and the ventilation mechanism that had managed to supply at least some fresh air was disengaged. The sea erupted further as the *Ticonderoga* reached the open water, beyond the protective lee of the southern tip of Ireland. Huddling in the lower decks, many passengers could scarcely believe that a ship of this size could be tossed so violently, like a toy boat on a river being tumbled in an eddy. Suddenly, the great ship's more than 1000 tons—which had felt solid and comforting—counted for nothing.

Then, for the hundreds on board, the ordeal of seasickness began. It is safe to assume that almost none of the passengers had experienced a voyage of any length, with the overwhelming majority never having been to sea in their lives. Now, suddenly, they were subjected to the fierce waters of the Atlantic on the longest journey in the world in conditions any present-day traveller would find utterly unbearable. As another ship's surgeon, a Dr Skirving, observed on board a similar emigrant vessel:

> Unused to the sea, seasick, homesick, cold, wet, fearful and battened down, few aggregations of human wretchedness could be much greater than was to be found . . . in the close dark 'tween decks of an outward-bound emigrant ship.[1]

The unfamiliar and debilitating bouts of nausea were bad enough, but in those first few days, the realisation dawned that it was in these few pitiful square feet of space that the indignities of illness as well as the myriad other aspects of ship life were to be endured. Married couples were allotted the berth's top bunk, measuring 6 feet long and 3 feet wide, permitting just 18 inches per person. The same dimensions were given to single women, who were likewise expected to share a bunk, with only the single men—who slept alone—given slightly more room, their bunks measuring 6 × 2 feet. Children occupied the lower bunks in the married quarters, and as two children under fourteen years constituted a single 'statute adult', they were expected to arrange themselves in any cramped and uncomfortable manner they could. There was no advantage to be had for married couples without children either, as their bottom bunk would be occupied by another couple, or even another couple's children.

In all cases, the space between the bed boards of the top and bottom bunks was a claustrophobic 18 inches, slightly less with bedclothes, meaning that virtually any raising of the head was impossible. To the side, considerably less than an arm's length away, was the neighbouring bunk, with the only privacy being provided by a flimsy board 23 inches in height, and affording no real modesty whatever. It was into these coffin-like dimensions that the *Ticonderoga*'s passengers were confined every night, or when rough weather arose. Then, as with that first storm just hours after leaving Birkenhead, the porous nature of a wooden sailing ship was revealed. On that occasion, as well as many more to come over the next twelve weeks, sea water would regularly seep, drip and occasionally gush in torrents into the passengers' living areas. Even on calm days, a wave or current could spring up unexpectedly and cascade in terrifying torrents down one of the open main hatches, making a river of the main and lower decks and soaking everything from clothing and foodstuffs to the bedding, whose straw interior quickly rotted and stank.

The *Ticonderoga*'s flushing water closets were indeed innovative, but at night or during a storm, they were difficult if not impossible to access, particularly for women in the voluminous skirts of the day who had to contemplate often two sets of ladders in virtual darkness. Instead, utensils of any kind were used to catch urine and other waste, and these often spilled with the movement of the ship. The smell of human beings permeated the whole ship. Sweaty clothes could only be washed sporadically, and then only in seawater tanks on the upper deck, fresh water being strictly reserved for drinking and cooking. Whale oil lamps in their braces nailed to the walls gave off at least some little light, but exuded a particular pungency of their own. Added to this was the stench of the rats—impossible to eradicate even in the newest vessels—as well as the cats assigned to catch them and their many associated stinks. Then there were the babies. Dozens upon dozens of vomiting, nappy-filling infants and toddlers crawled and cried all over the *Ticonderoga*. Their numbers in fact would be added to during the voyage, as pregnant women who had boarded at Birkenhead contributed no less than nineteen births at sea. It was said that the *Ticonderoga*'s crew, upon opening the hatches every morning, reeled back at the revolting miasma rising up from the decks below.[2] Later in the voyage, when the ravages of disease took hold of the ship, the stench would defy description.

Initially, though, as the *Ticonderoga* tracked far out into the Atlantic, a shipboard routine of sorts began to develop, with perhaps the greatest initial shock for people accustomed to the quietness of small village life being the sudden avalanche of noise on board a large and crowded sailing ship. The hundreds of voices of the passengers—talking, arguing, breaking wind, vomiting, copulating, snoring, all in alarmingly close proximity; the constant shouts and swearing of the crew and the officers; the babel of children yelling, playing, crying; then the array of sounds emanating from the ship itself. As soon as the *Ticonderoga* left the heads of the River Mersey, her timbers began their endless heaving, whining chorus as she began to be pulled and twisted by the elements. Even the clawing hiss of the sea seemed to be conducted upwards through every board and every beam, amplified in the limited confines of the 'tween decks. In a storm, the noise would come crashing from above in terrifying bouts, as if the ocean itself—like a monster at the door—was attempting to batter its way in. Then there was the continual jangling of chains, sails and rigging; the thumping of feet on the decks above; the wind playing its perpetual symphony through the rigging. It all combined to make the *Ticonderoga*'s aural landscape a blaring, multi-layered cacophony.

The one sound that governed the rhythm of people's lives on board, however, rang out from the ship's bell. Like the regulator on a gigantic clock, it was this brass voice that spoke the routine of life on the long journey. The bell sounded for the passengers to rise at 7 a.m., then at the other end of the day, at 10 p.m., to go to bed. It began the ship's day, not at midnight but at midday ceremony, as the captain and mate lowered their sextants at the sun's zenith and Boyle uttered, 'Make it noon, first mate', and then the response 'Ay ay Captain', as the bell was struck two times in quick succession. Then, the timeglass was turned for the sand to run exactly 30 minutes, at which point the bell would be struck once to sound the half hour, and the glass turned again. So this would continue, day and night, throughout the life of the voyage.

The bell also signalled religious services (of which there were many of various denominations), heralded announcements of news or decrees from the captain or the stewards, and alerted people to go below in the face of impending weather. Most of all, it drove the pulse of shipboard life: the daily meals, around which all other activities revolved.

Captain Patey and his officials at the depot had taken considerable care in appointing from the *Ticonderoga*'s passengers the important roles of stewards and constables, who would manage various necessary tasks, such as the messing and meal arrangements, conducting educational lessons, and to assist the ship's surgeons in maintaining levels of hygiene and cleanliness—a concept quite alien to some (and which, in the *Ticonderoga*'s case, would eventually prove impossible anyway). Nurses were likewise appointed to work in the two hospitals, particularly those whose written form demonstrated some prior medical or nursing experience. Among these were John and Mary Fanning, Presbyterians from County Coleraine near Londonderry in Ireland, travelling with their daughters, Mary and Catherine, and son, Patrick. Mary was listed as a midwife, a respected position in Irish society, and one of only two female professions to be listed in church records, the other being 'nun'.[3] Mary was thus asked to work as a nurse in the women's hospital while John was requested for the men's. Both readily accepted. The other skill of the Fannings was their knowledge of the Scots-Irish dialect, closely related to the Gael of the Highland Scots themselves.

Recalling the voyage to a newspaper reporter in 1917, passenger Christopher McRae from Inverness, who travelled as a teenager with his family, wrote:

> To carry out established rules and conditions imposed by the Captain and the Doctors, men suitable were elected to act as constables or stewards—the names of two of them I still remember—one being Andrew Dempster, a single man. The other—a young married man named Douglas Rankin. There were many others.[4]

Galley assistants had also been appointed to help the cooks, along with attendants for both the male and the female hospitals. Then there was the important role of ship's schoolmaster, who would provide daily lessons for the numerous children—and some of the adults—on board. This fell to 46-year-old Charles McKay who, as a professional teacher and a graduate of Aberdeen University, was one of the most educated of the *Ticonderoga*'s passengers, and who also happened to be fluent in the Highland tongue, Gaelic.[5] Christopher McRae believed him to be one of the most important figures on board the ship.

Far from being a destitute Highlander, McKay was travelling to Melbourne to take up the role of Vice Principal of the newly established boys' school, Scotch College, and boarded the *Ticonderoga* with his wife Margaret and five children, the youngest aged two. According to his grandson, Frank McKay, it had not been an easy decision and in a brief history of the family, he describes 'the many heart searchings before Charles McKay made the big decision to take his family to Australia and start a new life in a new world'.[6]

The shipboard lessons over which McKay presided were usually rudimentary in nature, offering basic instruction in English, reading, writing and simple arithmetic. For some of the children, however, these were of a higher standard than anything they had experienced at home, and for others it was their first taste of schooling altogether. A fair proportion of the adults, many of whom could neither read nor write themselves, likewise took advantage of McKay's instruction, picking up vital skills such as the writing of their own name, as opposed to the leaving of just a simple mark. Also listed as a sexton of a Presbyterian church—that is, one who has responsibility for the grounds and graveyard—McKay 'would minister to the spiritual needs of the Highland passengers by conducting services in Gaelic. This he did throughout the voyage, as well as after landing on the station'.[7]

At the rear of the ship were the single women's quarters, presided over by another of Patey's appointments, the single women's matron. According to the descendants of passenger Janet McLellan, the *Ticonderoga*'s matron was 38-year-old Miss Isabella Renshaw. It was into Miss Renshaw's care that the precious key to the single women's quarters was entrusted, which she used on a nightly basis to lock the girls in, preventing any illicit after-hours liaisons forming between them and the single men, or the crew. In the morning, they would begin their lessons in reading, arithmetic and Bible studies. Miss Renshaw was usually assisted by some of the abler and better educated girls, such as Annie Morrison from the Isle of Mull. Needlework and shirt-making were also taught, with the girls being able to keep the garments they made on the voyage.

Free time was allowed, and the sexes could in fact mix, but only on the open upper deck under the matron's supervisory gaze. An obsession with women's perceived 'virtue', particularly among groups of young and unattached females, was a feature of Victorian society, so it was replicated at sea. More than any other group on board the ship, all aspects of the young women's behaviour, appearance and demeanour were constantly assessed and judged by passengers and crew alike, with 'wantonness' suspected as the motive behind many of their actions.

One of those girls who would have been under observation was 22-year-old Janet Blair, a Presbyterian from Argyllshire whose clan, fiercely independent Protestant Covenanters, had been all but wiped out in the 'Killing Time' of the religious wars with England in the late seventeenth century. Thanks to a detailed account penned by her granddaughter late in her life, Janet Blair's personal story survives.

The eighth of fifteen children, ten of whom survived, Janet grew up on a farm of 320 acres on Loch Fyne in Scotland's west. When she was fifteen, 'the fever' took her father and two more of her siblings, at which point her older brother gave up the farm and moved with the rest of the family to Glasgow, where Janet became a housemaid to a wealthy family of gentlemen farmers from Argyllshire, the McPhersons. One of their three sons, Dugald, had become a successful sheep farmer in Australia and, impressed with the girl, Mrs McPherson began to encourage her to travel there herself to become Dugald's housemaid. Wages and conditions for a girl such as she, reminded Mrs McPherson, were far better than she could ever hope to receive at home. As Dugald was unmarried, Janet declined. Her enthusiasm to travel was sparked, though, and she even managed to convince a brother, a brother-in-law and two of her sisters to make the journey with her. At the last minute, they all backed out. Undeterred, Janet continued alone, and at Glasgow was seen off on the ferry in a tearful farewell by several members of her family.

At Birkenhead, she joined many other single girls likewise seeking a new and better life, and on 28 July was one of the first to board the *Ticonderoga*, several days before she sailed, bringing along her prized possession, a fine three-door oak trunk with 'Janet Blair' painted in elegant lettering on the outside. She even brought her own cutlery, and—quite contrary to the regulations—a blanket and pillowslip, together with as much warm clothing as she could carry. The journey, she had been told, would involve heading into some cold and icy weather to the south. Just how icy would only become apparent in the weeks to come. Although travelling alone, Janet was soon to make a firm friend of Georgina McLatchie, listed as 'Baptist', 25, from Edinburgh. As the voyage began, the two young women could have no idea of just how much each would come to rely on the support of the other.

Although many of the appointed steward positions were officially voluntary, a small gratuity was nevertheless usually forthcoming. It is not known what the *Ticonderoga*'s coffers offered, but a similar voyage taken a few years later on the emigrant vessel *Atalanta*, the schoolmaster and the matron were each paid £5, as were the galley assistants.

Perhaps the most important decision made about the *Ticonderoga*'s nearly 800 passengers was their arrangement into the 125 or so 'messes' of around six people each, in whose company they would share the experiences and travails of the voyage. An initial division had taken place onshore while still at the depot, but the process was refined during the first few days at sea by the stewards in consultation with the surgeons and the captain. Where possible, the bunks of the respective members of each mess were situated close by one another, as was their allotted 'desk', a 5-feet-wide oak table with raised edges to prevent plates and other utensils falling to the floor with the roll of the ship.[8] Space being what it was, several messes would in fact share the one desk, but it was within one's mess that the passengers tended to mix, 'as though each mess formed its own little village on board', according to historian Mary Kruithof.[9]

The object of the messing system was to encourage shipboard harmony; hence people of the same town, village or county were, where possible, placed together. Particular care was also taken to avoid potential flashpoints arising from those eternal sources of discord, religion and politics. The long voyage would provide more than enough idle hours for arguments to fester and ideologies to erupt, and religion—ever a sore point throughout Europe—was particularly inflammatory in the context of Scotland and its recent brutal history with England. With an emigrant's region and religion both stated on their form, those from opposing faiths, or people who had been observed to clash or squabble at the depot, were berthed as far from each other as possible. However, some may have been closer to their fellow passengers than they thought, travelling alongside distant members of their own large, clan-based families. There were, for example, three families each carrying the names Campbell, Herd, McKay and McPherson, four Camerons and no less than five separate families named McDonald. The names Bruce, Fraser, Morrison and several others were also represented multiple times among the *Ticonderoga*'s passenger list.

Indeed, genuine bonds and friendships—even romances—did form on the journey, to eventually form part of the emigrants' new life in Australia. There are at least two recorded cases of marriage between passengers, even though one of those—between a Cameron and a McRae—occurred much later in their lives, as the two were only young children at the time of the journey.

Much of the bonding between passengers inevitably occurred at mealtimes. Twice a day, in an exercise of mutual cooperation, the provisions for each meal were carefully doled out from the ship's stores by the stewards and the ship's third mate, who between them decided the daily menu, which in fact varied hardly at all. The ingredients were taken to the desk in a baking dish or lidded pot, where the 'mess captain'—elected by the members of the mess but rotated somewhat—was responsible for bringing them to the galley to be prepared by the ship's cooks as well as the passengers themselves. A chit would be received and, when ready, the cooks bawled out the number, and the meal was collected and then doled out to the mess on the tin plates and cups each person had been issued, and for which they were responsible.

The 'menu' varied only slightly from day to day and can hardly be described as exciting, or even particularly nutritious in the modern sense, but given the restrictions of the era prior to the advent of refrigeration, it was at least sustaining. Most main meals, taken in sittings from mid-afternoon, consisted of salted pork or beef (which would be all but inedible to a contemporary palate), supplemented by a pudding of suet (animal fat), flour and raisins. Other meat was dried and reconstituted into a sort of stew, as were some other starchy foods such as rice and potatoes.

Sailing to Melbourne from England at exactly the same time as the *Ticonderoga* in a smaller vessel, the *Emily*, Frenchman Antoine Fauchery, who would later set up a world-famous photographic studio in Melbourne, remembered the monotony of the shipboard meals somewhat sardonically:

> Each week our provisions allow us, and more than allow us, to have three or four meals a day if we see fit. In the morning, salted beef with dried potatoes; at noon, salt pork with rice; at two o'clock, dried potatoes with salted beef; at four, rice with salt pork. –Lord bless you, if we wanted it, we could at eight o'clock have both salted beef with potatoes and salt pork with rice![10]

There were no fresh vegetables and, being a government-assisted ship, the luxury of live animals carried for fresh meat was not forthcoming. Even a henhouse for fresh eggs—a not uncommon practice for ships of the time—seems to have been absent from the *Ticonderoga*'s inventory of provisions. Unlike on private-paying vessels, alcohol—except for medicinal purposes—was prohibited, with any liquor in a passenger's personal possession having to be surrendered upon coming aboard. The lack of fresh potatoes in particular was found by many of the Scots, as well as the handful of Irish, to be particularly irksome, forming as they did the starchy, bulky staple of their diet. In a later British parliamentary inquiry into many aspects of the 'double deck' voyages to Victoria, the difficulty of some passengers in coping with the lack of potatoes was specifically addressed:

> The potato has a small quantity of nutritive matter in a large bulk, and consequently extends the stomach largely; and those who have been accustomed to it, when they are put on a more nutritive and concentrated food, felt a sensation of sinking and emptiness. They attempt to remedy that by taking a larger quantity of food, which they cannot digest, and that immediately produces disease (sickness and diarrhoea).[11]

The greatest fault in the *Ticonderoga*'s meal system, however, was the complete lack of provision of food for the many infants, who were expected to be sustained solely by their breastfeeding mothers. This would have dire consequences throughout the voyage, not only with some babies wasting away due to the effects of malnourishment—or marasmus, as it was called—but also later, when many of the adults could barely sustain themselves.

After the meals, the routines established in the depot were resumed, with the women clearing and cleaning the utensils and the men sweeping the decks and dry hollow-stoning the desks. No fresh water was permitted for washing of any kind, so plates and eating utensils were covered with a permanent film of salt. Clothes, too, could only be washed on specified days in seawater tubs on the upper deck, unless supplemented by rainwater occasionally captured in specially erected awnings. Marine soap, made from palm or coconut oil and soluble in seawater, was issued; although today it would be barely recognisable as soap of any description, it was for many of the *Ticonderoga*'s passengers their first experience of it, due to it being heavily taxed as a luxury item. The daily discomfort of living for weeks in such clothes—itchy and salt-encrusted—is another aspect of conditions of the voyage that modern sensibilities would struggle to comprehend.

The single men in particular were kept busy on the ship, being allotted an array of tasks such as pumping seawater up to the flushing tanks above the water closet, sweeping decks and ladders daily, and keeping the ship's hospitals in good order. Several times a week, those rostered would venture through the lower decks, sprinkling and scraping away absorbent hot sand on the walkways and under the passengers' bunks. The young women, however, were required to clean out their own quarters.

Some men were even permitted to assist the crew in the running of the ship. This was a task many came to relish, eager to be intro-duced to the complex world of sail, delighting in the learning of nautical terms and the names given to the myriad knots, spars and sails: topgallants, royals, spankers and so on. What the ship's crew made of having to teach such a group of novices can only be guessed at and, inexperienced as they were, the danger of accidents was real. On the voyage of the *Hornet* from Southampton to Victoria in 1857, a male passenger had his hand crushed in a block while helping the crew to pull ropes. The ship's surgeon, a Dr Brownfield, was required to amputate two fingers and sew the skin back over the stumps, his patient's only relief from the pain being a large dose of brandy administered from the surgeon's medicine chest.[12]

At least at the beginning of the voyage, and if not riddled with seasickness or weighed down with children, for some the romance of the journey was still novel, and provided the passengers with experiences utterly removed from their lives hitherto and that they would remember forever. Despite the lessons, routines and other activities, there were many hours of free time on board the ship, which were theirs to pass as they pleased: long conversations with people with whom they would never otherwise have crossed paths; watching the undreamed-of sights of dolphins, porpoises, flying fish and the myriad seabirds following the slow pace of the ship. Then there was the ever-changing texture of sea and sky. On some afternoons and evenings, the sounds of fiddles and pipes resonated throughout the ship as the Scots lasses instructed some of the other girls in the art of Highland dancing. At other times, the girls would sing the plangent tunes of their home, which would quickly be picked up by the rest of the passengers, transforming the ship into a floating and melancholy chorus.

Then, night by night, as the *Ticonderoga* edged slowly south, the passengers could come out onto the upper deck and find a quiet spot to observe the heavens, watching those northern constellations with which they had been familiar for their entire lives gradually dip ever lower on the horizon, before finally disappearing forever.

12

Death at sea

Due to the low rates of literacy on board the *Ticonderoga*, as well as the lack of light in the accommodation decks—not to mention the disaster which overtook her on the second half of the voyage—no passenger diaries from the trip have survived, if indeed they were ever written in the first place. More strangely, nor have any detailed first-hand accounts compiled in the aftermath come to light. There are, however, a number of fragments—usually written long afterwards—that paint a picture of the *Ticonderoga*'s journey south.

Several of these make mention of one macabre incident early in the voyage, as word went around the ship one evening that a female passenger had thrown herself overboard. No further details could be gleaned, but a pall of horror was felt by all those on board. It was not until 1932 in an article in Melbourne's *The Argus* newspaper that some explanation of the incident was offered by one of the survivors of the voyage, Mrs Ellen Bentley. The woman in question had apparently recently eloped with her father's footman, a decision she soon regretted. 'Repentance came early,' recounted Mrs Bentley. Observed to be in 'deep distress' early in the voyage, the woman became more and more consumed with remorse until 'a leap overboard ended her suffering'.

Just eight days out of Liverpool, the first infant died—not of disease, but marasmus, a wasting condition brought on by lack of nutrients, especially protein. Little Samuel Ritchie was the youngest child of James and Mary Ritchie of Inverness. The news was not greeted as anything out of the ordinary: infants died routinely in the mid-nineteenth century of marasmus and many other ailments, and death rates at sea among the very young were particularly high. It was a requirement at sea that adults be buried during daylight hours to provide the proper decorum of prayers and service, but children could be given to the deep quickly, quietly and at night. The farewelling of the *Ticonderoga*'s first victim was nevertheless a solemn occasion, presided over by Captain Boyle reading the appropriate passages from the Bible and ship's order of service, standing beside the grieving Ritchie family as the pathetic white package wrapped in a patch of sailcloth was sent to the deep, weighed down with a small ship's iron from the carpenter's shop. For the Ritchies, as for many other families, the funeral of little Samuel would be only the first.

The high toll of babies and infants on board the *Ticonderoga* is not difficult to account for. The effect of the harsh and unfamiliar ship's diet on already weakened and under-nourished people began to take its toll, particularly in combination with the added debilitating effects of seasickness. Women, then as now, have a greater predisposition to motion sickness in general,[1] and on board the *Ticonderoga,* breastfeeding mothers were most vulnerable. For days or even weeks, they could be laid up, exhausted and incapacitated, barely able to look after themselves, let alone their suckling infants. With no special provisions for infants, feeding them the ship's diet could often make them sicker, so it was unsurprising that more babies and infants on board would waste away.

Just two days later, another child, Eliza Gardiner, four, likewise died of malnutrition, which again was regarded as standard. Then a bout of diarrhoea began to take hold, first in the single men's quarters but spreading throughout the ship. Many people simply could not adjust to the diet, and suffered accordingly. Christopher McRae caught it early and, in his words, 'suffered most of the time'.[2]

Then, around 20 August, Anna Maria Hando, sixteen years old and travelling with her parents, though residing in the single girls' quarters due to her age, came down with a high temperature and severe rash that covered her entire body. The Handos were one of several English families travelling from Somerset, a rural part of England that produced exactly the sort of skilled agricultural worker so sorely needed in Australia. William Hando, 44, was listed as a Church of England farm labourer from the village of Hutton near the seaside town of Weston-Super-Mare. Somewhat older than many of the passengers making the voyage, his skills were such that he and his family were accepted nonetheless, and both he and his wife Maria, 44, saw this as a God-given opportunity to begin a new life in the far-away, and quite unimaginable, colony of Victoria. Their family of seven was large, but by no means exceptionally so for the times. Their eldest son, Charles, also travelled apart from the rest of his family in the single male quarters in the bow, while William and Maria looked after Henry, ten, George, seven, and the youngest, Emma, aged four. The terrible condition being suffered by Anna Maria was recorded by Dr Sanger non-specifically as 'fever'. This was not unusual. As Major J.H. Welch points out in his history of the quarantine station where the *Ticonderoga* would spend the final chapter of her journey to Victoria, 'in 1852, there was no knowledge of the cause of any disease which was characterised by fever'.[3] Indeed, the symbiotic nature of fevers and rashes had been long observed, but their relationship was barely understood. They were seen to act upon the body simultaneously, as were the radical physical changes they implemented in what was often an alarmingly short time.

Such conditions were known by many names: ship fever, prison fever, camp fever, spotted fever, Brill's disease and others. Although the cause was a mystery, they were nevertheless observed to be in a terrible partnership with high fever, which itself changed and morphed in nature. It is likely that several different illnesses impacted the passengers on board the ship in the early stages—all of which Dr Sanger listed as fever, and the precise nature of which it is now impossible to determine. Later in the voyage, as a new and terrible strain took hold of more and more passengers, an equally terrible word would be settled on to describe it.

Over a few heart-wrenching days, young Anna Maria's condition deteriorated, her rash deepened, her joints and internal organs ached in agony and, as her fever raged, delirium set in. Drs Sanger and Veitch looked on, did what they could to cool and calm the girl, supplied her with comforting sips of wine, arrowroot and other accepted tonics and remedies of the day, but could do nothing to save her. After three days, she lay still. The funeral of Anna Maria Hando, the *Ticonderoga*'s third and oldest victim so far, signalled a terrible turning point on board the ship. In *Fever Beach* Mary Kruithof describes the poignant scene as the members of the Hando family, heartbroken and in shock, watch their beloved girl, taken on the cusp of life, descending to the deep:

> Passengers from the married quarters, single women and some crew gathered on the upper deck for the funeral. Anna Maria's shrouded and weighted body was placed on a wooden board which was carried to the upper deck and placed with one end slightly tipped over the side of the ship. With the ship's bell tolling during the service, the Captain and Mr McKay read the burial service together. On the words, 'We therefore commit her body to the sea', the board was tilted, tipping the body into the water. The ship sailed on. A terrible loneliness swept over the mourners and a sad company filed back down into their quarters below.[4]

For the Handos, like many other families, it would not be the last time they grieved.

13

A lonely encounter

As the *Ticonderoga* headed towards the equator, the weather and the ship began to heat up, which was another shock to those on board. Even the hottest day of the hottest British summer was nothing compared with this delirious, enervating onslaught that arrived with the dawn of each day, relieved only by the regular evening thunderstorm that caused the hatches to be battened down and water to once again leak profusely into the main and lower decks. The sea was at least mercifully calm, and as people gradually began to acclimatise to the motion, the incidence of seasickness dropped. But as the winds slackened around this part of the equator known to timeless seafarers as 'the doldrums', the ship's progress slowed and the risk of being becalmed—sometimes for weeks—was real.

Captain Boyle seems to have avoided the worst of the doldrums, but nonetheless put up every possible piece of canvas he could manage to catch what breeze was offered. Poring over the charts, however, he began to have concerns about his ship's progress. So far, there had been only a handful of deaths on board, and all the victims were young. In the Age of Sail, a fatality rate such as this was nothing out of the ordinary, and compared with some other voyages, it was even considered mild. Doctors Sanger and Veitch now began to elaborate somewhat on their earlier general diagnosis of 'fever' and reported that 'scarlatina'—or scarlet fever, as it was later to be known—was presenting in some young patients. This was a bacterial infection particularly prevalent in children and infants, especially those of fair skin—which in the Scottish Highlands was virtually everyone.

Though it was not yet an epidemic, more cases of scarlatina began to take hold. Parents could only look on helplessly as their infected children were racked by the terrible symptoms: crushing headache, sore throat, vomiting. Then the spreading of the tell-tale bright pink rash, first on the tongue, then across their creamy white cheeks and finally covering their entire bodies as their temperature soared to over 100°F. Associated infections of the middle ear and tonsils would break out, adding to the child's terror and misery. The doctors did their best to cool the burning, and though some did survive the few days over which the disease ran its course, it was the soaring temperature that carried the children away in those days before antibiotics.

Boyle began to sense that his ship, carrying more people—many of them children—on a long voyage such as this, was in fact dangerously overcrowded. For this floating twin-deck experiment to arrive at its destination without disaster, a good deal of luck would be required.

On these hot nights, the regulations were sometimes relaxed and some passengers stayed up on the upper deck under the stars, relieved to be free of the stultifying chamber of the lower quarters. Sometimes the Highland country dancing of the girls would be allowed to relocate to the open deck, creating something of a carnival atmosphere. Paying passenger vessels were usually accompanied by small bands of musicians—hired German bands being particularly popular—but those in the *Ticonderoga*'s single steerage class would have to make do with their own. There seem to have been a good number of fiddle and pipe players present to provide the tunes so beloved of the passengers from the towns, glens and villages. Above them, the canvas sails wafted—at times unconvincingly—watched always by the anxious eyes of the captain and crew, who willed the stronger breezes to come on. Boyle continually put up new combinations of sail, ordering this or the other rope to be pulled and that sheet furled or reefed, and the *Ticonderoga*, built to capture even the most insipid of winds, sailed on.

* * * *

Late on the morning of 4 September, after exactly a month at sea and as the ship's bow cut her way south, a cry went up from one of the crew, 'Sail!' Nothing on a long ocean voyage created so much excitement as the sight of another ship on the high seas. Instantly the word went around like an electric charge. A stampede of feet rushed from everywhere to the bulwarks to catch a glimpse of this precious connection to the outside world. 'There she is!' pointed out someone as a small white cloud of full sail was spotted on the azure sea heading almost straight for them from the opposite direction off the port bow. 'Raise the board!' sounded a command, and two seamen held up a large sheet of blackened timber. On this, in chalk, had hastily been written, '*Ticonderoga*—August 4—Liverpool'. The other vessel was a far smaller ship than the *Ticonderoga*, but the sight of her warmed the hearts of everyone on board. The closing speeds of the two ships amazed those who longingly watched her pass, agonisingly close, imploring the first mate and even the captain to stop and hail her, but Boyle, himself already alert and watching with his eye glued to his long glass telescope from his position up on the forecastle, politely pointed out that sadly this would not be possible. Sometimes, the passengers had heard, passing ships did hove-to and 'speak' in an exchange of news and even mail, but whatever hopes the *Ticonderoga*'s passengers may have had for such an exchange were not to be realised this day somewhere way out in the middle of the Atlantic.

The *Lima* under Captain A. Yule was tracing the *Ticonderoga*'s passage almost in exactly the other direction,[1] travelling to England with a cargo of wool and a single solitary passenger after an extended delay in Port Melbourne. Having shipped a cargo of coal from Sydney, the *Lima* was forced to join the growing number of ships in Port Phillip Bay lying idle at anchor, abandoned by their crews who had absconded to the goldfields. She managed to set sail in late April, but the reason for her taking four months or so to reach the *Ticonderoga*'s position is unclear. Still, peering intently through his glass, Boyle tried his best to steady himself on the binnacle and focus, cursing under his breath at the rocking of the ship. 'Mark her as . . .,' he called at last to his Mate, '*Lima* . . . 130 days out'. Across the narrow stretch of water, the crew of the *Lima* had likewise raised their board, but heading north, were able to impart to the *Ticonderoga* one vital piece of information Boyle did not want to miss.

'Four days up from the Line,' he read. 'That puts us . . . where, First Mate?'

'I'd say about eight points north, Captain.'

'I concur,' said Boyle.

'She is doing well, Captain,' said the Mate.

'She is doing *very* well, first mate. Very well indeed!'

In a time-honoured tradition, the two ships had exchanged their names and estimated positions, still in this age determined by nothing but a doubtful ship's clock, the position of the sun and mental arithmetic. The *Lima*, having gradually watched the sun's zenith rise and fall, could report that it had crossed the important 'line' of the equator just a few days earlier. The news pleased Captain Boyle immensely. The *Ticonderoga* was racing down the world, making excellent time.

The passengers listened to the exchange as the *Lima* passed by then quickly vanished from view, swallowed up in the endless blue seascape. That same day, another child, four-year-old Robert Moorhead, travelling with his family of nine, died—again of scarlatina. His mother, Eliza, was beside herself at the death of her youngest, but her grief would be short-lived. Soon, she too would be joining him.

This fleeting glimpse of the *Lima* would be the *Ticonderoga*'s only contact with the rest of the world for her entire voyage. Following the Great Circle route to the bottom of the world, she would sight no other vessel until she reached Port Phillip.

On the deck, the passengers began to disperse quietly, but a number lingered, still trying to keep the *Lima* in sight even long after she had disappeared. The initial flurry of excitement was soon eclipsed by a sense of loneliness—even dread. Once more, the terrible heat of the day weighed in upon them, and people—even the women—loosened or even removed as much of their clothing as they dared. Some prayed for the relief of a cool breeze, wondering whether this heat would ever end. They need not have been concerned. Having sweltered through the tropics, the mercury would now plunge as the *Ticonderoga* continued south, and her passengers would once again be afflicted by conditions beyond their imagination—this time, in the frigid latitudes of the Roaring Forties.

14

The Great Circle

From the time of the passage of the First Fleet to the gold rush more than 60 years later, the route from England to Australia was prescribed by the Admiralty and not a subject anyone thought required much debate. And it was slow. In stately fashion, ships leaving British ports and travelling the 13,000 or so nautical miles to the Antipodes would call in at the island of Tenerife off the north-west coast of Africa, then drop in further south at the Cape Verde Islands, saunter across to Rio de Janeiro, restocking once more before heading east again to Cape Town on the southernmost tip of Africa. From here, after a stop enjoying the gentle climate of the famously beautiful town, ships' masters would steer their vessels straight across the Indian Ocean at the Admiralty's recommended course of 39 degrees latitude.[1] Across this final leg of 7000 miles of empty Indian Ocean, sailing roughly equidistant between the Indian subcontinent to the north and the mass of Antarctica to the south, landfall would eventually be made somewhere close to the southern tip of Western Australia.

After 1817, Rio was finally given up, but the sojourn in Cape Town remained. As ships became faster, however, and the demand for speed greater, all this was to change. On each side of the Atlantic, two brilliant minds—one a watchmaker's son from Plymouth, the other an American naval officer whose sailing days were over due to a badly broken leg—would usher in a revolution on the high seas.

Anyone observing an atlas could be forgiven for deducing that the shortest distance between two points should be a straight line. The Earth being spherical, however, makes this a delusion. It was the Englishman, John Thomas Towson, who first proposed using the Earth's curvature to significantly shorten long shipping routes such as that from England to Australia, along roughly the same principle that determines that travelling from A to B around the base of a mountain can sometimes be shorter than going over the top.

Towson's genius was indeed wide ranging: he had earlier discovered many of the principles of early photography, including the method by which an image can be preserved on a sheet of glass, the use of the reflective camera and the development of photographic paper. Having exhausted his interest in this field, in 1846 he turned his attention to the principles of navigation, presenting his 'Great Circle' theory in a compact but enormously important book, *Tables to Facilitate the Practice of Great Circle Sailing,* which he convinced the Admiralty to publish in 1847. For the first few years after its release, it remained little more than a tantalising theory, with no ship's master actually daring to follow Towson's radical path, as it required them sailing to parts of the world to which neither they nor anyone else had ever ventured—or particularly wanted to.

Instead of leisurely hugging the coast of Africa down the Atlantic, then turning left and following a line straight to Australia, Towson's theory permitted a ship travelling to Australia from England to make no stops whatsoever, the route being sufficiently shortened for the ship's provisions to last the distance. His Great Circle by-passed Teneriffe, ignored Cape Town completely, then continued way south before swinging to the north-east along a line that still left the south-west corner of Australia thousands of miles to the north. Although covering a much shorter distance, this Great Circle meant that ships needed to touch latitudes of 40 and even 50 degrees south, where the winds howl in an endless easterly gale around the bottom of the globe, unencumbered by any feature of land, propelling the ship like a slingshot across to Australia and beyond. If his theory was correct, the speeds that could be attained would allow a ship in the last third of the journey to cover the same distance in nautical miles as it had during the first two-thirds.

Towson's Great Circle was not perfect in practice, however, as the theory in its purest form required following a single curve across Antarctica. Instead, he broke it down into a shorter series of smaller curves, or 'rhumbs'. However, as a compass needle was not able to follow a curved course, great navigational skills were required by the master to determine the precise moment the ship needed to change direction. For this reason, Towson's Great Circle remained unattempted for a full three years after he revealed it to the world. Finally, in 1850, a Captain Godfrey backed both his ship, the *Constance*, and his navigational acumen, and attempted the journey. He reached Adelaide in a new record of just 77 days.[2] The Admiralty, though impressed, still demurred, unwilling to alter its official route. For this, it required more proof, which was duly provided by the great American navigator Matthew Fontaine Maury, the man dubbed the 'Father of Modern Oceanography', or even 'Pathfinder of the Seas'. He wrote, as part of a ground-breaking study of oceanic wind and current patterns:

> The Admiralty route to and from Australia is one of those tedious old routes, but very difficult to break up, because of the weight and authority which everything with the imprint of that ancient and renowned board upon it has with its navigators.[3]

This study provided him with a theory that would bolster that of Towson.

Maury had spent a good deal of time at sea, fascinated by the patterns of the winds and currents he observed. At 33 years of age, however, a stagecoach accident broke his right leg and condemned him to a shore job for the rest of his career. Not really knowing what to do with him, in 1842 the US Navy put him in charge of its Depot of Charts and Instruments in Washington, where he essentially became a librarian. The posting was a perfect fit.

In dusty vaults and forgotten trunks, Maury discovered thousands upon thousands of ships' logs, dating back to the very beginning of the navy, compiled by long-dead captains who recorded winds and currents across all the world's oceans during all times of the year, going back nearly a century. Maury categorised them and, most importantly, studied them, poring over countless notations on winds, sea drifts and currents. In the days before computers, Maury's achievement of assembling the information into a coherent pattern was extraordinary. Slowly, he began to understand what was taking form in front of him, and in his ground-breaking 1847 study *Wind and Current Chart of the North Atlantic*, put it all together. Later, he would even use information gathered from the diaries of whalers to determine that these creatures actually migrated from sea to sea—a previously unknown fact—and from that deduce the likelihood of a north-west passage across the top of the American continent.

Perhaps most significantly of all, Maury's work confirmed that not only was Towson's Great Circle the most efficient route to Australia in terms of distance, but that the winds south of 40 degrees were far more favourable to easterly bound ships than those further north.

In the end, shipowners and masters took matters into their own hands and began to follow Towson's and Maury's advice on their own. Only in 1854 did the Admiralty acknowledge the superiority of the Great Circle and adopt the route. The average trip from Britain to Australia was reduced from 120 days to around 80, and for his efforts, Towson was awarded £1000 and Maury became established as one of the greatest oceanographic scientists of all time.

For those on board ships heading to the Antipodes, however, the price paid for Towson and Maury's Great Circle shortcut was high indeed. If the *Ticonderoga* had baked like an oven as it limped across the equator, now her passengers were to be subjected to another extremity: the wild and freezing latitudes of the Great Southern Ocean. It is here, at the end of the world, that sub-Antarctic gales howl endlessly across the dark and mountainous seas swirling around the coldest place on Earth. At this precise moment, a new and terrible epidemic—brewing now for weeks in the seams of the passengers' clothing or even on their bodies—would burst upon the *Ticonderoga*'s human cargo with unspeakable consequences.

15

Surgeons at sea

The Colonial Land and Emigration Commission (aka the Board) stipulated that all ships carrying over 50 of their assisted passengers must be accompanied by a surgeon. Laden with around 800 people, the *Ticonderoga* seems to have been significantly under-catered for, although this was not thought so at the time. The surgeons were well remunerated for their services, with the experienced Dr Sanger being paid £200 and his assistant, James Veitch, on his first voyage, receiving £80 pounds, though this would increase quickly with experience.

To a modern observer, the contents of the *Ticonderoga*'s medical kit appear somewhat curious. Listed under 'medical comforts', the inventory has survived courtesy of the Public Record Office in London. What, today, are we to make of 'Box—125 packages, patent groats', or the '100 gallons, vinegar' it was felt necessary to bring along? The list is long and includes apparently large quantities of what was otherwise banned completely on the *Ticonderoga*: alcohol. For strictly medicinal use, no less than three dozen cases of Hollands gin were included, as were six dozen cases of sherry and double that of port wine. There were large supplies of brandy and porter (stout) as well as 80 gallons of oil, although the type is not specified. Other supplies included '62 jars, 5 gallons each, lime juice', '160 lbs arrow-root', boiled beef, boiled mutton, eight barrels of raw sugar and so on.[1]

In the sailing ship era, ship's doctors, or 'surgeon superintendents' as they were also known, were regarded as being just as proficient, if not more so, than their counterparts on land, despite their popularity with the passengers varying from individual to individual. Occupying a unique position on board ship, they were expected to fulfil a wide variety of roles, some of which had little to do with the practice of medicine itself. As historian Robin Haines points out in her extensive study of medicine in the Age of Sail, surgeons were the chief contact between the passengers and those in charge of their destiny on the voyage—the captain and crew—performing the role of 'agent of the state at sea'.[2] They soothed quarrels, passed on passenger grievances to the captain, instigated and oversaw washing and cleaning routines, and were explicitly responsible for the general health of every passenger under their care.

However, most doctors with any experience of working at sea in emigration vessels were under no illusions about just how difficult the journey facing the men, women and families under their care would be. Dr Robert Scot Skirving, surgeon superintendent on the emigrant vessel *Ellora*, who would go on to become a prominent medical practitioner in Sydney, observed that:

> It was horrid, even indecent for decent married people to be herded like beasts, with almost no privacy to dress or undress, and where, in the close and stuffy double beds they slept in, only a thin board separated each couple . . . The ventilation was very poor, and in the tropics, with a temperature of 90 degrees, the air was mephitic.[3]

Or, as author and historian Don Charlwood put it,

> Surgeon-superintendents were just as responsible as ships' masters for bringing emigrants safely to the new land . . . they needed as

much skill in human relations as they did in medicine . . . most voyages would have been intolerable without their arbitration, and losses of life would have been very much higher without their devotion.[4]

It had not always been so. In the early days of convict transport, the rate of deaths on board convict vessels was high, but after the infamous 1814 arrival of the transports *Surry, General Hewitt* and *Three Bees*, in which together nearly a hundred convicts, crew and even some of the guards had died of 'a malignant fever of a very infectious nature',[5] it was agreed that something needed to be done. Assistant Colonial Surgeon William Redfern, who himself had arrived as a convict sentenced for mutiny (though he soon earned a full pardon from Governor Macquarie, who desperately needed his skills), was asked to submit a report on the voyage. His ground-breaking recommendations made a major contribution to colonial public health. Competent and qualified surgeons, said Redfern, should be sourced and installed on all future convict transports, and be given powers to insist that ships be kept clean, fumigated and ventilated—even to the point of overruling incompetent or drunken ships' masters. Being a navy man himself, Redfern suggested such surgeons be selected from the ranks of the Royal Navy. In a short time, convict mortality at sea plummeted from 11.3 to 2.4 per thousand per month.

Besides preventative measures and administering treatments for everyday conditions such as indigestion, constipation, sore throats and diarrhoea, a surgeon's practical skills were paramount. They would set broken limbs and bandage sprained ankles, sew up wounds and perform minor surgery for hernias and other 'internal obstructions'.[6] They would also become obstetricians for the many babies they would inevitably be called upon to deliver, treat and even bury at sea on a long sea voyage such as the *Ticonderoga*'s.

As well as a daily visit to as many parts of the ship as they could manage—much like a current-day hospital doctor making the rounds—they held clinics that were enthusiastically attended by the many passengers for whom medical attention had been a previously unaffordable luxury. Once a day, too, they would report to and confer with the captain, keeping each other abreast of all that was happening on board—particularly the mood and state of the passengers—always presenting a united front of authority. Of particular importance was their task of keeping the vessel clean.

At a time in which little could be done to cure everyday diseases, the surgeon's primary focus was prevention. Routines of health and cleanliness, it was believed, could remove the conditions where such ailments could thrive, particularly with regard to those most vulnerable on a sea voyage: children. Although the feeding of infants and newborns was the responsibility of their mothers—sometimes with tragic consequences should they be unable to do so—it was up to the surgeons to ensure that older children received adequate rations, that their berths were adequately lit and ventilated, that they could exercise, and that their clothes and bodies were washed regularly. This, of course, often came up against the physical limitations of the ship itself, but in any case involved instigating unfamiliar hygiene routines for both children and parents, and directing the sanitation of the vessel itself.

Dr Joseph Charles Sanger was one of the most respected doctors at sea of his time, and a favourite of the Board, which had several times commissioned him to accompany migrants on the long journey to Australia: 'Dr Sanger has already given great satisfaction in four previous voyages in our service',[7] they stated in correspondence regarding his appointment to the *Ticonderoga*. With fifteen years at sea already under his belt, the most dramatic moment of Dr Sanger's career thus far had occurred just the previous summer, in July 1851, when his ship, the 919-ton emigrant vessel *Marion*, struck a reef on the southern tip of South Australia's Yorke Peninsula, barely hours from its destination of Adelaide following a gruelling 128 days at sea. Keeping the 350 terrified passengers on board as calm as he could, Sanger stayed on the deck as the ship's longboats ferried the passengers back and forth to the shore a few miles away. Miraculously, not a soul was lost, and Sanger was commended for his cool-headedness. He would eventually complete twenty voyages in total, almost all for the Board, and was still sailing in 1866.

At twenty years his junior, his assistant, James William Henry Veitch, would be undertaking his first ever sea appointment with the Board—or, for that matter, anyone else. He was a young man whose star was on the rise. A descendant of two generations of naval doctors and a graduate of the London School of Apothecaries, he had already come to the attention of physicians of influence by demonstrating both high standards and calmness during a recent cholera outbreak in Portsea, near the naval base of Portsmouth. About to turn 27, with a coveted contract with the Board, he had good reason to anticipate a long career in the footsteps of not only Sanger, but his own father and grandfather—both respected and well-connected naval surgeons. However, it was not to be.

James Veitch's voyage to Melbourne—like that of the *Ticonderoga* herself—would be his first as well as his last. There is no evidence to suggest that Veitch had any intention to settle in Australia when he departed Birkenhead in August 1852, yet within weeks of his arrival he had forfeited his passage money home, travelled far from the sea to inland Victoria, and for the remainder of his long life did not set foot on board a ship again. What his father made of his son's decision can only be guessed at. James Veitch, however, no doubt had his reasons.

James William's father, also named James, was born in 1783 in Selkirk, Scotland, and had retired by the time his son left for Australia on his first appointment with the Board, a position he unquestionably helped his son to secure. As a young assistant, he had served at sea with distinction in the Napoleonic Wars, taking part in various engagements such as the Battle of Cape Ortegal, the final chapter of the Trafalgar Campaign of 1805, then as surgeon on several ships, and finally running naval hospitals in the British territories of the Caribbean, such as at English Harbour in Antigua.

At sea, Veitch worked in the horror of the ships' surgeries, small rooms painted red from floor to ceiling to hide the blood. And of blood there was a great deal indeed. In naval battles, cannon balls tore off heads and limbs, or sprayed shards of wooden splinters that cut through human flesh as if it were butter. Anaesthetic was a rope clenched between the teeth and, if the screaming patient was lucky, a swig of rum. The primary instrument of surgery was the hacksaw. At the height of a battle, buckets of blood and amputated limbs were emptied over the side, to be returned and filled again. More often than not, what was left of the mangled seaman was buried at sea a short time later, or after the infection had set in.

James Veitch descended from a long line of lowland Scots of Norman extraction, 'Veitch' supposedly being a corruption of 'La Vache', French for cow, derived from one William La Vache, a minor noble of the thirteenth century whose family proceeded to own cattle for the next few centuries. There is even a Veitch crest featuring a trio of long-horned Highland bulls above the Latin *Famam Extendimus Factis*, 'we spread our fame through our deeds'. There is—or rather was—a castle at Dawyck on the Scottish borders which was demolished in 1830 and replaced by a somewhat gaudy house of the early Victorian style.

As his career went on, James observed enough of the horrors of primitive amputations and the horrendous associated loss of life to begin to experiment with replacing the coarse threads traditionally used to stitch wounds and arteries with fine gut sutures. As a result, he achieved both a higher survival rate and lower incidences of infection.[8] His findings were put into a book somewhat gruesomely titled, *Observations on the Ligature of the Arteries, Secondary Haemorrhage, and Amputation at the Hip-joint*, which was published in 1824 and changed naval surgery forever. He became surgeon to the Royal Naval Hospital at Plymouth, was admitted as a member of the Royal Medical Society of Edinburgh, then as Licentiate of the Royal College of Physicians in 1822, and eventually rose to 'deputy inspector of hospitals and fleets' before retiring to a fine house in

Ovington Square, Brompton, in the heart of London's very fashionable West End. His travels with the Royal Navy saw him publish extensively on a wide variety of medical subjects, such as his 1818 'Letter on the Non-contagious Nature of the Yellow Fever', based on his observances of that disease in the West Indies, as well as some more nuanced papers like 'Remarks on the Necessity of Attention to the Surface of the Body in the Treatment and Prevention of Several Complaints; With a Recommendation of the more General Employment of the Vapour-Bath', in which he espouses such notions as 'Temperature, acting on the surface of the body like opium, and wine acting on the stomach, is capable of imparting vigour to the human frame'.[9]

James married one Jane Booker, and their first child, James William Henry, is listed as having been born in September 1825 in the parish of Stoke Damerel, just beside the great naval depot of Portsmouth, where James would have been stationed. The young man seems to have followed his father into medicine early, being apprenticed to a surgeon from the ages of sixteen to 21, and in 1849 the census records him as having his own practice in either Commercial Road or Commercial Way, Peckham, a suburb in London's south-west.

While in London, James William was admitted into the prestigious Worshipful Society of Apothecaries, an institution devoted to the compounding and dispensing of medicines and a precursor to present-day pharmacy. With a lineage reaching back to the early seventeenth century, it still operates from a magnificent baroque hall built immediately after the Great Fire of London in 1666. Fully qualified as an apothecary, and with his father's influence, James William then gained a position near his parents in Portsmouth as one of the physicians at the large Portsea Island Union workhouse, a substantial institution whose large infrastructure had been thoroughly rebuilt and upgraded by 1846. Several hundred impoverished inmates were housed in its large and intimidating rows of red-brick dormitories, with one section being designated as a workhouse asylum. An 1844

report paints a typically unsympathetic nineteenth-century assessment of its unfortunate inmates:

> 26 Lunatics; 15 Females and 11 Males. 7 were Epileptics and 2 Idiots.
> Many of the Patients, although not strictly speaking, imbecile persons,
> were individuals of weak intellect. Some of them, however, were
> decidedly Insane, and occasionally violent and unmanageable unless
> restrained, and some of them were labouring under delusions.[10]

It is unknown in exactly what section of the Portsea Island Union
the young Dr Veitch worked, but it was here that he would face his
first test as a physician in an outbreak of one of the most brutal and
least understood diseases of the time. In July 1849, a series of inmates
began to exhibit certain symptoms that sent a deep chill through the
doctors of the Portsea Island Union workhouse. One after another,
both men and women began to experience nausea, then vomiting,
quickly followed by terrible diarrhoea and drastic fluid loss. Every
sign pointed to the dreaded *cholera morbus*, the unstoppable disease
that fifteen years previously had swept Britain in a pandemic lasting
two years and killing more than 50,000 people.

First noted among the troops in Bengal in the early nineteenth
century, cholera spread across India, Asia and Europe before arriving
in the north of England by boat. It spread quickly across the British
Isles—believed, like many other ailments, to be spread by airborne
miasma, due to its terrible associated stench. It was not until the discovery of germs in 1864 that its true nature as a water-borne disease
was understood.

By the time of the next outbreak in 1849, some improvements
in sanitation had occurred, even though another 50,000 would
again perish across England and Wales, exacerbated by the arrival
of already weak and under-nourished Irish fleeing the effects of the
recent potato famine.

Portsmouth at the time was lamented as having some of the most
dire poverty and poorest sanitation conditions in the country, due in

part to it being a walled and fortified island town with a compressed network of dank and narrow streets compounding any illness that took hold. Set a little way back from the fine high street along which the wealthy wives of senior naval officers would regularly promenade, Portsmouth's poorer houses were badly built, allowing damp to permeate into badly clothed human bodies through broken windows and dilapidated cellars. Rates of poverty and malnutrition were high, with mortality rates—particularly for children under five—being well above the national average. Out in the harbour, rotting convict hulks housed their own cargo of human misery.

In just two months, the epidemic tore through the Portsmouth area, taking 676 victims. The confined spaces of the Portsea Island Union were not immune, but the resident doctors did their utmost to limit the impact on their inmates. In the crisis, James Veitch proved himself a resourceful and capable physician, his tireless efforts in reinforcing cleanliness and seeing—to the best of his abilities—to the comfort of his patients at great personal risk coming to the notice of the medical authorities. Letters praising the young Veitch were written, the most effusive being that of the district medical officer, countersigned by six other prominent members of the medical establishment of the day:

> We the Committee of Public Health in the Portsea Island Union, do hereby certify, that Mr James William Henry Veitch, Surgeon, was engaged by us as an additional medical assistant in consequence of the prevalence of Cholera in the union in the months of July, August and September last, and that during the whole period of his engagement he shewed very considerable skill and was most attentive in the performance of his duties; and we accord to him our best thanks. Dated the first day of October, 1849, JT Pratt, Chairman[11]

The commendation, as well as his prestigious name, brought Veitch to the attention of the Board. In particular, his proven ability in the face of an epidemic led them to conclude that he was the perfect candidate to assist one of their most respected surgeons, Joseph Sanger. In the middle of 1852, an offer was made to the young Veitch and, to the delight of the Board, it was accepted immediately. Should this first appointment go well, he was told, there would be many more such appointments, as competent and reliable physicians were highly sought after. For this initial journey, the fee would be limited to not more than £80, but—the Board was at pains to point out—this could escalate quickly.

Veitch was told he would be travelling on board the *Ticonderoga*, a fast American double-decker clipper, one of four such vessels hired by the Board to sail to Port Phillip this year, each carrying close to 800 passengers to cope with the acute demand for travel to the Australian colonies due to the discovery of gold.

The regulations regarding the amount of children, it was explained, had recently been relaxed, so there would be a large number of youngsters on board and the risk of disease would be high. The ship, however, had been meticulously fitted out with many new innovations to ensure the highest standards of cleanliness and hygiene, and her master, Captain Boyle, was as capable and as conscientious a master mariner as could be found anywhere. Only when pressed, James Veitch said that he indeed felt himself qualified for the role, and the men of the Colonial Land and Emigration Commission wholeheartedly agreed.

Eight hundred people did, however, seem rather a lot for one ship.

16

The first cases

'Captain, I believe we have a case of typhus on board,' said Dr Sanger to Captain Boyle, bringing him out of earshot of a group of passengers standing nearby on the upper deck. Boyle's blood ran cold at the news, but he maintained his demeanour, not wishing the passengers to observe his unease. After all, everyone seemed to be enjoying the party.

In the first week of September, at latitude 3 degrees 19' north; longitude 20 degrees 24' west, the ship's company of the *Ticonderoga* was in a festive mood, preparing in the next day or so to cross 'the line' of the equator—a significant moment on any sea voyage. Despite the heat of the tropics and at times enervating humidity to which no one was accustomed, the mood of the passengers was high. The day before, the first of the monthly scheduled changes of clothes had taken place, and the crew, assisted by many of the single men, had hauled up some of the hundreds of colourful boxes and trunks to allow people to reacquaint themselves with their possessions, transforming the *Ticonderoga*'s normally functional upper deck into something resembling a lively and colourful market.

For many, handling again something that was personal and familiar seemed like a brief but blessed return to normality.

Meanwhile, some of the sailors were busy preparing their costumes for the time-honoured ceremony of the line crossing. In reality, these amounted to little more than bits of whatever scraps and flotsam that could be found around the ship, but the stage was soon set to welcome the King of the Deep, Neptune, his 'wife', Amphitrite, and several of their cohort, who would be ushered aboard and, with great flourish, interrogate the captain. 'Where are you from?' the sea god would ask rhetorically. 'How long have you been out? For where are you bound?' The captain would also be asked how many 'children' he had on board in need of a 'baptising' to mark the occasion of their first crossing. The assembled passengers, enjoying this moment of levity, ooh-ed and aah-ed at all the appropriate moments, as if watching a music hall show.

Then there was an announcement from the top of the wheelhouse through a loud hailer that those who had never before crossed the line would now be sought out and should prepare themselves for the 'ceremony'. In the case of the *Ticonderoga*, this was almost everyone, so the practicalities of performing the often revolting 'initiation' of being shaved, covered in tar or other filth or, for the ladies, simply soaked to the skin were quietly abandoned in favour of a good deal of noise, cheering and parading around the upper deck as the equatorial sun blazed high overhead. For good theatrical measure, a few first-timers were rounded up and locked into the forecastle for a while.

Dr Sanger's urgent words, delivered to Captain Boyle as he too was preparing to enjoy the colour of King Neptune's antics, were met with a dread. 'Typhus?' he could only repeat. 'Not scarlatina?' But Dr Sanger was certain. The scourge of typhus had come to the *Ticonderoga*.

A day or so later, his grim prognosis was borne out when 28-year-old Jane Gardiner joined her daughter, Eliza, the *Ticonderoga*'s second victim, who had perished three weeks earlier at just four years of age. She left behind her husband, Alexander, and their sole remaining child, Robert, five. One of the *Ticonderoga*'s English families, the Gardiners had left their home in Northumberland full of hope for a better life. Now, barely a month later, only a shattered widower and his son remained.

There had already been a regular procession of death on board the *Ticonderoga*. Besides Anna Maria Hando, the infant son of Alexander and Ellen Mercer, Andrew, had been buried at sea, as had one-year-old Mary Ann Ross, Christina Jenkins, also one year of age, and tiny Margaret McJames. In at least two cases, the children's grief-stricken mothers had thrown themselves overboard as well. As ghastly a toll as this appears to a modern reader, it was still not regarded as very much out of the ordinary in this age of prevalent disease and short life expectancies.

The three other double-decked ships hired by the Board in 1852 to make the run to Australia had also experienced a high loss of life. In the case of the large 1495-ton *Borneuf,* which was in fact still on its way to Geelong as the *Ticonderoga* set sail, 88 of the 754 passengers had not survived the voyage. All but four of these were children—mainly Scots—and all under the age of seven, with the average age being much younger. Most of these deaths were attributed to the typical wasting diseases of the poorer classes of the day: marasmus, scarlatina, measles, diarrhoea and chicken pox. Despite this, the *Borneuf*'s journey was regarded as a success.

The death of an adult, however, was another matter, and the passing of Jane Gardiner—an ostensibly healthy woman in her twenties—represented a grim turning point in the *Ticonderoga*'s voyage. Drs Sanger and Veitch had watched, helpless, as over a few days the terrible symptoms had worked their damage on the young mother: first the rash that spread from her chest then across her entire body, sparing only the palms of her hands; the temperature that raged through her constitution at up to 105°F; the nausea, exhaustion and vomiting; the terrible aches in limbs and joints. Then, almost unbearable for her husband and child to watch, the delirium.

As the fever set in, the woman's mind became unhinged in a verbal rampage that terrified those around her in the lower deck's claustrophobic quarters, then in the ship's hospital. After this, she fell into a coma. Attempts to both cool her down or administer any kind of medicine were fruitless. The awful smell then led the *Ticonderoga*'s doctors to realise exactly what they were dealing with. It could only be typhus, and they were powerless to stop it.

* * * *

For centuries typhus had been one of the great scourges of Europe. Entire armies had been laid waste by the disease. During the wars against the Moors in 1489, it is estimated to have wiped out 17,000 Spanish soldiers during the siege of Granada. In Napoleonic times, it accounted for more French troops than did the Russians during the retreat from Moscow in 1812. In the 1830s, 100,000 Irish died in a series of severe outbreaks and during the Crimean War of the 1850s, war wounds accounted for no more than one in six soldiers' deaths, the rest being attributed to a variety of diseases, principally typhus.

Even as late as World War I, 3 million deaths were attributed to typhus, and despite the advances of medicine at the dawn of the twentieth century, no one had any idea how it was transmitted. It was, however, observed to act upon large amounts of people living in close, often unsanitary conditions, and hence became known by many descriptive names, including prison fever and camp fever.[1] It could tear through the populations of army barracks, slums, prisons, hospitals and particularly overcrowded ships such as the *Ticonderoga*.

The closest anyone could come to explaining the spread of typhus was via the generally accepted 'miasmatic theory', by which greatly feared diseases such as cholera, the Black Death and even chlamydia were spread not by infection and contact with germs, but rather by the foul air that seemed to accompany the rapidly expanding cities of the Industrial Revolution, and that appeared to emanate in rotting organic matter. Until the advent of powerful microscopes in the late nineteenth century, the contagion vs. miasma theories competed with one another for years, with even such luminaries as Florence Nightingale believing fervently that diseases she herself witnessed wreaking death and destruction on troops in the Crimea had nothing to do with proximity to others carrying the infection, but instead were carried on the breeze. It was an enduring theory, and it accounted for the notion that fresh, clean air was the key to health in crowded situations like hospitals and ships. In such a light, the *Ticonderoga*'s canvas air vents were seen as a most forward-thinking innovation. Towards the 1880s, the miasma theory would gradually be overtaken by weight of evidence of germs and bacteria, but the exact causes of some diseases, including typhus, remained a mystery.

Discovering the causes of infectious diseases had been a lifelong quest for Brazilian physician Henrique da Rocha Lima and his friend, Czech pathologist Stanislaus von Prowazek, with both men taking a particular interest in typhus. At great risk to themselves, they followed outbreaks and epidemics right across Europe, travelling to Serbia in 1913 to study one outbreak, and observing another in Constantinople the following year. In the winter of 1915, as war raged across Europe, they worked to contain a sudden and devastating outbreak among Russian prisoners of war in a camp near Berlin. Here, both men became infected, and von Prowazek quickly died. Da Rocha Lima recovered, however, and became more determined than ever to track down the cause.

In 1916, after a period of intense research, he announced the discovery of an entirely new group of bacteria that, once introduced into a person's bloodstream, induced the familiar symptoms of high temperature, aches, rashes, delirium, sensitivity to light, often coma and, above all, the terrible stench—all the indications of typhus. In honour of his late colleague and another prominent victim of the disease, an American researcher named Ricketts, da Rocha Lima named his new strain of bacteria *Rickettsia Prowazekii*, and further announced to the world that the means by which it had, for thousands of years, been introduced into the human system was via one of mankind's oldest companions, *Pediculus humanus humanus*, the common body louse. The discovery revolutionised the treatment of typhus. Lice were hunted down and destroyed with purpose and vigour like never before and by World War II, when DDT and later a vaccine had been developed, the incidence had been so reduced that the vaccine's production was actually halted.

For the passengers and crew of the *Ticonderoga*, however, such developments were far in the distant future and in 1852, doctors Sanger and Veitch lacked the benefit of any such knowledge. Nor could they have had any idea as to the pathology of the disease: how it will eventually kill the louse itself; how the bacteria contained within its faecal matter will keep living on the surface of human skin for several days; how the unbearable itching of the louse's bite will cause the patient to scratch, forcing the bacteria directly into the bloodstream; how the incubation period can last up to two weeks; how one single louse can lay up to 200 eggs; and that the ideal environment for the creatures to propagate was in humidity above 40 per cent and in temperatures between 29 and 32°C—precisely the conditions the *Ticonderoga* had been experiencing as she sailed slowly south over the warm waters of the equator.

A lack of real knowledge of the disease notwithstanding, when Jane Gardiner died on board the ship in the early days of September, Sanger and Veitch had a terrible suspicion that there would soon be more to follow.

17

Typhus takes hold

The word 'typhus' derives from the Greek word *typhos*, meaning smoke or fog, and was originally used in the context of the disease by the great Hippocrates himself to describe the stupor and 'confused state of the intellect' he observed in its victims.[1] What would not be observed—neither by Hippocrates nor anyone else—for another 2000 years was the relationship between the disease and the common body louse, *Pediculus humanus humanus*.

As research into the twentieth century revealed, typhus is spread when the louse feeds on the blood of a person already infected with the disease. After several days, the *Rickettsiae* bacteria thus introduced into the louse's system will in fact kill it, but not before the louse crawls off to find a fresh victim whose body is neither too hot with infection nor cold from death. Prior to killing the louse, the bacteria multiplies exponentially inside it, to be excreted onto a person's skin in the creature's faecal matter, where it can remain viable and infectious for many days. The itching of the bite compels a sufferer to scratch, thus infecting themselves by forcing the bacteria into their own bloodstream via tiny cuts and abrasions. After an incubation period of about ten days, the first signs of the disease will start to appear, thus perpetuating the gruesome cycle.

A victim's clothes would also become great spreaders of the disease, with garments not carefully removed from the victim releasing clouds of lice dust, eggs and faecal matter, which would reattach and infect again, partially vindicating the prevailing theory that the disease was wholly spread by stale and 'infected' air. The *Ticonderoga*'s innovative wind sails, which in fair weather distributed at least some air throughout the fetid lower decks, ironically helped to spread the disease.

How the typhus came on board the ship in the first place will never be known. Despite the best efforts of the staff at the Birkenhead depot, and the spick and span condition of the ship that Captain Boyle had gone to such lengths to present to Captain Patey and the inspectors of the Colonial Land and Emigration Commission; despite the washing and re-washing of the passengers' clothes before embarkation, someone—most likely in the seams of a jacket or shirt or bonnet or perhaps even in the smuggled blanket of young Janet Blair, had unknowingly brought on board the seeds of disaster in the form of a tiny colony of lice or their eggs. In her exhaustive research, Mary Kruithof believes that it was unlikely to have been Jane Gardiner, one of the first of Dr Sanger's 'fever victims', who was incubating the disease when she came aboard, and that it was more probable that she caught it from another person in the married quarters—possibly someone she knew from her own part of Northumberland, quartered with her on the ship.[2] Without knowing anything beyond an awful itch and a terrible headache, Jane Gardiner would first have become aware of the bites on her body a fortnight or so earlier. She may even have noticed them, in shock and grief at the recent loss of her daughter, Eliza, just ten days after setting sail from Birkenhead. The incubation period being at an end, the symptoms took hold of her quickly. Then, as her temperature rose, the lice themselves either died or vacated her overheated body for newer, cooler premises—and in the cloying proximity of the *Ticonderoga*'s passenger decks, such newer premises abounded.

The following day, another tragedy unfolded for the Appleby family from the Somerset village of Baltonsborough. Silas Appleby, 28, was listed as a literate, Church of England agricultural labourer, and was undoubtedly anticipating a better life for his family with significantly improved wages and conditions for his work in Australia. He had boarded the *Ticonderoga* with his wife, 23-year-old Sarah, their daughter, Emma, and son John, three. Little Emma had already passed away on 24 August, mere hours after contracting the raging fever that could not be contained. By 9 September, Sarah herself had contracted the disease and died. Mercifully, perhaps, she did not live to see the death of her remaining child, John, who would be buried at sea three weeks later on 2 November. Silas Appleby, having walked onto the *Ticonderoga* the head of a family of four, would depart it a grieving widower, entirely alone.

The next day, 10 September, 28-year-old Mary Ritchie from Inverness died after what seemed like a pathetically short battle with the disease. Her little Samuel had been the first infant to perish on board, and the very next day after her own death, the second of her children, two-year-old Alexander, also passed away. This left, once again, only the father, James Ritchie; having set out with his family of four, he was now also all on his own. He would soon be joined by others facing a similarly wretched situation.

The day Alexander Ritchie died, so did twenty-year-old Jane Dempster, a Scots girl housed in the single women's quarters. By the middle of September, Sanger and Veitch realised that a full-blown epidemic was breaking out around them. Dreadful enough in itself, it was to be greatly exacerbated as the ship continued on to the Great Circle, ploughing into colder waters and freezing winds. The *Ticonderoga*'s passengers, already weakened by sea-sickness, a foreign diet and the claustrophobic ordeal of ship life, having been exhausted by weeks of sweltering heat and humidity utterly beyond their experience, would now be forced to endure the freezing latitudes of the sub-Antarctic. To keep warm in the icy gales and endless storms that would soon follow, families would huddle even closer together in the berths, sharing what warmth they could in their inadequate clothing. This scenario of prone bodies lying side by side would, over the next few weeks, present the most ideal conditions imaginable for the spread of typhus, and the *Ticonderoga*'s doctors would be tested beyond their limits. A particular burden, however, would fall on the shoulders of the young assistant surgeon on his first voyage, Dr James William Henry Veitch.

Dr James William Henry Veitch and his wife, Anne, in the late 1880s. These two unlikely heroes of the *Ticonderoga* saga met on board ship and the experience of the voyage bonded them for life. Author's collection

No image of the *Ticonderoga* herself exists, but the 1087-ton *Alnwick Castle*
was said to be a near replica. This photograph was taken around 1869.
State Library of South Australia (SLSA)

THE AUSTRALIAN CLIPPER-SHIP, "MARCO POLO."

One of the giants of the clipper era, the *Marco Polo*—under James 'Bully' Forbes—
stunned the world with a record passage to Melbourne of just 68 days.
National Library of Australia (NLA)

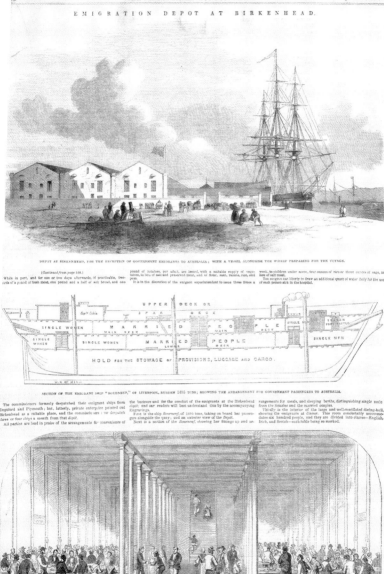

The Birkenhead Emigration depot, from where *Ticonderoga*'s passengers embarked, as reported by the *Illustrated London News* in July 1852. NLA

The claustrophobic interior of an emigrant vessel, as depicted in the *Illustrated London News*, August 1850. For women in particular, mobility was a virtual impossibility. NLA

Sketches drawn on board an emigrant ship, 1875. State Library of Victoria (SLV)

SCENES ON BOARD AN AUSTRALIAN EMIGRANT SHIP.

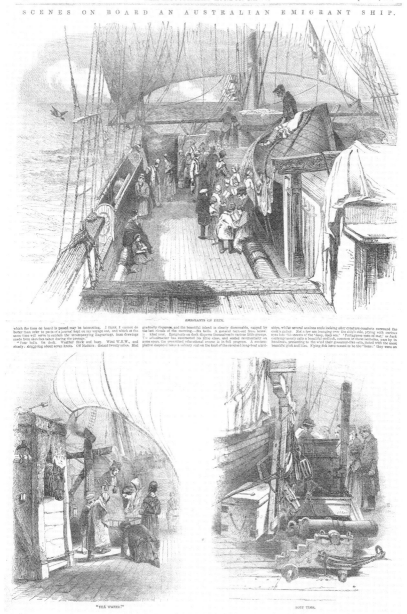

EMIGRANTS ON DECK.

which the time on board is passed may be interesting. I think I cannot do better than refer to parts of a journal kept on my voyage out, and which at the same time will serve to explain the accompanying Engravings, from drawings made from sketches taken during the passage.

"Forty bells. On deck. Weather thick and hazy. Wind W.S.W., and steady, ship going about seven knots. Off Madeira—distant twenty miles. Mist

gradually disperses, and the beautiful island is clearly discernable, capped by the last clouds of the morning.—Six bells. A general turn-out from below. Breakfast over. Emigrants on deck disperse themselves in various little groups. The schoolmaster has summoned his little class, and seated reverentially on some spars, the prescribed educational course is in full progress. A contemplative shepherd takes a solitary seat on the knol of the reversed long-boat amid-

ships, whilst several anxious souls looking after creature comforts surround the cook's galley. Not a few are lounging over the ship's side, prying with curious eyes into the secrets of the "deep, deep sea." "Portuguese men-of-war," as Jack contemptuously calls a beautiful mollusk, common to these latitudes, pass by in hundreds, presenting to the wind their gossamer-like sails, tinted with the most beautiful pink and lilac. Flying-fish have roused to be the "lions!" they were on

"TEA WATER!"

SOUP TIME.

Further sketches of life on board an emigrant ship, published in the *Illustrated London News*, January 1849. Australian National Maritime Museum (ANMM)

QUARANTINE GROUND,
PORT PHILLIP BAY

Melbourne's first quarantine station at Red Bluff, Elwood. The gold rush city began to expand so quickly that a new one had to be established at Point Nepean. *Ticonderoga* was its first customer. SLV

The author at the now abandoned Point Nepean quarantine station. It was onto this lonely beach that the *Ticonderoga* unloaded her sick and dying passengers.
Author's collection

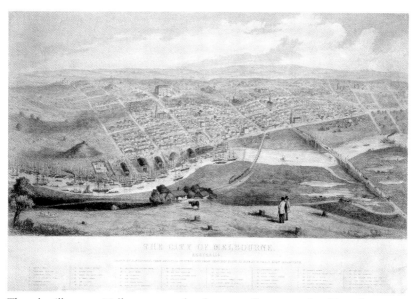

Though still young, Melbourne was already a sprawling town when *Ticonderoga*'s passengers finally disembarked in December 1852. (This image was drawn in 1855 from official surveys and sketches taken in 1854.) SLV

An early image of Melbourne, from Emerald Hill, 1855. SLV

Henry Veitch, the youngest child of James William Henry and Anne, who lived until 1962.

Author's collection

QUARANTINE STATION CEMETERY
1852 ~ 1854

The original burial place of those who died while in quarantine. Sea erosion over the years caused graves to collapse and storms uncovered the remains. In 1952, the quarantine station staff moved all that was identifiable to Pt. Nepean cemetery. The first burials in this cemetery were of the immigrants of the sailing ship Ticonderoga.

TICONDEROGA

An American registered sailing ship of 1089 tons, 169.8 ft, chartered by the British Emigration Commissioners to transport shepherds and farm workers with their families, to replace workers in Australia who had deserted for the goldfields. The Ticonderoga sailed from Liverpool on 4 August, 1852, with Captain Boyle, Surgeon Dr J C Sanger, Assistant Surgeon Dr James W H Veitch, 48 crew and 795 immigrants from the Highlands of Scotland, North England, Somerset, Gloucestershire and Ireland. Provisions were plentiful and water was of good quality.

On 3 November, 1852, the Ticonderoga arrived at Port Phillip Heads. During the voyage 100 immigrants died and 19 births were recorded. In quarantine at Pt Nepean about 400 were seriously ill mainly of typhus fever, a number of births and a further 70 deaths occurred on shore. The official death toll is 168 passengers and 2 crew. The ship was released from quarantine on 22 December 1852, deaths which occurred after this date were not considered as having taken place during the voyage. The number of these deaths is not known because there were no statutory civil records at the time but at least ten further deaths can be reliably inferred from contemporary sources.

The names on this stone were obtained from the Public Records Office. With additional information from Descendants, minor changes were made. Our thanks to the Descendants who helped us fund this Memorial, and to Jack McRae for research. Friends of the Quarantine Museum   10 NOVEMBER, 2002.   Nepean Historical Society Inc.

Quarantine Station Cemetery's memorial plaque to the *Ticonderoga* and the 170 of her passengers who would never complete the journey from Birkenhead.

ReadThePlaque.com, a project of 99% Invisible

18

The box with the dull pink ribbon

Late one morning in 1983, aged twenty, I sat at a table in a modern, well-lit reading room as a librarian placed before me a shoebox-sized document container. I remember no more details of her, except that she wore a bottle-green cardigan and, save for the soft clink of her two very fine, very old-looking gold bangles, went about her work in complete silence. Mouthing a silent 'Thank you', I directed my attention to the box. It was secured by a dull pink ribbon, a little like a legal document. More than its appearance, however, I remember its smell: musty, with a hint of musk or cedar.

Earlier that day, I had taken the main line train from Waterloo station, preferring it to the underground as it allowed me to take in more of the London which, as a hopeless young anglophile, I'd pictured incessantly since childhood. Arriving at Kew Gardens station, I had been overawed by London's gargantuan Public Record Office, a sprawling postmodern labyrinth of concrete and glass situated on the outskirts of the city.

As I entered the PRO's looming grey facade, it occurred to me that somewhere amongst these miles of rooms and corridors, built to house the millions of documents recording the rise and decline of a nation and an empire—from luminous thousand-year-old parchments, to scribbled musings on Cabinet notepaper of long dead Prime Ministers—something pertaining to my own family lay hidden. My job was to find it.

As I began to tackle the complicated knot of ribbon, I pondered how many years had passed since some unknown hands had first tied it. Ten? A hundred? I felt myself to be at the end of a long, but private, quest. In fact, it was just the beginning.

* * * *

My father, who I resemble in myriad ways both good and bad, but particularly physically, enjoyed a successful career in newspapers, though I suspect he preferred to think of himself more as a writer rather than a journalist. His forte was human interest. Even in such roles as court reporter he had a knack of bringing the emotional drama of a trial to life, rather than simply offering the usual dry procession of witnesses and judgments. Inheriting that gene myself, at school I found writing was the only thing I was remotely good at, and my father agreed. My writing became to him something of a project. In high school, he would mark up my essays and stories with the mysterious signs and symbols of a newspaper subeditor. He was ruthless, but when praise came, I knew it was genuine and hard-earned. In the end, writing became a bond—perhaps the only bond—between us.

One night he told me a story of his own. It was a true story, that of the terrible journey of the 'plague ship' *Ticonderoga*, and the dramatic arrival of the first of our family, our clan, in this country— my great-great-grandfather, James William Henry Veitch. In solemn tones, he spoke of the awful disease which erupted on board the over-crowded vessel, how death stalked the passengers, carrying off entire families, and the miracles our revered ancestor performed among the sick and the dying, both at sea and later in quarantine. It sounded like a dark and heroic epic, which of course is how it had been told to him. 'This is your story too, you know', he said. 'You should write about it'. I agreed with him wholeheartedly. But I never did.

It was only several years later I came to appreciate just what the *Ticonderoga* story must have meant to my father. In all, Dr James William Henry Veitch and Annie bore nine children, six of whom survived. Their last, Henry, lived to the venerable age of 92, dying only in the year I was born, 1962. For reasons long forgotten, however, a family feud had split him from my grandfather, Alfred, and the two were not reconciled until late in life.

It was only well into his adulthood therefore, that my own father encountered his grandfather, Henry. Although he had always been aware of the *Ticonderoga* story, it was for him inchoate, and in fragments. Only after meeting Henry did it become something of an obsession for him.

A gentle and, by all accounts, beautifully spoken man, Henry Veitch told my father of his life growing up in central Victoria in the late 1800s, of his father, then a respected councillor, of his mother's lilting Highland brogue which never left her, and of the harrowing account of their journey to Australia on board the *Ticonderoga*. Why my father did not seek out Henry earlier—feud or no feud— remains a mystery to me, as is the reason why he never attempted to write the story himself.

Many years later, as I prepared to leave for Europe as a twenty-year-old backpacker, my father requested that I chase down some of the original documentation pertaining to the *Ticonderoga* and James William Henry Veitch, which he suspected to be held in London. I gave him a half-hearted assurance that I would try, though in fact barely intended to keep the promise. In the weeks leading up to my departure, however, it was virtually all he talked of. Over the previous weeks, he had corresponded furiously with the Kew Public Record Office via mail, tracking down files and catalogue numbers, distilling them all into a folder, which he pressed solemnly into my hand a few days before the flight. As I passed through the airport gate, the look of expectation in his eyes made me realise that, like it or not, I too had now been burdened with the saga of the *Ticonderoga*.

A few weeks later, I lifted the lid of the box marked '54829 Colonial Correspondence—Victoria—Colonial Land and Emigration Society, 1852–53'. Inside was a pile of official letters, folded longways into rectangles and all written with a steel-nibbed pen in the long-vanished hand of copperplate. Some were bound by more pink ribbon. I opened the first one, smoothing out the century-and-a-half-old crease, quietly amazed that I was not required to wear special white gloves, or at least be watched over by the librarian. My own enthusiasm for the quest now thoroughly awakened, the contents of the box seemed far too precious to be handled by someone such as myself.

Although exquisite, the handwriting was at first almost impossible to decipher. Only after a few minutes could one word be made out, then another. Then, gradually, like cracking a code, the sentences appeared to almost shift into place and come alive. The first few documents seemed of little relevance, being written by one or other unknown government official concerning such topics as schedules and ships' insurance tables, but a third of the way through the pile, one word on one letter leaped off the page. 'We have to acknowledge the receipt of your letter of the 17th instant, enclosing a Despatch from Lieutenant Governor Latrobe relative to the mortality which occurred among the Emigrants by the "Ticonderoga" both during her voyage and in Quarantine.'[1] It was written by Sir Thomas William Murdoch, the Board's then chairman, to Herman Merivale, Permanent Under-Secretary for the Colonies, and dated June 29, 1853. It runs for fourteen pages, without a single mistake or correction, and represents the Board's initial reaction to the report of the *Ticonderoga* disaster, which Murdoch had received only a few days earlier direct from Victoria and penned by Governor Charles La Trobe himself.

When La Trobe's report had hit Merivale's desk, it was like an explosion. The barely controlled panic in Murdoch's words to his superior is palpable. In it, he quotes La Trobe's report extensively, choosing those passages that could be turned to ameliorate any responsibility on the part of the Board. The impression was of a man trying to position himself in the best possible light before an impending disaster. The very next letter in the pile was Governor La Trobe's report itself.

It is referenced with the number CO 309/13 and dated 26 January 1853. Addressed to the Right Honourable Sir John Pakington, 1st Baron Hampton, member of the Privy Council and Queen Victoria's Secretary of State for War and the Colonies, who would later rise to First Lord of the Admiralty, it begins,

> My despatch No 163 of November 9, 1852 apprized you of my having received intelligence of the arrival of the Government Emigrant Ship 'Ticonderoga', the lamentable loss of life by disease which had been experienced during the passage and the great extent to which the sickness of a very serious character still prevails . . .[2]

Holding in my hand the personally written words of the first Governor of my home state of Victoria, after whom one of Melbourne's main streets is named, was something of a thrill; that he was writing about the arrival of my ancestor's vessel was doubly so. What I craved, however, was some direct reference to James William Henry himself, and this did not seem to be forthcoming. Several other letters again seemed to be of no relevance, then at the very bottom of the box, a two-page document written in the far less legible, almost hurried-looking hand of Dr Joseph Charles Sanger, offering the dramatic heading,

> Ship Ticonderoga, Thursday, Midnight, November 4, 1852.

> Sir, I have the honour to announce the arrival of the Ship 'Ticonderoga' from Liverpool with a large number of Government Emigrants on board under my superintendence—I deeply regret to have to inform

you of the serious amount of formidable sickness prevalent during the whole voyage especially the. latter part, and of the long list of fatal cases resulting therefrom.[3]

Sanger's letter, written at midnight on one of the worst days of the saga, is a desperate cry for help, the first official description to the wider world of the still-unfolding tragedy. Then, about two-thirds down the first page,

There are at present at least 250 patients requiring treatment, and both my coadjutor, Mr Veitch, and myself are almost wearied out by the constant demand for our services, especially as it is impossible to get proper nurses for the sick in sufficient numbers.[4]

Although no shadow of doubt had ever clouded my appreciation of the story, seeing my great-great-grandfather's name, written in such dramatic fashion, as proof of the part he played in the drama of the *Ticonderoga*, nevertheless sent a surge of relief coursing through me, sitting that day in the little room in the great building on the other side of the world. Much of the excitement I felt was for my father.

I thanked the librarian, before arranging for as many photocopies of the letters as the few pounds in my pocket would allow. On the train journey back to my digs in Islington, I pictured my father opening the big yellow envelope that I intended to mail him, and his eyes scanning the hand-written lines, revealing the story of the terrible second half of *Ticonderoga*'s journey to Australia.

19

The Southern Ocean

To the best of their efforts, the authorities at Birkenhead organised the *Ticonderoga*'s passengers in berths as close as possible to others of similar national, ethnic or religious backgrounds. Beyond that, it was pure chance that determined exactly where, and with whom, they would spend the voyage. The luckiest passengers were the 103 families assigned positions on the ship's main accommodation deck.[1] As claustrophobic as their tiny berths may have seemed as they settled themselves into them at the Birkenhead depot back in August, it was with a shudder of horror—and no little relief—that they had watched those other families—56 in all—shuffle past to line up above the dark, yawning hatch that led down to their own berths in the Stygian bowels of *Ticonderoga*'s lower deck. It was here in these gloomy confines that the epidemic that seized the ship at the end of September would wreak its most terrible havoc.

Meanwhile, the passengers were forced to deal with another tormenter, one that visited all decks and did not discriminate on the basis of class, sex or age: the weather. From five weeks into the voyage until almost the very end, it had begun to seem to all on board that it represented nothing but a long and continuous torture.

A few days after dropping below the equator, excitement rippled through the ship as the voice of one of the crew, high in the rigging, announced 'land to starboard!', and all on the upper deck rushed to the rail. There, about 20 miles distant, rising from a blueish sea mist, stood a tall and majestic finger of rock pointed directly at the sky. Captain Boyle appeared on deck with his officer of the watch and the two consulted closely. Dr Sanger was beckoned over and handed the spyglass. The captain seemed pleased:

> Sir, you may inform the passengers that we are passing the island of Fernando de Noronha—a little over 200 miles from the coast of Brazil. The ship is making excellent time. Tell them also, if you will, that this is the last land we shall see for some time.[2]

The last comment sent a slight shudder through those who heard it, and all eyes strained for a better view of the distant and mysterious island—in fact, a Portuguese prison colony—surprised at how hungry they had become to step foot upon something solid after so many weeks at sea.

A day or so later, on 12 September, the mother of one of the English families, Mary Sharpin, 35, listed as 'Wesleyan' from Norfolk, succumbed to what Dr Sanger again noted simply as 'fever'. She left behind her husband, Robert, and three daughters, aged four, seven and ten. Nor would this be the final tragedy to visit the family.

An eighteen-year-old girl, Christine Rankin, plus two more infants, Lawrence Fulton and Helen Gartshore, were all buried at sea a few days later. In just over a week, from 10 September, Sanger and Veitch had lost fourteen passengers, in equal numbers of children and adults. Any notion that the epidemic now starting to rage on board the *Ticonderoga* could be confined to children was now confounded, and it was becoming clear that a catastrophe was looming.

With no understanding of the true cause or origins of the disease, and with its relationship to the bacteria carried in the common body louse not to be revealed for another half-century, the common treatment for typhus in the mid-nineteenth century revolved around the supposed invigorating qualities of wine. In one of the most respected naval medical texts of the time, William Turnbull's *The Naval Surgeon Comprising the Entire Duties of Professional Men at Sea* (a copy of which Dr Veitch's father, James, would undoubtedly have pressed into his son's hand, entrusting it to him like a precious tome), the primary method of treatment for typhus fever was described as 'wine, in liberal quantity, suited to the circumstances of the case, but given in small doses at once and judiciously repeated'.[3] This was preceded by a period of induced purging and vomiting brought on by the administration of a compound of antimony, a metallic element that had a particularly violent effect on a patient's bowels and stomach. Though unpleasant, the treatment was not uncommon.

Only after this ordeal could the already suffering patient be rested and kept warm, after which 'a nourishing diet is to be administered in the most soluble form, and such as is most grateful to the patient'.[4] By this general plan, assures Turnbull, 'a cure will, for the most part be effected'.[5] As the two struggling doctors were to witness on board the *Ticonderoga*, Turnbull's breezy optimism was grotesquely misplaced.

A few days later, as the south-east trade winds pushed the *Ticonderoga* far out into the South Atlantic, the first of the storms hit. None of the passengers had experienced anything like it. In just two weeks, they had travelled from the cloying sauna of the equatorial tropics to the storm-tossed fury of a southern hemisphere winter. They had, of course, been warned to expect the weather to turn, and many had taken the advice of packing warmer clothing for the second half of the journey, but the winds and the seas that picked up the great ship, and seemed bent on tearing her apart, were beyond imagining.

As stated, no direct first-hand account of the journey survives from any of the *Ticonderoga*'s passengers, but writing at around the same time, another emigrant on a similarly assisted passage, Englishwoman

Fanny Davis, described in vivid detail her experience on board the *Conway,* an emigrant vessel of just over 1100 tons but carrying only half the number of passengers as the *Ticonderoga.* Fanny likewise sailed from Birkenhead and experienced the hardships of the Great Circle, but her extensive and descriptive diaries give us an insight into what effect the experience of storms, hundreds of miles from any land, had on the passengers. Two months and ten days into the voyage, somewhere out in the Atlantic, Fanny Davis records:

> We had a most fearful night, it has blown a perfect hurricane . . . Nearly every minute a large wave broke on our deck and the wind sounded fearfully. All we could hear besides was the Captain and mate shouting to the men all night.[6]

And the next day:

> Another very cold day, the wind cuts down our hatchway and nearly blows the hair off our heads and we are obliged to sit with a thick shawl on and even then we cannot keep a spark of warmth in us.[7]

The following day's entry was even more dramatic:

> It has been a most terrific night, such a one as makes young people old in one night for it was a regular night of horrors, the wind blew a perfect hurricane and every now and then the ship seemed perfectly under water and it poured down the hatchway in a perfect deluge. It is at such times as that we feel the comfort of having a top berth for the people in the bottom ones get washed out of their beds. The screams of the people as each wave comes down the hatchway was enough to make the stoutest heart to tremble.[8]

According to Mary Kruithof, throughout the last month of the voyage, the *Ticonderoga* was 'overtaken by storm after storm . . . each one lasting for days at a time'.[9] Memories of warm equatorial evenings spent in calm and cordial conversation on the upper deck were now so distant that many of the passengers questioned whether they had taken place at all. Then, the heat had sometimes seemed unbearable, but what would they now give to have just one of those evenings back again?

Shivering with cold as well as fright in their dank beds, the *Ticonderoga*'s passengers endured hour after hour, day after day huddled in the confines of their berths, feeling the ship tossed and pummelled by the screeching wind that drove the seas before it into a monstrous frenzy. The awful seasickness that they thought they had left behind now returned. It seemed the sea was determined to invade the confines of the ship, and even tightly closed scuttles shrieked and whistled as water pushed its way through every inadequate gap and seal.

During the big storms, the galley system all but broke down. Coppers were upset and fires were extinguished as soon as they could be lit by the exasperated cooks. Besides, moving about the ship—for anyone—under such conditions was perilous. Those who did so frequently came to grief on ladders or simply slipped on the icy deck. Skulls were thrown against bulkheads, elbows and ankles cracked as the lurching ship threw everything inside against its wooden interior. Those who risked getting up from their cots to answer the call of nature had to grip hard with both hands to avoid being hurled as a wave struck. People tripped and skidded on the swirling mass of water and all the possessions tumbling around on the floors. Some intrepid souls who could no longer bear the confines of the lower decks occasionally ventured out onto the top open deck and described it as akin to trying to walk on a pitched roof.

Even the single men, who had assumed their recent roles as sailors with such gusto—even to the point of starting to affect the talk and manners of the real old salts—were stunned into silent terror. From their quarters in the bow of the ship, the dreadful lurching of the vessel as it plunged down the troughs of 15- and 20-metre waves was at its most extreme. Like a train plummeting over a precipice, their hands—white knuckled—would grip the wooden rails of their cots as the ship lurched forward, throwing everything not bolted down into a cacophonous clatter of pans and cutlery. Foot-lockers burst open, spilling their contents. Then came the great crash as the ship's bow hit the bottom of the trough, burying the upper deck under metres of sea water before the ship miraculously recovered once again. As terrifying an ordeal as this was, the men knew that above them, somewhere, the real seamen were at work, on the deck and in the rigging, climbing the mainyards and somehow managing to stay upright to grapple with the ship in the face of the storm. For them, the real terror came from the mighty swells that rose up from the *Ticonderoga*'s stern, stealing her wind before breaking over her in a deluge and turning her bursting sails into sagging sheets of sodden canvas.

Captain Boyle was up there too, somewhere in his sou'wester high up on the forecastle. Between the bouts of wind, they could occasionally hear him barking out his orders, encouraging his helmsman, driving his army of men trained to fight this impossible struggle against the raging elements—one he could not afford to lose. The *Ticonderoga* was strong, and her raked bow could slice apart the fiercest of waves, but should she allow the wind to turn her side-on, to slip into the lee of one of those monstrous swells, Boyle knew that the sea could overcome her in seconds, her yardarms turned turtle into the water, her leaden sails dragging her over as another wave pounded across her decks. Then, in moments, she would be pulled to the bottom like a stone. It happened all the time, he knew, to finer ships manned by finer crews than his.

While no list remains of the *Ticonderoga*'s crew, they were believed to have numbered 48 in total, and were all experienced sailors. But although the runs across the Atlantic could be fierce at times, none had seen seas comparable to the ferocity of these oceans swirling around the bottom of the globe. Boyle had done his best to make them aware back in Liverpool that conditions further south would be rough, but no one had envisaged this.

George Pollock Russell, a Scotsman whose journal of his 1854 voyage has survived (due to the diligence of his granddaughter, Eunice), was likewise shocked by the severity of the weather:

> It is quite out of the question to walk on deck it is leaning at about an angle of 45 degrees . . . at half past seven in the evening a wave struck the ship with such force, we thought for certain the ship was going down. The storm is now raging fearfully; some are going to bed, others are stopping up . . . the sea is washing over the decks and into our beds . . . our table is broken in a heap in the middle of the floor . . . I turned into bed about 1 O'clock but did not sleep.[10]

To compound the passengers' misery, in such seas the innovative fresh air canvas ventilation system scooping fresh air from up top and distributing it below was disengaged, lest it become a conduit for seawater—which was everywhere in any case for those people cocooned in the lower decks. Hatches that were easily battened down and secured in calm seas burst and tore away, allowing cascading torrents to gush into the bowels of the ship. Waves crashing onto the deck forced water down through every deck board, gap and opening. Diarist William Johnstone, sailing the Great Circle route on the *Arab* a few years later, recalled that:

> The between decks where the Emigrants were all stowed away (sometimes a man and his wife and two children in the one bed) were in a most horrible condition. The seas washed down the hatchways and the floor was a complete pont, many of the beds drenched through and through. In addition to these delights, with four or five exceptions, they were all violently seasick—some of the women fainting, and two going into convulsions—all call out for Brandy, which they had been told by the Emigrant Agent had been put on board for their use—but which they now found 'non est inventus'. The squall had come on so suddenly that their boxes were all adrift,

flying about from one side to the other, with nearly 50 whining sick squalling children to complete their misery.[11]

Patience and caution were attributes not highly sought after in sea captains of the emigrant clippers during the gold rush. Dash, nerve and the skill to drive their great vessels to a quick passage through the high seas and gales of the Great Circle and Southern Ocean were qualities far more sought after by shipowners and agents. Apart from the wonderful headlines generated by a quick passage to Melbourne, it delivered passengers to the goldfields faster, and could cut short the inevitable spread of disease. 'Hell or Melbourne!' had been Bully Forbes' audacious response when asked to slow down the *Marco Polo* a little for the sake of his passengers.[12] So driven was the famous mariner that it was rumoured he padlocked his sails in storms to prevent the more timid of his crew hauling in some of the dangerously strained canvas. Captain Boyle, though, as Christopher McRae remembered, was a different man entirely:

To show how very solicitous the Captain had been for the comfort of the passengers and to prevent any panic amongst them, he had frequently been known, when coming on deck and finding the ship carrying full sail—which the second officer was given to do—gave order to shorten sail. Not so much because the ship could not carry it, as concern for those on board. There was no doubt of the ship being overcrowded.[13]

The sole advantage of the *Ticonderoga*'s arrival in southern waters was that her speed picked up considerably. Dropping roughly two degrees in latitude every day, three weeks was all it had taken for her to exchange the balmy equator for the fury of the Roaring Forties and beyond. Now, large Southern Ocean whales, unlike any seen further north, began to surface beside the ship, eying her curiously. Unfamiliar southern latitude birds, such as cape petrels and shearwaters, made their appearance, and albatross stalked her for any scraps she might leave behind in her wake. The upper deck, recently the scene of languid evening promenades, now became the setting for children's snowball fights in the day or two of respite between storms. Down in their beds, however, the passengers huddled for warmth, wearing every scrap of clothing they could find.

On calmer days, the departure of the wind often gave way to the Southern Ocean's famous fogs, which rolled across the seas like a wet and freezing blanket. At these times, visibility was cut to almost nothing, at least equalling the thickest 'soups' dished up by the English Channel. Through the cloying mist, sailors on watch strained their ears to pick up a new and unsettling sound: ice. The icebergs that drift up from the Antarctic ice shelf in the southern autumn are far greater in size than those in the northern hemisphere and frequently measured in miles, with ice of significant size being not unheard of as far north as 40 degrees. The *Ticonderoga*'s route took her well inside Antarctica's northern ice zone, making the danger of sudden and catastrophic collision real, with the iceberg's unseen mass below the water being capable of splitting a ship's timber hull like balsa wood, particularly travelling at strong speed before the southerly gales. Nor was it only the larger ice that presented danger.

Smaller, melting 'growlers', clear and almost impossible to see, also lay in her path. Only the strange hollow wash of the sea breaking over them, or the popping and sizzling as ancient air bubbles were released as the ice melted gave their positions away, prompting the lookouts to shout frantic course corrections for the helmsman to steer around them. Such caution was only possible on calmer days. During the storms, when the ship was bolting through the water, there was almost no chance of receiving warning of them, and simple luck had to be relied upon.

In the days of the clipper, the farther south a master steered into the Great Circle, the shorter was his route and the faster his time. Some captains, driving their ships as far south as 60 degrees, could cut as much as 1000 nautical miles off the route to Australia, but here the danger of ice increased exponentially. When ships began sailing the Great Circle, the Board had been advised by the Secretary of State to prohibit such vessels employed by them to drop below certain southern latitudes. This, however, prompted such a fierce outcry against perceived government interference in the sacred freedoms of navigation from shipowners and masters wanting to set ever-faster records to Australia that the provision was dropped. In any case, they realised, it was impossible to prescribe rules for each charter due to the different seasons and accidents of weather. The choice of route therefore continued to be left to the discretion of individual masters.[14]

Assuming the *Ticonderoga* followed roughly the same route as previous emigrant clippers such as the *Marco Polo*, which had left Liverpool exactly a month earlier, on 4 July 1852, Captain Boyle would have steered his ship as low as 55 degrees south—below the remote French territory of the Kerguelen Islands, below even the ice-covered sub-Antarctic rock of Herd Island, to well under a thousand nautical miles from the coldest place on Earth, the great icy mass of Antarctica.[15] Then, finally, with the second half of the entire journey completed in just a few weeks, he would begin to climb back towards the north-east and Australia.

In the meantime, a full outbreak of typhus fever had erupted across the length of the ship.

20

Hell Ship

Although largely poor, the *Ticonderoga*'s 800 or so Scots and English emigrant passengers had been selected by the Board for their general intelligence, hardiness and willingness to adapt to the travails and privations of a long voyage at sea. Embarking on their one-way journey in a spirit of gratitude and adventure, they endured conditions that would be completely and utterly abominable to any traveller today. Nevertheless, they accepted the horrendous cramping of their quarters, the seasickness, the stifling heat and drenching downpours of the tropics, the monotonous and largely inedible food, the storms, the leaking and the general terror of the voyage with good grace and few or no complaints. Even in their most challenging moments, most remained conscious of the fortune that had smiled on them in being handed this once-in-a-lifetime opportunity to escape destitution of their homeland and begin a new and more prosperous life on the other side of the world.

In the first month of the *Ticonderoga*'s journey, deaths had indeed occurred—largely among infants—but this was an accepted part of the risks they had undertaken. The strange and challenging routines of ship life were largely adhered to, allotted tasks were performed with diligence, and consideration and respect for the needs of their fellow passengers were generally observed.

No one, however, could possibly have been expected to withstand the terrible confluence of circumstances that overtook the great clipper as the month of October arrived. It was at this stage—over the last third of her journey—that the routines of ship life would begin to break down, that order and morale would collapse and that, despite the best and most strenuous efforts of Captain Boyle and his two steadfast doctors, Sanger and Veitch, as well as the stewards, death and chaos would stalk the decks of the *Ticonderoga*. Now she would begin to earn the terrible epithet she would be ascribed when, disease-ridden and desperate, she finally limped to her destination: 'Hell Ship'.

Captain Boyle faced a dilemma. The *Ticonderoga* was living up to her promise as a fast and well-built vessel, and for a while was even keeping pace with the *Marco Polo*'s record-breaking run to Melbourne of just 68 days. What, however, would be the cost in taking full advantage of these southerly gales? As more of his passengers and crew became sick, Dr Sanger reported that the terrible tossing of the ship in the rough weather was making the situation far worse, not only for the patients themselves but also for his and Dr Veitch's ability to care for them.

The two men consulted at length about striking a balance between delivering their increasingly sickening passengers to Melbourne as soon as possible and not causing even more deaths in the process. Because now death was everywhere.

The married quarters—first on the lower deck, then the upper— were the hardest hit. Freezing families huddling together became breeding grounds for colonies of lice, which moved from one warm body to another. Always the same pattern emerged, presenting particularly quickly with the children and infants: the pink rash that grew to blister almost the entire body, the terrible fever, the skin of loved ones almost unbearable to touch. With adults, a ranting delirium set in; with children, it was a coma then death.

In these terrible days of October, the *Ticonderoga*'s exhausted doctors were given barely a moment's rest. As Christopher McRae recalled in a letter to *The Argus* in January 1917, 'I remember the Captain accompanying the Doctor, going through and seeing that things were in proper order, that is, as far as it was possible, under the circumstances.' Cries for help rang throughout the ship, and Drs Sanger and Veitch answered all those they could, fighting the pitching of the vessel to make their way across the increasingly chaotic mess of the decks to another bunk, and another red and heaving patient staring with fixed, glassy eyes. Veitch carried the heavy medical chest, offered a sip of brandy or sweet wine to the deathly white lips of the patient, regardless of their age, while Sanger, in the half light and cloying atmosphere, set up his bottles and made up a tincture. Wet cloths were applied to cool the burning brow. Sometimes it seemed to work, with the patient's overheated brain gaining some respite, even occasionally recovering. More often than not, though, it was all for nothing.

The Campbell family, listed as Presbyterians from Argyllshire, were all but wiped out in a month. John, 44, and his tiny daughter, two-year-old Jane, died within hours of each other on 5 October. Allan, an otherwise healthy lad of eighteen, would join his father and sister on 18 October, to be followed by another sibling, Peggy, a short time later.

The ship's hospitals—both male and female—were soon overflowing into the narrow and inadequate corridors. Sanger and Veitch had to virtually force their way through to reach bodies prone on the floor, or in makeshift cots, to administer at least some semblance of treatment. Both knew that their medical supplies were running dangerously low. Soon, with the postponement of funerals due to the rough weather, the hospitals became morgues, filled to capacity, making them resemble an overflowing charnel house. The sick were ordered to stay in their bunks and wait to be treated there, only to be moved to the hospital once a patient had died. Those occupying neighbouring bunks watched with horror as the terrible symptoms took the patient closer and closer to death, and wondered when their turn would come.[1]

The pace of sea burials increased—now a far cry from the early dignified ceremonies presided over by the captain. They were now hasty affairs, conducted quickly between breaks in the weather, watched over by almost no one. Now it was one of the ship's mates or even the redoubtable schoolmaster and impromptu minister of religion, Charles McKay, who was called upon to repeat the same few desultory words as yet another deadweight was tipped over the side, making a brief white splash into the slate-grey water as shocked and sobbing family looked on. The *Ticonderoga*'s sail-makers, in whose canvas the bodies were sewn, had permanent work as the ship's undertakers. There was a pervasive and morbid fear of who would be next, with no one daring to contemplate how much worse the epidemic could become. Then another squall would roll in, and everyone but the crew would be ordered below.

A macabre backlog started to evolve, with more and more victims needing to be disposed of simultaneously. Years later, in January 1909, in one of just a handful of first-hand accounts given in a letter to *The Argus*, James Dundas recalled travelling as a nine-year-old with his family of five from Aberdeen:

> I saw, more than once, ten buried in one day. They were tied up in bedding and mattresses, all together, and thrown overboard, to float away, as there was nothing to weight the corpses with. If we had not got to land when we did, I do not think there would have been many left to tell the tale.

On 11 October, Dundas watched his two-year-old sister, Elizabeth, burn up in a fever and expire in a matter of hours. The sounds of the sobbing of his father Lewis, 34, and mother Isabella, 36, would haunt him the rest of his life.

A graph prepared in 2002 by a diligent amateur historian of the *Ticonderoga*'s grisly journey plots the frequency of deaths over the course of her 90-day voyage.[2] Over the first few weeks of August and into September, the curve is mainly flat, with one or two rises and falls representing the ship's handful of early fatalities. Then, as the 60th day of the voyage is reached, around the first day of October, the graph begins to rise. The curve is gentle at first, but it increases dramatically as the month proceeds, attesting that almost half of the *Ticonderoga*'s approximately 104 deaths at sea occurred within the last two weeks of October.

One of the reasons for this was discovered by Sanger and Veitch early one evening when called to attend a sick Englishwoman in her bunk on the lower deck. Even in daytime, the poor light made vision difficult, but at night the few swinging whale oil lamps offered only the most pitiful spluttering gloom. This perhaps afforded the patient at least a modicum of comfort, as one of the symptoms of the disease is an agonising sensitivity to light.

Having attended the woman in this cave-like atmosphere, the two doctors made their way back to the gangway when they noticed a family huddled over their child. Dr Sanger interjected to inspect the mite, finding her to be already in the advanced stages of a raging fever. Astonished, he looked at the parents and inquired angrily why he hadn't been informed of her condition. They shrugged, but seemed reluctant to engage him any further. Dr Veitch was astonished that a parent would fail to report a sick child under such circumstances, and sought to remonstrate, but Sanger restrained him. Leading him away, he assured his less experienced assistant that it was an all too depressingly common occurrence.

The Scots Highlanders, warily looked upon as dangerous outsiders even by their fellow countrymen in the south, were unused to outside interference or assistance of any sort—particularly medical attention from those not connected with their small community. For centuries, the traditional home remedies of their village and extended family had, for better or worse, sufficed. Added to this were a language barrier and a deep suspicion of outsiders, including those from the southern parts of Scotland, and particularly the

English, as 800 or so years of conflict between the two kingdoms, followed by the recent Clearances, attested.

As Dr Sanger had found on previous voyages, what he represented to many of these people was a gulf too vast to bridge, even in the face of dire sickness and ultimately death. Now, however, both he and Veitch began to peer more closely into the dark nooks of the lower decks where those quiet Gaelic families huddled in their berths. Soon, both found that the epidemic was more widespread than even they had thought. By the time Sanger and Veitch had attended to one of the sick children, the other members of the family were also usually harbouring the disease and would soon present with the symptoms of typhus. Charles McKay worked tirelessly beside Drs Sanger and Veitch as translator, doing his best to convey the gravity of the situation that many of the Highland families were facing. Reluctantly, some of them gave their sick members over to the doctors' care, but little could be achieved in any case. The hospitals were already full and there were almost no medical stores left to treat the patients. As always, the disease remained particularly brutal on children.

On 18 October, Janet Gillard perished, just a single summer into her life, as did another infant of the same age, Agnes Welch, following her mother Mary, who had died two days earlier. Baby James Smith perished the next day, and on 21 October, yet another of the McRae family died: little Elizabeth, who was just two years old.

Soon the funerals themselves became almost redundant. Now, more often than not, a father, or even a sympathetic member of the crew, or even Dr Sanger himself, would spirit away the tiny bundle from the bedside of the grieving family and drop it quietly over the side to spare them further torment. Even with the adult funerals, hardly anyone now attended outside the immediate family. The sail-makers ran out of canvas in which to sew up the bodies. Weights of iron to pull the deceased quickly below the surface also became scarce. As young James Dundas recalled decades later, anything that could wrap a body to offer some dignity was now used: bread bags, tablecloths, even the bedding in which the patient had died. Previously, this was disposed of separately, but now it doubled as the funeral shroud.

As the *Ticonderoga* finally began to leave the ice to proceed towards the north-east, she encountered fierce headwinds, into which she was required to tack back and forth to make any headway at all. Then, climbing back through the Roaring Forties, a new horror arrived. Under a leaden sky one afternoon as the ship made its way across the Southern Ocean, another two passengers were hastily buried at sea. The tiny group of family members could barely look as their bodies were given to the waves, but then a gasp went up as all watched a series of grey fins attack the half-floating bundles slowly receding in the ship's wake. Sharks, the ocean's great scavengers that traditionally follow the refuse trail of ships, large and small, had found another reason to stay close to the *Ticonderoga*. Mourners and crew likewise looked away; attending children were quickly ushered below. To avoid this horrific spectacle, some burials—contrary to the custom—began to take place at night. The pall of grief sweeping the ship was immeasurable.

Meanwhile, the entire system of the ship, practised and refined successfully in the early weeks of the voyage, was breaking down. Although less infected than those in the married quarters, the single men in the ship's bow also suffered, reducing the numbers of hands capable of keeping the ship relatively clean. Even those still fit enough to be rostered to such duties were soon overwhelmed by what they saw in the degenerating lower passenger decks and abandoned their tasks. Dr Sanger and Veitch, their wines, spirits and other medical comforts now virtually exhausted, were at their wits' end. Now, often accompanied by Captain Boyle, all they could offer was sympathy, kind words and a little comfort. For those who had already given up hope and were resigned to the fate of either themselves or their loved ones, however, such displays of care and dedication counted for much.

The intricate meal system around which so much of the ship's life had revolved was now in chaos. The galleys may well have coped with the battering dealt by the Southern Ocean—many of the stoves were gimballed and could cope with all but the fiercest tossing of the ship—but in the face of the disease, all semblance of order collapsed. While the *Ticonderoga* did not run out of food, the means to prepare it collapsed. Stoves went cold as more and more passengers became debilitated, first with fear of the storms, then with sickness. Those unaffected with either had to make do independently, conducting scavenger parties to the now often deserted galleys or gathering handfuls of soup tins and other sustenance from the stores. Biscuits and water became the staple for many.

By late October, even those who still had an appetite could not avoid one of the disease's most confronting symptoms: the ranting shouts of delirium. The severely high fever associated with typhus scorched the minds of its helpless victims, sending even the most demure into bouts of screams, shouts and random abuse. For children witnessing their parents in such a situation, or vice versa, it was particularly harrowing. One woman was reported in the *Geelong Advertiser and Intelligencer* later in April of 1853 as dementedly shrieking, 'We are done for! We are done for!', convincing those around her that, fever or no, she was forecasting a prophecy. This, amplified dozens then hundreds of times, made the ship resemble a floating prison for the insane, from which there was no escape.

Even worse, perhaps, was the terrible stench. Emanating from the breath and the myriad red and gangrenous sores that cover the body, it has been said that the stench of a single typhus patient is strong enough to be detected at the other end of a hospital ward, or even behind a closed door. Even today, typhus patients will be isolated for just this reason: the disease utterly lives up to one of its many names—'putrid fever'.

Historical accounts of typhus's awful stench are legion, but perhaps one of the most graphic was penned by a local priest recording an outbreak in eighteenth-century Guatemala:

> The filthy smell and stench which came from those who lay sick of this disease was enough to infect the rest of the house, and all that came to see them. It rotted their very mouths and tongues and made them as black as coal before they died.[3]

Doctors who treated typhus patients also reported on their 'cadaver-like breath', and how the dreadful smell 'provided a sensory aspect to the disease that was almost impossible to escape'. Descriptions of the smell of typhus vary from source to source, but most agree that it resembles advanced rotting flesh or vegetable matter, and can easily make a person not used to it retch violently. As we have seen, the interior atmosphere of the *Ticonderoga*, with her full load of passengers, was volatile even before the disease took hold. Even the crew, inured though they were to the challenging olfactory standards of a nineteenth-century sailing ship, reeled back in disgust upon removing the night covers at dawn. What she then began to smell like with dozens suffering various stages of typhus can scarcely be imagined. The smell reached into everything on board, pervading clothes, bedding, even the very timbers of the ship herself.[4] Nor was the disease the only factor contributing to the ship's rank atmosphere.

With passengers either ill or physically or emotionally weakened, and with morale and possibly even sanity collapsing, fewer and fewer had the strength or presence of mind to make the climb from the lower decks to use the ships' water closets. Night utensils became filled to overflowing, and other receptacles began to be used for human waste, urine, vomit and ordure: soup tins, pots and other cooking utensils, drinking mugs—anything that could be found. With the rolling and pitching of the ship, the floors of the decks became awash in filth, further compounding the hellish atmosphere.

The lower deck was in an even more indescribable state, as effluent began to seep down the walls and through the floorboards from the equally chaotic main deck above. Those who were still well enough to eat left food scraps, putrefying, where they lay.

At one stage, Captain Boyle ordered his second mate to venture below to the passenger decks and attempt to organise some kind of clean-up. He at first flatly refused but further pressure eventually compelled him to do so. His report to Boyle about conditions below deck so appalled him that he immediately appointed a number of the still fit men from the single men's quarters to become cleaning constables. This supposedly, led to some improvement, but the descriptions of the ship when it was inspected after it arrived in Melbourne indicate that little was in fact achieved.

Now, in mid-October, the ship was heading on a course roughly 140 degrees east, making fast for the entrance to Bass Strait. As the *Ticonderoga* closed on her final destination, however, the rate of mortality from the disease increased. Death, it seemed, was making a final lunge as the finish line drew near. The end of October was particularly grim.

On 23 October, Margaret Stewart, 22 years of age and travelling alone in the single women's quarters, died along with her dreams of meeting a husband with good prospects in Australia. The following days saw a gaggle of little children perish: Jane Smith, three; Mary Rutter, two; Elizabeth Drinnan, one. Nor were mature patients spared. James Dochard, 22, left his wife Mary, 23, and younger brother, William, eighteen, to finish the journey alone. A young mother, Mary Ann Henderson from Ross in the heart of the Highlands, joined her infant son, David, leaving behind her husband and a two-year-old, James. Another Scot, Jane Kay, died, leaving her husband and five children, all under the age of eight. A few weeks later, their youngest, William, would die in quarantine.

The *Ticonderoga*'s crew also became sick, but as they berthed separately, the rate of infection among them was not as severe as it might have been. Some estimates of ten seamen falling ill have been quoted, which represents slightly less than one-fifth of the 48-member crew. One of those was William Boyle, the ship's third mate and younger brother of Captain Boyle. Deep in a coma, the captain knew his brother was in a parlous state, unlikely to recover.

The group that seems to have been least affected by the disease was older children and teenagers, only 5 per cent of whom died from the typhus, despite many more than that contracting the disease. Most of those who did fall sick usually recovered and survived. Apart from a naturally robust constitution, many may have been spared, ironically, by being compelled to man the ship, particularly in the trials of the Southern Ocean. Captain Boyle seems to have encouraged many of the young men in the single quarters to learn as much as they could about the art of sailing, and he drew upon their help when the ship needed all the manpower that could be mustered during the storms. It was dangerous work—although not nearly as dangerous, it would seem under the circumstances, as staying below deck.

Undaunted, the two doctors continued to make their presence felt in the dreadful lower decks of the ship alongside Captain Boyle, who in every recollection of this terrible part of the voyage to have survived, is remembered by all to have displayed the utmost consideration for his ailing passengers: 'Captain Boyle was as careful as possible for the wellbeing of those committed to his charge,' recalled Christopher McRae. 'From a sense of duty and the possession of a human and kindly disposition, he used every means at his command to prevent such a condition of filth.'[5] Simply observing the regular presence of the foremost authorities of the ship—the captain and his two surgeons—seems to have given many people the sense that, at the very least, they had not been completely abandoned. Boyle would do his best to assure people that the ship was making good time, and that any day now they would arrive at Port Phillip, where the best of care would be arranged for them—a promise he quietly prayed he could honour.

Drs Sanger and Veitch, now overwhelmed, sought more help among the passengers, as some of those recruited earlier had become sick and even died. Few came forward. An exception remained the Fannings—John, his wife Mary and now their son Patrick, sixteen— who throughout had served as nurses and attendants amid the chaos of both the male and female hospitals. This steadfast family all risked their health—indeed, their lives—to assist their fellow passengers in dire need, and remained until the end of the voyage, and even well after, battling at the forefront of the disease.

Two young women put forward their services. Mary Dochard, a young Scot from Stirling who had recently lost her husband, James, to the disease, was travelling with her extended family, including her late husband's parents and several siblings and in-laws. Perhaps she felt obliged to assist the surgeons, if only to offer some protection for the rest of her family. The second young woman had lost no family, as she travelled alone in the single women's section. She also appeared to be in good health and, being somewhat older than most of her companions, possessed a maturity that Sanger and particularly Veitch found compelling. Rather than sit out the weather and hope to remain free of illness, Annie Morrison, who had farewelled her father from the ferry at Tobermory, stepped forward to offer her limited experience of nursing.

In the putrid decks and in the ship's hospitals, the small band of two doctors and a handful of volunteer nurses and other assistants worked tirelessly among the *Ticonderoga*'s sick, which in the latter stages of the voyage was estimated to be around 300 wrestling with various stages of the disease.

One morning, after another dismal night of broken sleep, Dr Veitch arose to once again proceed with Dr Sanger to the hell of the lower decks. Undoubtedly, there would be more grief and sickness than they had seen just the previous evening, and there would be little they could do to relieve the passengers' suffering, but both felt it was their duty and purpose to make their presence felt, and to try. A knock on the door of Dr Sanger's small cabin did not meet with its usual answer, however. Veitch called, but still no response came. Another entreaty was at last met with a hoarse response. Veitch quickly pushed open the small wooden door to find Sanger, still on his small bed, covered in sweat, his temperature sky high. His worst fears realised, Veitch began to administer what he could to his superior, even managing to retrieve some of the medicinal wine he had kept in reserve for just such an emergency. Sanger was presenting with the early stages of typhus and seemed utterly incapacitated. The mantle of care would now pass from one of the most experienced doctors in the emigration service to a virtual novice on his first appointment, facing one of the greatest disasters ever to have taken place in the history of peacetime emigration.

Veitch comforted Sanger as much as he could, but privately had little faith that he would recover. He seemed to be alarmingly advanced. No red rash had yet appeared, but Sanger was definitely febrile, nauseous and showing early signs of delirium. He managed, however, to impress on Veitch that he should carry on the work they had started, and that even with little medicine to administer, they were still of great value. Besides, they could not now be too far from Port Phillip and must surely soon be weighing anchor. Then, he said, help on a grand scale would be at hand.

Feeling a dread weight of responsibility, Veitch gathered his handful of nurses and assistants and got to work. After a short time, he asked the dependable Annie to inform the Captain—but no one else—of Sanger's condition. She did not flinch.

Amazingly, amid the chaos, somewhere between twelve and nineteen (sources vary) babies were born during the voyage—mostly to Scottish women. It being impossible, particularly in the latter stages, to use the female hospital, most of these births took place in the mothers' own bunks in the married quarters, where they were attended by Mary Fanning or others acting as midwives. Utterly against the odds, each of these newborns, though surrounded by death, survived not only the birth, but the remainder of the journey. Amid the terrible jangle of the dying, the grieving and the demented, the cries of just-delivered life could also be heard on board the *Ticonderoga*, contributing to an already surreal symphony. To the further encouragement of all, some of the patients—particularly the older children and youths—began to show signs of recovery, their fever dropping, and the rash and delirium abating. Those who had been lucky enough to be washed, largely removing the infestations of lice from their body and clothing, stood a better chance of recovery. These incidences were, however, some of the few moments of joy.

The tragedy that befell the Robertson family from Inverness unfolded on 26 October, when both Daniel, 40, and his wife Isabella, also 40, died within hours of each other. A few days later, their now orphaned baby daughter, Ann, would also pass away, leaving their eldest, eighteen-year-old Mary, to care for her three younger siblings, one of whom would also die a few weeks later in quarantine. Having left Birkenhead a family of seven, the Robertsons would finally disembark in Melbourne just three strong. In the last few days of October, the death toll on board rose to a terrible crescendo with around 25 passengers perishing within a few days. On 28 October, 32-year-old Sarah Bell from Somerset died, leaving a husband and three children, although she had begun the journey with four. The next day, James McKean, 24, also passed away, making a widow of his 22-year-old wife Margaret. On the last day of the month, Margaret Rutherford, 28, died. Exactly a month later, she would be followed by her husband. That night, as the ship pitched in a stiff breeze towards the north, yet another funeral for two of the infants who had died over the past two days took place. It was a pathetic affair, with barely a word spoken above a mumble of the few lines of the prescribed service and the endless wash of the sea. There were simply no words left to say.

Then a triumphant voice sang out somewhere high in the rigging: 'Light! Port bow!' Forgetting everything—even the melancholy reason they were on the deck—the funeral party rushed to the side of the ship and peered into the darkness. There, in the distance, a pale yellow beam stoked the blackened sky to the north.

Instantly, feet were heard from everywhere rushing onto the deck. Captain Boyle appeared, his first mate clutching a heavy ledger, hurriedly opening it to a particular page under the dim light of a hurricane lamp. 'Yes, First Mate, yes?' Boyle urged impatiently. 'A moment please, Captain,' said the excited young officer, running his eye over the myriad lines of information in front of him. Then, finding what he was so frantically seeking, 'Three by three seconds, Captain!' The two men peered again at the stabbing shaft of light, each counting quietly to themselves. To those watching the late evening scene, the suspense was almost unbearable. 'I think we have it, First Mate, please note the time,' said Boyle finally, with an excitement in his voice that even he could barely contain. 'Please feel free to inform passengers and crew that we have just sighted the Cape Otway light, on the coast of Victoria.' It was early on Monday morning, 1 November, 1852.

21

Arrival

Four days later, an alarming headline would greet readers of the late morning edition of *The Argus* newspaper: 'Terrible State of Affairs on board an Emigrant Ship at the Port Phillip Heads!'

Their attention well and truly grabbed, groups of people going about their business stood still alone or in huddles along busy Bourke and Elizabeth Streets, holding open the large sheets of newspaper, close by the paper boys and newspaper stands where they had just been bought and, with growing alarm, read on:

Intelligence was brought to Williamstown, on Wednesday evening last, by Captain Wylie, of the brig *Champion*, from Adelaide, that a large ship named TICONDEROGA, ninety days out from Liverpool, with upwards of 900 Government emigrants on board, had anchored at the Heads. A great amount of sickness had occurred amongst the passengers, more than a hundred deaths having taken place, and almost a similar number of cases (Typhus fever) being still on board. Nor was this all. The doctor's health was so precarious that he was not expected to survive, and the whole of the medicine, medical comforts, etc., had been consumed . . .

Passers-by, or those who could not afford the thruppence for their own copy, paused and shuffled close to hear the words spoken aloud by readers who found themselves with an instant and captivated audience. In colonial Victoria, where the single artery to the outside world was the arrival of ships, any new emigrant vessel was worthy of attention. Who was on board? What news, fashions and innovations would soon be arriving from the place that, although on the far side of the globe, was the colony's cultural and economic epicentre: Britain? Ships also brought other, less welcome things, however, and as they listened, one word stuck like a thorn, compelling people shake their heads and raise a protective hand to the throat. *Typhus.* Muttering quietly, the shock felt by some quickly hardened to a sense of anger. This, they said, had long been predicted.

* * * *

Having sighted the Otway light, Captain Boyle could momentarily relax. He had, after all, managed to steer his large ship, undamaged across the ferocious seas of one of the longest and most dangerous shipping routes in the world. Moreover, despite neither he nor any of his crew having ever sailed these waters before, he had managed it in 90 days, which—while not a record—was an excellent time nonetheless. As navigators, Boyle and his first mate had proved themselves to be exemplary, missing not a mark, and successfully negotiating by far the most dangerous part of the voyage: the final days before reaching Port Phillip. It was at this point that the dreaded 'threading the needle' needed to be negotiated, with the approach to Bass Strait requiring seamen to slip through the narrow gap between the north-west–south-east running line of the Victorian coast and the rocky northern tip of King Island, Cape Wickham out in Bass Strait. After emerging from the whiplashing of the frigid Southern Ocean, this was no easy feat.

As Boyle, and every other seaman afloat, would have been all too aware, the coastlines of both places—Victoria and King Island— were strewn with the remains of both ships and lives. Seven years earlier (as he would have been reminded during many meetings held leaning over charts, protractor and compass in hand, with the representatives of the Board), the emigrant vessel *Cataraqui,* a large barque, had slammed into a rock shelf on King Island's south-west shore, her skipper having erred tragically in estimating his position, convinced himself that he was actually much further to the north. Over three ghastly days, in a fierce storm, the ship was torn to pieces by the breakers, and though just metres from shore, no more than a pitiful four survivors remained alive from a passenger and crew list numbering 500 souls. The *Cataraqui* was, and remains still, Australia's worst peacetime maritime disaster. Amazingly, a lighthouse at Cape Wickham was not built and activated until 1861.

Any glow of self-congratulation was short-lived, however, as Captain Boyle was brought back to reality by the sobs of the grieving and the wailings of the demented among his poor afflicted passengers and crew. As much as he would like to believe otherwise, his ordeal was far from over.

Staying on deck for the rest of the night to navigate the remaining 70 or so nautical miles to the entrance of Port Phillip Bay, Captain Boyle took the *Ticonderoga* north-east into a stiff spring breeze. After a few hours, almost in front of him, the first signs of his first day in Australia became visible on the eastern horizon.

Being completely unfamiliar with Australian landscapes, he took in the rich dark olive of the foliage, the undulating hills and the sweeping beaches of the Victorian coastline as it became slowly visible with the dawn—not unlike, he thought, some parts of America, with which he was far more familiar.

A new stirring began to be heard among the passengers. Finally, after weeks of the most terrible turmoil, of praying constantly for this nightmare voyage to be over, all sensed that they were finally nearing its end. Those in good health came onto the upper deck, braving the chilly wind to take in for themselves the first sights of their new country, no longer confined to the imagination but now real, there in front of them.

People who had lived and worked on farms all their lives came on deck and gripped the handrail. It was lush land, they thought to themselves, green and fertile. After what they had been through, this at least they needed to believe.

On a clear and bright early morning, after a journey of nearly 13,000 miles, the *Ticonderoga* arrived outside the entrance to Port Phillip Bay. Negotiating the formidable Heads was not a task to be taken lightly, particularly for those unaccustomed to its tricks and peculiarities. Beyond its entrance stretched a vast, almost entirely landlocked, inland bay measuring nearly 800 square miles. But first, the infamously treacherous passage between its two guarding promontories, known appropriately to sailors everywhere as 'the Rip', needed to be navigated. Although 2 miles of water separated the Heads—Point Lonsdale on the west and Point Nepean on the east—the intervening Rip was riven by a chaotic pattern of reefs reaching out from both points, reducing the true navigable distance to a gap little more than half a mile wide. A mistake made here would not be forgiven. So treacherous was the Rip, in fact, that even the government pilot vessels were reluctant to traverse it to bring vessels in. That risk, in most cases, would have to be undertaken by the captains themselves. According to his Notes to Mariners, Boyle was required to make his own way through the Rip to a small outcrop on the western arm near the fishing village of Queenscliff named Shortland's Bluff. Once here, he was to signal for a pilot to guide him through the fairways to the shipping channel and eventually up to the port of Melbourne, Port Phillip itself. With the sandy floor of the bay at an average depth of only 26 feet, this was not a course Boyle wanted to tackle unaided.

He would have appreciated that same help with tackling the Rip itself, where unpredictable waves, eddies and currents abounded. Then there were the tidal streams that ran through it at up to 6 knots, and vastly differentiating depths—between 5 and 100 metres— making for surges that had already trapped scores of vessels, such as the 500-ton *Isabella Watson*. Eight months previously, this passenger barque had come to grief, taking nine lives with her, executing exactly the manoeuvre that Boyle, in a much larger ship, was now about to attempt. He could clearly see the *Isabella Watson*'s broken carcass washed up on a tiny cove just inside Point Nepean, as if placed there as a warning of the dangers that confronted him.

Boyle had studied his Notice to Mariners for the approaches to Port Phillip. Likewise he recalled the warnings to take particular care with the Rip. Slack water between the surge of the tides, he had been advised, would be the safest time to make his approach, but even then a sudden squall or current from below could drag a ship onto a reef or into the infamous natural feature of Corsair Rock, which lay guarding the Rip's entrance like a sentinel.

Until deemed safe, it was customary for ships to pause outside the Rip, sailing back and forth under half-sail several miles out into Bass Strait, awaiting the most opportune moment to enter, then picking up the pilot to Melbourne. Captain Boyle, however, did not have time on his side. With his passengers dying like flies and 300 suffering various degrees of illness, his priority had to be delivering them to better care, and quickly.

A mate then announced that one of the sailors had in fact sailed to Melbourne several times previously—albeit not recently. Conditions were not ideal, but the water looked calm, a breeze was blowing in his favour and so Boyle decided to make the attempt. Even approaching the entrance from the ocean side was dangerous, as jutting nearly a kilometre into Bass Strait was the Rip Bank, another obstacle that needed to be avoided. A brief conference took place on the upper deck, with charts and notes consulted once again. Standing by the captain and behind the helmsman stood the unnamed seaman who, several years before, had likewise attempted the passage, the weight on his shoulders now feeling much heavier than he would have liked. Boyle looked up and ordered more sail. When all was ready, he then gave the command to bring the *Ticonderoga* about, and with men placed fore and aft giving soundings, in the great ship went.

Even in calm weather such as this, Boyle felt the surge of eddies tugging at the ship as it negotiated the bottleneck. Around him was a true patchwork of ocean temperaments: white water here, a smooth glassy upsurge from deep below there. Shadows flitted by as she glided over alternating patches of dark reef and pale sand. Boyle quickly appreciated the reputation of this torrid piece of water among sailors the world over. Running before the wind, the shore now began to move past. A line of little white stone cottages became visible, the first signs of habitation of this new land.

Then the soundings indicated more water beneath them and the sea settled to its dark bluey grey. They were past the Heads and through the Rip of Port Phillip Bay. Rounds of 'Well done! Well done!' made their way along the upper deck from the captain and first mate. Boyle trimmed the yards as the *Ticonderoga*'s bow edged towards the low hump of Shortland's Bluff. Then came the order that every soul on board had, for 90 agonising days, longed to hear, 'Come to anchor!'

'Ay, Cap'n,' came the response, and the magnificent clanking of the great anchor chain, finally released, reverberated throughout the ship. Finding a sound bottom, the *Ticonderoga* swayed for a moment, then rode at her anchor, still.

* * * *

Henry Draper had been part of the Port Phillip pilot service for less than a year, but his time thus far had been anything but uneventful. As first mate of the barque *Nelson,* he had arrived in Melbourne from England in 1851, disembarked a load of privately paying passengers, and was preparing to load up for the return journey with a cargo of 2600 bales of wool and 9000 ounces of gold, which arrived under escort by steamer. After loading, his skipper, a Captain Wright, unwisely chose this moment to go ashore for a last carouse before their departure the next morning. Riding at anchor at Hobson's Bay, Draper was awakened in his cabin during the night by sounds of scuffling on the deck. Emerging, he soon found himself surrounded by an armed gang who were preparing to liberate the ship's store of gold. In the drama, a pistol was discharged at one of the mates, the ball missing him but grazing Draper's hip. The bandits then locked the entire crew up and made off with the gold.

The ship's cook, who had escaped attention by hiding under his bunk, released Draper, who then swiftly raised the alarm upon rowing ashore. The bandits were soon rounded up. Draper would have liked nothing better than to have simply left as planned the next morning, but as a witness to a robbery, he was now compelled to cool his heels for several weeks awaiting a trial. He was in the meantime feted as a minor hero, awarded a total of £170 for his troubles and visited by Port Phillip's Chief Harbour Master, Charles Ferguson, who promptly offered him a job. 'I received the request with astonishment,' Draper later wrote, 'as I considered my position far above that of a pilot's.' His pride quickly recovered, however, when told that his salary would be in the range of £100 per year.[1]

A year into the job, Draper was being kept busy at the pilot station at Shortland's Bluff. The discovery of gold had seen a huge increase in shipping entering the bay, but his small group of pilots still had just two oared whale boats and a cutter at their disposal to guide as many as ten vessels a day both through the Rip and into the shipping lanes that cut their way through the shallow sandy banks up to the busy port of Melbourne. Early November was a particularly active time, and the records show that on the day the *Ticonderoga* came in, another nine ships also entered, many needing assistance. Few days of his career, however, would be as dramatic as this bright November morning when he answered the request of a large, dark emigrant ship lying at anchor off Shortland's Bluff. She was, he could see, an unusually fine clipper, but as he approached her in his pilot's cutter, he sensed all was not well. He could see people on deck, but they were few in number and appeared unsettled. Then, as he came within earshot, a series of desperate shouts could be heard, 'Don't come on board, pilot,' he was told. 'We are dying of fever!'

Standing off, Draper assessed the situation. The large ship could not remain where it was, but to come aboard to steer her into the lanes was apparently a risk. After examining her formidable sides, he directed his helmsman to come close. Making a perilous grab for one of the mizzen chains and shields on the side of the hull, built to take the great strain of the mizzen mast shrouds and stays, he hauled himself up. Avoiding setting foot on the deck, he continued scrambling up into the network of ropes, which took him eventually into the rigging from where he then looked down upon a scene of despair.

Under a tarpaulin lay a group of bodies. Passengers stood or lay around, their faces pale, red-eyed and exhausted beyond caring. The ship herself was unkempt, the deck a mess, the rigging around him untidy, the yards badly reefed, as if done by amateurs. Then there was the smell: a terrible, decomposing stench that rose up sickeningly into his nostrils. What on earth, he asked, had these people been through?

Captain Boyle appeared below him, explaining the terrible sickness that had broken out on the voyage, which had already taken a hundred of his passengers. More were bound to die, he said, and even more remained ill. The senior ship's surgeon, too, was incapacitated, his medicines exhausted. Supplies of fresh food and water, as well as proper care, were desperately needed. 'I was informed they had 1000 passengers and that they had lost 102 on the passage,' Draper later recalled in a brief memoir, although his memory may have exaggerated the numbers slightly.[2]

In an instant, Draper knew that the *Ticonderoga* would not, for the foreseeable future, be going anywhere near Melbourne, and that it was of the utmost urgency that news of her arrival be sent to those in authority as quickly as possible. He explained to Captain Boyle that, given the grave situation on board, he could not permit her to proceed to Melbourne and that, regretfully, she would have to remain here until further instructions were received. On hearing this, a further wave of despair washed over the small group of passengers. Not wanting to stay on board a moment longer than necessary, Draper climbed back down towards his waiting cutter. 'And Captain, Sir,' he added solemnly as he departed, 'I would advise you to hoist the Yellow Jack.' Boyle said he understood, and thanked the pilot.

Returning to his cutter, Draper proceeded as quickly as possible back to the shore station to seek the advice of his colleagues. The *Ticonderoga*, meanwhile, would continue to lie at anchor, the situation on board deteriorating by the hour. Boyle called over his first mate and a brief but solemn conversation took place. The mate nodded, and proceeded immediately below to a storage locker containing the ship's signal flags, rolled up neatly in their respective wooden pigeon holes. At the very bottom, the mate drew out the one flag no ship's master ever wanted to give the order to fly, the dreaded 'Yellow Jack', a simple square of yellow signalling catastrophe. Returning to the deck, he instructed one of the crew to climb the mainmast and hoist it at its highest point. Now every passing vessel, as well as everyone on shore, would see that the mighty clipper *Ticonderoga* was a ship of disease, a plague ship, which should under no circumstances be approached.

With Sanger in the grip of the fever, it was now Dr Veitch, the young physician on his first sea voyage and the only fit surgeon on board, who would take on the mantle of his superior. For the time being, it was he Captain Boyle would consult on the daily updates of the passengers' state. Sadly, however, Veitch could offer his captain no good news.

Since the ship's arrival the previous day, death had continued to ravage the *Ticonderoga*. Helen Bowie, the only child of a young couple from Edinburgh, George and Helen Bowie, died on the first day of the month, making their arrival into the bay a melancholy affair. Two-year-old Jemima Grant, whose family had travelled from Inverness, at the other end of Scotland, was next. Nor was the new month's tally confined to the very young.

With the death of her husband, John, twenty, Jane Sievwright was suddenly a widow. Janet Stevenson, 35 from Stirling, left her husband, Alexander, and their two daughters, Christina, seven, and Jane, four, to face their new world without a wife or a mother. Three or four deaths were now taking place each day, and with burials at sea forbidden inside the bay, the bodies could only be laid out on the deck under canvas. However, even more horrifying to Henry Draper than this macabre tableaux he had spied from his perch in the rigging was the apparent disinterest shown by the other passengers. It seemed to Draper that they were people pushed to a point beyond caring.

A desperate Dr Veitch remonstrated with Captain Boyle. Surely, he pleaded, they were not expected to simply sit there as a floating morgue while the fever took even more victims? But Boyle's hands were tied. For the time being, there was nowhere for them to go, and no one to take them.

Henry Draper had in fact been doing all in his power to help. Soon after returning to his shore station, he reported to his colleagues what he had seen on board the *Ticonderoga*. None of them had faced a situation like it, and felt further instructions from Melbourne were urgently required as taking a ship in her wretched condition into Hobson's Bay was out of the question. All agreed that the passengers needed to come ashore, but to where? Port Phillip was a full day's sailing away. Draper again regarded the eerily still ship, which seemed to have taken on a more menacing appearance. As the small group of men spoke in urgent circles about the ship and her plight, Draper went to the window and with a spyglass surveyed a long low stretch of beach and scrub that stretched away a mile or so from the bay's eastern head, Point Nepean. 'There,' he announced. 'There is where she will go.'

* * * *

A short time later, by luck, the familiar sight of the 225-ton *Champion*, a coastal brig that regularly plied the southern coastal waters between the ports of Fremantle, Adelaide and Melbourne, came into view. Making one of her regular entrances into the bay, she was this day carrying six passengers and a load of general cargo.³ Her skipper, the well-known Captain Wylie, needed the help of no pilot to slip into the fairways and up the lanes to Melbourne. Upon spotting the small two-masted brig, Draper hailed him with a signal that he should prepare to be approached. A short time later, the pilot cutter came alongside the surprised Captain Wylie.

Indicating the big dark clipper anchored of Shortland's Bluff behind him, Draper told Wylie what he had seen on board, just as the older man caught sight of the Yellow Jack fluttering from her topmast. One hundred already dead, said Draper to an increasingly shocked Wylie, with many more sick and no medical supplies. The harbour authorities must be informed, he continued, and help must be sent—urgently. Wylie did not need to be told twice. Putting on more sail, he set off and made his way north to Melbourne as quickly as possible.

The next morning, 3 November, Draper again approached the *Ticonderoga* and, by the same means he had employed the previous day, came aboard. Another night spent out on the water had not improved her situation. After requesting that the captain weigh anchor and put on some sail, Draper directed the helmsman to the other side of the bay, and into the small cove that had come to be known as Abraham's Bosom, from where the two lime-burners, William Cannon and Patrick Sullivan, watched her stately but eerie approach.

In a decision the Governor of Victoria, Charles La Trobe, would later praise, Henry Draper took it upon himself to direct the *Ticonderoga* to an area of land that he understood to have only recently been set aside as a future quarantine station. There were as yet, he knew, few resources to be found there: only the two limestone cottages built by the lime-burners themselves, and one or two other small structures, but fresh water wells had been sunk, and a secure anchorage was to be had not far off the beach. From here, the sick could be evacuated and help could be delivered relatively easily. Getting those people off that ghastly ship, he had decided before approaching the *Ticonderoga* that morning, had to be the first priority. As he later recalled—indeed, with some pride—in his memoir:

I piloted her to the Quarantine Station at Point Nepean, let go the anchor, gave her 60 fathoms of chain, came down the rigging, and slipped back into my boat . . . by taking the precaution of going into the mizzen-top I could state to the Health Officer that I had not had any communication with the ill-fated people. Getting up into the mizzen-top was considered quite a masterpiece of ingenuity and forethought.[4]

Closer to the shore they may have been, but if the poor passengers on board the *Ticonderoga* had thought that their ordeal was nearing its end, they were sadly mistaken.

22

Protecting the colony

Despite the ever-increasing confidence of nineteenth-century medicine, despite the delivery of intelligent and highly trained graduates from ancient universities such as Oxford and St Bartholomew's into British hospitals and surgeries, despite the volumes written about new advances in medical treatment of all kinds, most of the virulent and destructive diseases of the day remained essentially mysterious and completely incurable. With typhus, for example, despite the millions it killed there is no evidence to suggest that anyone, anywhere—prior to its pathogen being finally described by Henrique da Rocha Lima and Stanislaus von Prowazek in the early 1900s—had so much as suggested the possibility of its cause being linked to human body lice.

In the 1850s, therefore, doctors such as Sanger and Veitch, despite their best intentions and tireless concern for their patients, could barely even scratch at the symptoms with the knowledge and medicines at their disposal. Prior to the modern comprehension of infection, a disease having taken hold was simply left to run its terrible course. The only bulwark against its spreading was avoidance, in the form of isolation or quarantine.

With the advent of the gold rush, the colonial backwater of Melbourne, founded only seventeen years previously by John Batman (a syphilitic conman and slaughterer of Tasmanian Aboriginals, described by artist John Glover as 'a rogue, thief, cheat and liar, a murderer of blacks and the vilest man I have ever known',[1]) suddenly began to burst its established boundaries, even up to the threshold of its hitherto isolated quarantine station at Little Red Bluff. This had been established by the government in 1840, its hand forced by the arrival of one of the unluckiest vessels ever to set sail, the *Glen Huntly*. This purpose-built 450-ton barque departed Greenock on her maiden voyage from Scotland under the command of a Captain Buchanan in December 1839, laden with 157 mainly Scottish emigrant passengers bound for Victoria. On her very first night at sea, she collided with a coastal vessel, then in the English Channel as fog set in, she missed a marker and struck a submerged rock, which damaged her timbers even further. A few days later, despite being in the open waters of the North Atlantic, the hapless Buchanan managed to plough into yet another vessel, this time an American packet ship, which tore away the *Glen Huntly*'s masthead and lower spars. Then, while crossing the equator, typhus broke out, resulting in her arrival into Melbourne with 50 cases of 'fever' and ten passengers fewer than had embarked.

When the unfortunate ship limped into Hobson's Bay with the yellow flag at her topmast, the people of Melbourne, already spooked by a recent outbreak of typhus that devastated Hobart and reports of the disease in Sydney, went into such a panic that the then Superintendent of the Port Phillip District, Charles La Trobe, was later reported by *The Age* of 1931 as becoming 'considerably perturbed and anxious to avoid the introduction of what might prove to be a serious menace to the well-being of the small but flourishing community'. He ordered the *Glen Huntly* to depart forthwith to a small sandstone promontory known as Little Red Bluff, 4 miles south-east of the city. It was a lonely, windy place, isolated in the bush but bordered by a swamp on one side, which had been a former meeting place for the now dispersed Bunurong Aboriginal people.

To accommodate both the *Glen Huntly*'s sick and healthy passengers, a hospital of sorts was set up in tents along the fore-shore, which evolved by default into Melbourne's first quarantine or 'sanitary' station, as it was dubbed initially to dampen public fears. In any case, it was a facility for which the burgeoning city was long overdue. Accepting its sudden establishment as a *fait accompli*, La Trobe appointed Dr Barry Cotter, Colonial Surgeon and the man described on a family biographical website as 'Melbourne's first doctor', to oversee its proper development. Cotter decided that the sick would remain on board their anchored ships to either recover or die, while those still healthy would be housed in canvas tents along the shore and up on the bluff. These twin camps were named, appropriately enough, 'Sick' and 'Healthy', and the arrangement apparently worked, as only three more deaths eventuated from the *Glen Huntly*. To bolster the station's position of isolation, La Trobe also provided a contingent of soldiers to prevent any contact between the patients and the outside world, as well as a water patrol in rowboats to deter any notions those confined to their ships may have had about swimming ashore. Cotter's diary of April 1840 captured some of the scene:

> The remainder of the emigrants were landed yesterday from the Glen Huntly, with an addition of six fresh cases for the sick camp. There are at present in the healthy camp one hundred and eight, including children; many of them appear much emaciated from long and continued illness but I have every reason to hope that the change of quarters and diet will soon restore them.[2]

Despite Cotter's efforts, and the considerable interest shown by La Trobe, who became a regular visitor, Little Red Bluff was, by all accounts, a miserable place. Cold and windswept by the souther-lies slicing up the bay in winter, baking hot in summer, it remained for more than a decade no more than a flimsy canvas city filled with miserable people who desperately wanted to get out of there. Hemmed in by the sea on one side and a swamp on the other, and under permanent armed guard, its inmates would have felt little better than convicts. Nor was the gloomy atmosphere alleviated by one part of the camp evolving eventually into one of the city's first burial grounds.

However, as Melbourne's southern seaside residences expanded further southwards, the camp became untenable—particularly when gold was discovered, at which point even the guards proved unable to prevent the escape of those determined to head inland and try their luck in Bendigo and other places. In September 1852, the *Wanata*—one of the twin-deck clippers that preceded the *Ticonderoga*—likewise having had a terrible journey with many cases of typhus, arrived; she was followed two days later by HMSS *Vulcan*, a Royal Navy frigate recently converted into a steam-powered troopship. She carried several hundred Somersetshire soldiers of the 40th Regiment of Foot, arriving for their second tour of duty in Australia, who were destined to see a good deal of action fighting off bushrangers on Cobb and Co. stagecoaches as well as storming the Eureka Stockade in 1854. First, though, they had to make it off the boat, and as one of their ranks seemed to be presenting signs of the dreaded smallpox, they were all ordered into quarantine at Little Red Bluff, which was now struggling to cope. The entire regiment was placed on board the hulk *Lysander*, an ageing veteran of several runs from England, currently sitting idle and empty in Hobson's Bay. The *Lysander* was quickly fitted with 50 beds and a generous amount of stores, and the men of the 40th were told to settle in for a long wait.

A new quarantine station was obviously needed, and Charles La Trobe, recently elevated to the position of Victoria's first Lieutenant-Governor upon the colony becoming independent the year before, demanded that another location be found, accessible by sea but preferably a long way from the city. In early 1852, he sent his Port Health Officer, Dr Thomas Hunt, on a surveying mission.

Two possible sites were decided upon, one at Swan Island on the west side of the Port Phillip Bay, the other on a section of the long sandy peninsula which made up one arm of the bay's eastern entrance. Hunt eventually concluded that Swan Island was too marshy, too hard to land at and generally too depressing, but the bright little cove over on the eastern shore around from Point Nepean had potential. In a report to La Trobe, he described this area as

> admirably adapted for the purposes required; its position isolated, its anchorage good and easy of access both from inside the Heads when a vessel takes a pilot there and from Shortlands Bluff. The soil is sandy and at all times dry, the air pure. Water is procured by sinking wells to the depth of 12 to 15 feet, in abundance and sufficient purity, although somewhat aluminous and impregnated with lime. A root resembling sarsaparilla, wild parsley, and a root known here as pennyroyal, grow wild and cure scurvy in a short time.[3]

The site in fact already had its own short history of White settlement. Edward Hobson, a sailor turned grazier (and cousin of Captain William Hobson, a recent Governor of New Zealand and in whose honour Hobson's Bay had been named), was probably the first European to establish himself in the area, arriving overland from Parramatta in 1837. Seeing the potential of the area as cattle country, he used his connections to secure permission to graze across two large runs he established around the southern part of the large spit of land stretching south-east from Melbourne known as the Mornington Peninsula. He gave his runs two Aboriginal words, *Kangerong* and *Tootgarook*, the latter being the local Aboriginal Bunurong word to describe the croaking frogs in the many nearby swamps.

Over the next decade or so, a handful of other hardy families arrived and set themselves up along the peninsula's southern and western ends—including Point Nepean—taking out pastoral, fishing and lime-burning leases or squatting. Patrick Sullivan, who with his brother-in-law William Cannon had observed the *Ticonderoga*'s arrival from across the other side of the bay, was part of a large family of ten who had been evicted from their ancestral land in County Kerry, Ireland, by their English landlord (who at least agreed to pay their passage to Sydney, where they arrived, as free emigrants, in 1839). Before long, the Sullivans had ventured south to the Port Phillip District, where they liked what they saw, taking out several leases, constructing modest dwellings and generally living completely removed from interference by government—or, for that matter, anyone else. Other families arrived and likewise established themselves into a tight-knit and inter-marrying community. As Crown Land leaseholders, however, their tenure to the land they had come to regard as their own was uncertain, and in faraway Melbourne, those in power were preparing to bring that tenure to an abrupt end.

Throughout 1852, with Little Red Bluff's time as a quarantine station coming to an end, a stately procession of paperwork passed between the desks of Lieutenant-Governor La Trobe, his Port Health Officer Dr Hunt and the Victorian Surveyor-General Robert Hoddle. In October, La Trobe requested that due diligence be applied in establishing exactly what rights the lessees at Point Nepean may have:

> what are their expected tenures, and what power the Government possesses of removal, now or at the expiration of lease, whenever that may be.[4]

On 27 October, Surveyor-General Hoddle replied that with one month's notice, and a balance on the remaining leases—roughly £12—being refunded to each individual leaseholder, such lands as His Excellency might require may indeed be secured without too much fuss. He suggested that the Harbour Master, Charles Ferguson, might be granted sufficient legal and administrative powers to execute such an arrangement. La Trobe thought it an excellent idea. In this fashion, the bureaucratic wheels slowly revolved, and the plan for a new quarantine station to protect the people of Melbourne began to take shape—at least on paper.

A few days later, on the morning of 3 November, Ferguson sat in his office in Williamstown when the wild-eyed figure of Captain Wylie burst in. The two men knew one another, but Ferguson had never seen his old friend like this. He had sailed at haste all through the night, he said, and was wrung out and exhausted. He stammered:

> A . . . ship has come. A large one. From Liverpool. A hundred . . . yes, a hundred! . . . dead on board, many more sick. You must inform the Governor . . . and send help.[5]

The leisurely progress of the planned, but entirely prospective quarantine station had been overtaken by a very real emergency.

* * * *

Meanwhile, the passengers on board the *Ticonderoga* were close to despair. Three days earlier, believing their arrival into Melbourne would lead to better care, or at the very least the chance to get off this wretched ship, the passengers had felt that the worst was over. Those well enough and not numb with grief could finally allow themselves the luxury of contemplating some kind of future. When instead they dropped anchor off a lonely bluff with little signs of habitation, bar a couple of cottages, some tents and a signal station, then the pilot ordered them to remain there for an entire day, then another, followed by a third, they once again began to lose hope. Finally, though, the pilot boarded once more and as the sound of the anchor being raised reverberated through the ship, hopes rose again. But these too would be dashed when, instead of heading north to Melbourne, the pilot took them just a short way across the bay to an even more desolate-looking location, and left them there.

At this small and seemingly deserted little cove, where all that could be seen was scrub, sand dunes and empty beaches, rumours began to fly that they were to remain here for the foreseeable future, in quarantine.[6] When this was confirmed by the sight of the pilot once more departing, many began to curse their decision to leave their beloved homeland to travel on this death ship to the far side of the Earth, only to be left alone and forgotten by the rest of the world. Nothing, however, could have been further from the truth.

23

A colonial crisis

After hearing Captain Wylie's account of the *Ticonderoga*, and relaying what the pilot, Henry Draper, had seen of her horrific state, Harbour Master Captain Charles Ferguson started a chain of events that would electrify the upper echelons of Victoria's young colonial government. An urgent note was dispatched immediately to Governor La Trobe, but Ferguson had no intention of waiting for his answer before deciding to act.

A short distance from Ferguson's office in the small port of Williamstown, just a few miles from Melbourne, HMS *Empire* sat tied up and ready. This fast little ship served as an emergency vessel of sorts, scooting around the coast of Victoria and beyond, pulling stranded ships off reefs, rescuing survivors from shipwrecks and intercepting incoming emigrant ships to ensure that their captains were in compliance with the *Passengers Act* (one such master would later be fined almost £500 for supplying inadequate provisions to his passengers).

Ferguson planned to sail the *Empire* as soon as possible to Point Nepean to deal with this new emergency and to take along with him one of the most important medical men in the colony, his colleague and Port Health Officer, Dr Thomas Hunt, whose new quarantine station, Ferguson had told him, might be happening considerably sooner than planned. In the meantime, he arranged for the ship to be packed with as many fresh stores as she could carry: eleven live sheep, 276 pounds of fresh beef, 53 loaves of freshly baked bread, 24 bags of fresh potatoes, four cases of porter, one case of wine, 9 pounds of arrowroot, and six iron pots. The list was a long one, but whatever had to be done to see it filled, Ferguson saw that it was done.

The rest of that day, orders and requisitions raced out of the Harbour Master's office to suppliers across Williamstown and Melbourne. Their response came swiftly in the form of wagons arriving at the dock heavily laden with provisions. The most important acquisition of the day was the full medical chest to replenish the exhausted supplies of Drs Sanger and Veitch, but what Ferguson desperately needed was another doctor to travel with it. This same person would be then required to relieve the ailing and exhausted ship's surgeons, distribute supplies, then stay on to organise the quarantine station, which at this moment existed only on paper. Such a person would not be easy to come by—particularly at short notice—but these were desperate times. Hurrying down the corridor to Thomas Hunt's nearby office, the two men struggled to think of a suitable candidate.

Ferguson then fetched the list of ships currently in port and, running his finger down the column, stopped at the *Ottillia,* another large emigrant vessel that had recently arrived from Liverpool, currently undergoing repairs for lightning damage, and whose surgeon was listed as a Dr Joseph Taylor. The two men looked at each other. Perfect, they agreed, before hurrying out the door. A short time later, they stood beside the handsome *Ottillia* as she was tied up at the wharf, inquiring of her officers whether the surgeon superintendent might be available for a brief word. As it happened, Dr Taylor was in his cabin, and more than a little surprised to have his presence requested by no lesser figures than the Chief Harbour Master and

Port Health Officer, who greeted him in the warmest of terms despite neither having met him before in their lives.

After extolling his well-known reputation as an exemplary practitioner of medicine, Ferguson and Hunt came quickly to the point. A brand new government quarantine station was being set up a little way from Melbourne and Dr Taylor was just the man to run it. A handsome salary of not less than £300 was on offer, as well as accommodation and excellent rations for himself and his family. Did he by chance, Dr Hunt inquired, happen to have any experience with fever? Absolutely, replied Dr Taylor, a veteran of several long voyages who in fact had treated many such cases. 'Excellent!' exclaimed Ferguson. Lieutenant-Governor La Trobe, he added quietly, is most pleased that you might consider the position favourably. When Taylor's head had stopped spinning, he wondered whether he might be allowed a little time to consider the Lieutenant-Governor's most generous offer. Unfortunately, insisted the two gentlemen, time was such that the Lieutenant-Governor was most anxious to see the position filled without delay, and so an answer was required, well, immediately. As soon as a stunned Taylor nodded his assent, he felt his hand pumped vigorously and was told to pack his bags to be ready to sail to Point Nepean in precisely . . . at this point Ferguson checked his fob watch . . . two hours' time. Oh, Dr Hunt added, you would be advised to bring with you all the medicine and drugs you might have in your possession, as well as all those you can get your hands on at short notice. Then, thanking him profusely and wishing him a good day, Ferguson and Hunt were gone.

* * * *

Sitting in the wooden cottage he had had dismantled in England and brought out in pieces to be re-erected on his estate in Melbourne, which—in a touch of nostalgia for his French heritage—he had named *Jolimont*, news of the *Ticonderoga* hit Lieutenant-Governor Charles La Trobe like a lightning bolt. Immediately, he knew himself to be facing the most serious crisis in his role of running this new colony. Not only could such a disaster have serious ramifications for the flow of able-bodied people willing to come to Victoria, but if the disease itself was allowed to gain a foothold in Melbourne itself . . . it was a picture that did not bear thinking about.

The *Empire,* he knew, would soon be on its way to Point Nepean along with Hunt and Ferguson, but with nearly 700 desperately ill people stranded on a beach, whatever relief she could bring would, he knew, not last long. He urgently inquired about what other provisions were available to be sent to the *Ticonderoga.* He then learned that, by remarkable fortune, the old *Lysander* had once more become available, on account of the initial diagnosis of smallpox among the men of the 40th Regiment of Foot now being declared a false alarm. Advanced syphilis, it transpired, was the disease in question. While undoubtedly ghastly for the sufferer involved, this was nonetheless a far cry from smallpox. The relieved men of the 40th had been allowed to disembark the *Lysander*, and the ship was given *pratique*—permission to enter port—a day or so later. Even better, 50 new beds had just been installed in her holds, and her stores of fresh water and other provisions had yet to be returned to the warehouses. She would therefore immediately be dispatched to Point Nepean, where she would distribute her goods, offer what help she could and remain as a hospital ship until the quarantine station could erect more permanent facilities. This would have been welcome news indeed for the people on board the *Ticonderoga*, as down at the little cove, help could not come fast enough.

* * * *

Unlike just about everybody else on board the *Ticonderoga*, Dr Sanger was showing some signs of recovery. Having been acting as his plenipotentiary these past few days, Dr Veitch conveyed his superior's instructions when he was well enough to actually issue them, doing his best to reassure the passengers that a period of quarantine was a blessing in disguise—it was not only essential to stop the spread of the disease, but the enforced rest it entailed, not to mention the fresh food and medicine that would soon arrive, would provide the greatest incentive to a cure that could be asked for. In truth though, Veitch had shared his passengers' shock at realising that they were headed not for port, but rather for a lonely beach, and for an indefinite period of time.

The pilot, Henry Draper, had not said much beyond delivering them to the sanitary station, but when Boyle searched the shoreline for evidence of such a station, all he could see in front of him was sand and scrub. Draper may at this point have quietly qualified his earlier remark with the words 'future sanitary station'. He assured Boyle that help would be arriving, and that they must wait here until it did.

Boyle informed Veitch of the situation, adding that as far as anchorages went, this secure and sheltered little cove was not too bad. Wherever they found themselves, however, both agreed that the passengers—starting with the very sick—must be evacuated off the ship as soon as possible. Without waiting for instructions, Boyle directed those able-bodied of his crew to go ashore and begin to construct whatever shelter they could from the ship's spare spars and sailcloth, which were hauled out from deep in her holds. In the bright sunshine, the working parties rowed ashore and toiled in front of the lime-burners' cottages and further back among the dunes, using the hardy ti-tree branches as supports for makeshift tents.

Patrick Sullivan, William Cannon and a small group of local lime-burners and fishermen were more than alarmed to see a group of seamen storming ashore towards their homes like a small invading army. Confronting them, they demanded to know what exactly was going on. The crew of the *Ticonderoga* had no time for niceties, however, and relating what they had been through these last weeks—for the first time to outsiders—while they worked on the shelters, the little crowd, as well as those family members whose curiosity had overcome their fear to emerge from their dwellings, gathered around their uninvited guests in deepening silence while the story of the ship of death unfolded.

As they listened, Sullivan and Cannon, who had watched the vessel's ominous approach from the other side of the bay the day before, realised that their worst fears were unfolding. None of it came as a complete surprise. It had now been months since the small surveying party led by the important doctor from Melbourne, Thomas Hunt, first arrived to inspect their beach and its environs. From that moment, the brothers-in-law realised that the clock was ticking on the day the government would take it back from them. For Sullivan, whose parents had already suffered exile back in Ireland when people of power decided they would leave their land, it seemed that history was repeating itself.

With some rudimentary shelters established, Veitch made an assessment of the little hospital ward taking shape on the beach and was pleased by what he saw. Delivering his patients to shore, however, would be a far more difficult matter. Except for the very worst cases, though, the risk must be taken to remove them from the ship, where he knew only too well there was no hope for them whatever. Again, the crew of the *Ticonderoga* would carry out the task, being instructed to extract people as delicately as possible from their berths or from the ship's hospital and carry them, literally on their backs, to the deck then down the long gangway to the waterline, where rowboats would take them to shore. Some of the sick could walk, but not many.

Reporting back to Sanger, Veitch was told to delay not a moment further. It was a long, miserable and enervating process for all concerned, but by the end of the first day at the cove, 40 of the *Ticonderoga*'s most feverish and delirious passengers had been taken off and laid down on dry land for the first time in three months. Some, however, were simply too sick to move and were compelled to remain on the ship. For those who came ashore, it was all they could do to crawl into the shady nooks and shelters that had been provided for them by the sailors. Passenger James Dundas recalled years later that 'there was very little canvas for tents, so they had to make bush mia-mias for us to camp in them . . . like black fellows'.[1] Here, at the very least, they could look up at a clear sky, released finally from the dreadful smell, the deathly, suffocating atmosphere and incessant rocking of the ship.

The ship's doctors, by contrast, could indulge in no such relief, faced as they were with an entirely new set of problems. Veitch estimated to Sanger that upwards of 250 people still required treatment and that not enough of anything was available to help them. To start with, there was hardly any bedding left on board that was not putrid, that of the dead having been thrown overboard after them, and much of the spare sailcloth had gone as well. And how were they expected to feed this burgeoning beach hospital? Time would be needed to remove stoves and other facilities from the ship and relocate them on to land. Nor were there any medical comforts remaining, with both Veitch and Sanger having now exhausted their own stocks as well as the ship's. Then there was the question of who was to bury the dead, mounting up perilously on the deck in the warm spring sun. For it was now, upon arriving at her destination, that the *Ticonderoga*'s death toll reached its terrible zenith.

In the first few days of November, within clear sight of land, no less than fourteen people died on board the *Ticonderoga*. Alexander Mercer, 32, from Edinburgh followed his infant son, who had been one of the ship's earliest victims back in August, leaving only his wife and six-year-old boy. The infant Elizabeth Wilkie perished—mercifully the only member of her family of five to do so—but the very opposite was the case for the Appleby family, which saw the death on 2 November of John Appleby, three, following his younger sister Emma and his mother Sarah to the grave, leaving Silas Appleby, 28, alone in a new and unfamiliar world.

The list continued: Euphemia Reid, 36; John Spinwright, 30; Janet Stevenson; and Mary Bunton, 31. Little James Isbister would be the first—but not the last—to die from his very large family of twelve, who had possibly travelled the furthest of anyone on board the *Ticonderoga*, having left their home in the remote Orkney Islands off Scotland's north-east coast.

The worst day of the voyage was 4 November, when seven people died. One of those was Elizabeth Harcus, twenty, who the very next day would be joined by her sixteen-year-old sister, Mary, as the disease tore through the single women's quarters. By the end of the voyage, her father, George, would have lost all the women in his family as well as a son. There would be more deaths the next day, and the day after that until the warm spring sunshine and healing rest would gradually begin their work. Meanwhile, the ship continued to be awash with misery, but the focus of Drs Veitch and Sanger had to be on the living. Without the continued assistance of their volunteer nurses, Mr and Mrs Fanning and the steady Highland lass Annie Morrison, the doctors could not possibly have coped.

When dusk came, a good number of the sickest passengers had been placed ashore in their hastily constructed quarters. It being too risky to continue transferring patients after dark, Captain Boyle called a halt to the proceedings as the sun started to set. As he did, he was approached by one of the more senior passengers on board, 49-year-old Malcolm McRae, who had travelled with his wife, Helen, 39, and their seven children ranging from seventeen-year-old Christopher to Malcolm, two, who was currently sick. As McRae would later recall in his letter in *The Argus*, he politely explained to the captain in his soft Highland accent that his only daughter, Janet, ten, had died that afternoon and he would like permission to go ashore and bury her. To Boyle, he looked as utterly worn out as a man could be, but he was at pains to maintain his dignity as well as his manners. The captain had no doubt a refusal would be met simply with a nod, a 'Thank-you, Captain', and a quiet departure. Despite the last of the rowboats having returned for the night, some light still remained on the western horizon. Boyle looked around for one of his crew. 'You would need to be quick, Sir,' he said to McRae. 'I cannot have you returning in the dark.' McRae shook his hand. 'I thank you, Captain,' he said, with just a hint of a failing voice.

With the help of her eldest brother, Christopher, the girl was retrieved from below and her father carried her out, under a cloth, her small body appearing to weigh little more than the cold, damp clothes that clung to her. He was led down the side gangway and waited there while the sailor retrieved the small rowboat. Doyle watched them as they set off for the nearby shore, the rich red rays of a dazzling sunset lighting his expressionless face.

A short time later, at the very edge of the dusk, they returned to the ship, where yet more grief awaited Malcolm McRae. His son, Malcolm, had also now died. Once more, he politely requested permission to bury him, but this time Boyle had to refuse. 'Thank you, Captain,' was the man's only reply, as he nodded and turned quietly away, having lost two children in a single day. His son would be buried beside his sister the next morning, in a dry plot behind the dunes that the first mate had pegged out that afternoon. The boy would not be the last member of his family that McRae would have to bury before the ordeal was finally over.

24

The *Lysander*

Sick and bewildered, not understanding why help from Melbourne had failed to arrive, Dr Sanger that evening dictated a midnight letter to James Veitch (which, 131 years later, I would find in the Public Record Office in Kew). He intended it to be read by the highest authorities in the colony, but not knowing exactly who they were, he addressed it somewhat generally to 'the Colonial Secretary', who at that time was also Port Phillip's first police magistrate, William Lonsdale.

> Sir,
> I have the honour to announce the arrival of the Ship *Ticonderoga* from Liverpool with a large number of government immigrants on board under my superintendence.
>
> I deeply regret to have to inform you of the serious amount of formidable sickness prevalent during the whole Voyage, especially toward the latter part, and of the long list of Fatal cases resulting therefrom, in the greater numbers from Scarlatina and other Febrile diseases, nearly the whole of which have assumed a Typhoid character . . . which appears rather on the increase than otherwise and

I fear will continue to do so as long as the emigrants are in the vessel. The Deaths have been 100 in number and Births 19. No. of souls dispatched from Liverpool 795. There are at present at least 250 patients requiring treatment, and both my coadjutor Mr Veitch and myself are almost wearied out by the constant demand for our services, especially as it is impossible to get proper nurses for the sick in sufficient numbers.[1]

He then requests

sufficient supplies of medicines including, Porter and Ale, Wine and Brandy sufficient for the Emergency; also a quantity of beds and bedding as those belonging to the majority of the patients seriously ill are completely spoiled. As the state of the Emigrants demands steps to be taken instantly for their relief, the Captain and myself have made arrangements for the removal of a portion of them on Shore, a covering of a temporary nature being in the course of erection. From the statement of the Pilot who directed us to proceed to the Quarantine ground, and informed us that the Emigrants might go on shore, we expected to have been visited by the health officer to-day, but as no less than seven persons have died within the last 24 hours, and many more are in a very precarious state, we have deemed it indispensably necessary to apply for the articles annexed without delay.[2]

When, a few days later, Lonsdale put the letter in front of Lieutenant-Governor La Trobe, the worst of his earlier fears for the *Ticonderoga* were confirmed.

* * * *

The morning following Sanger's late-night missive, Captain Ferguson, along with the new sanitary station superintendent Joseph Taylor, finally arrived aboard the fully laden *Empire*. Having sailed through the night, he pulled up in the *Empire* and stood off from the much larger ship lying quietly at anchor in the little cove called Abraham's Bosom. 'What ship is that?' Ferguson called. At first there was no response to the prescribed maritime ritual. He hailed her again. 'What ship is that?' If the captain was not on deck, the officer of the watch would normally be the one designated to make the response. But the great black clipper was as quiet as the grave. Eventually, a weary voice hailed back in the dawn light across the glassy still water, '*Ticonderoga*'.

Taking a risk that pilot Henry Draper refused to even consider, Ferguson went straight aboard, accompanied by Dr Taylor, to meet with Boyle, Sanger and Veitch. As they listened to what these three exhausted men told them of the voyage, as well as what they could see for themselves, Ferguson realised things were even worse than he had thought. Boyle appeared spent, a man utterly at the end of his tether, Veitch not much better and Sanger still ill.

The deaths on board had now well exceeded 100, Boyle continued, with more people dying every day. More than 200 were still sick. More than a dozen bodies were lying here on the deck—some had been there for days—and their immediate burial was of critical concern. Looking around at this scene of horror, a suddenly very pale Joseph Taylor began to glean what he had so hastily signed up for. One of the most recent deaths, Boyle then said, was his very own brother, the *Ticonderoga*'s third mate, William Boyle, who had succumbed to the fever just hours earlier. The visiting men offered their sincerest sympathies, and from that moment, Harbour Master Ferguson took charge of the situation.

In his report penned to Governor La Trobe a few days later, which has survived, Ferguson recounts a whirlwind of activity that he instigated in the days following his arrival. His first and most urgent task was to bury the dead. Then he needed to transfer the large amount of stores from the *Empire* to the shore, working the two ships' crews hard in the November sunshine. He soon realised that the little *Empire*'s holds were not nearly generous enough for this emergency. The *Lysander*, he knew, was being prepared for sail and should arrive soon, but even with what she held, more would be needed. Leaving an increasingly alarmed Dr Taylor to gather a thorough understanding of the state of illness on board, as well as to sort out the stores, Ferguson and Veitch ventured ashore to inspect the makeshift hospital under canvas and ti-tree branches, as well as the patients it contained. Here, Veitch explained, they—as had he—spent their first night off the ship, accompanied where possible by members of their families and some of the remaining nurses, such as Annie Morrison and the indefatigable Fannings; however, more properly trained medical and nursing staff were sorely needed. Ferguson wrote, 'I landed and found about forty of the sick people in temporary tents near the lime-kiln and houses occupied by Mr Patrick Sullivan.'[3]

Sullivan would not occupy them for long. In his hand, Ferguson brandished an order for the eviction of all tenants within the proposed quarantine area, the boundaries of which would now be outlined. They would, he added, be generously compensated for the breaking of their leases, as well as the requisitioning of their dwellings. He trusted that there would be no trouble. Enlisting some of the burlier members of the crews of the *Empire* and the *Ticonderoga*, he made his authority clear to the assembled families and delivered the news. It was all here in black and white, he said, signed personally by the Lieutenant-Governor himself, that he, Charles Ferguson, Harbourmaster

> holds an authority from me . . . to take such steps as may be found desirable in withdrawing from licensed occupation such portion of land as may be required for the purpose of the immediate formation of a quarantine station at the Heads . . .[4]

Then, heading off into the bush with a small pot of whitewash, Ferguson paced out what he considered to be the reasonably accurate boundary of the station. It was not by any standards a fastidious measurement, and would not have met with the approval of his colleague the Surveyor-General, Robert Hoddle, but this was far from a normal situation.

Sullivan had built a series of wattle and daub cottages, including a reasonably substantial one of three rooms and a small dairy cellar, albeit in disrepair, which lay in the middle of the proposed station. This, explained Ferguson, would now be requisitioned and occupied by the sick, for which Sullivan would be compensated £200: 'I also arranged with Mr William Cannon who holds a lime-burner's licence within the limits of the proposed quarantine ground to remove to the Westward of the boundary line.'[5]

The more of the area Ferguson explored, the more he believed Hunt's initial recommendation for the site to have been a sound one. As well as bush, he reported a large area of

> dry open country, a large portion of which is capable of immediate cultivation, with abundance of timber, and from the statements of the Pilots, and those who have resided there for many years, plenty of fresh water can be got at all seasons by sinking wells at a moderate depth. The anchorage is quite secure, any vessel can lay in safety within a quarter of a mile of the beach.[6]

There was also an area of several acres under cultivation with oats and potatoes, which would be of good use.

Red marker lines were laid out to delineate various other necessary aspects of the station, and by making all who were there again walk over the boundaries with him, Ferguson made sure everyone understood exactly the new parameters of their changing world. Failing to respect those parameters, he added, would lead to severe consequences. Then, satisfied with the rudimentary layout, Ferguson ordered two 30-foot timbers to be taken from the ship's carpentry stores and brought ashore. Two holes were dug several yards apart, and the timbers were erected as flagpoles, marking out in the boldest terms the entrance of the station—directly off the beach, facing the water, so that any who approached would be in no doubt that this was no longer simply a quiet piece of beach.

The next morning, to Ferguson's considerable relief, the great hulk of the *Lysander* hove into view. Three vessels of size—a small but impressive fleet—had now dropped anchor inside the previously quiet cove of Abraham's Bosom. More stores were offloaded, then Ferguson requested that Captain Boyle assemble all his able-bodied passengers. In terms that invited neither question nor equivocation, Ferguson informed them that all joiners, carpenters, stonemasons— in fact, every man skilled in a useful trade—were as of now employed by the government at a rate of 5 shillings a day. A quarantine station needed to be built right here, he told them, and they were going to build it. Those who had not travelled with their own tools would be provided with them from the *Ticonderoga*'s stores, or those of the *Lysander*. The men, slightly dumbfounded, looked around at each other briefly, then nodded in assent. The stonemasons went ashore first, and were told to begin work on a couple of simple storehouses utilising the abundance of limestone that surrounded them. Aside from the pay, which was at a rate greater than they could expect doing similar work at home, most were happy to finally be of some use after the ghastly voyage when all they could do was wait for death to stalk yet another victim.

Apart from the practical advantage of an instant labour force, Ferguson, who had worked with men all his life at sea, on no account wanted idle and potentially disgruntled hands lying about with nothing to do but brood on their ill fortune. In his report, he dared to

respectfully suggest that the Colonial Architect send down at once a plain plan or sketch of a large airy barracks or depot, as there is an abundance of materials on the spot for its construction, which would furnish immediate work for the healthy Emigrants, who ought on no account to wander about the station in idleness.[7]

Realising that sick people could endure only so much sleeping on a beach, and that an alternative quickly needed to be found, Ferguson drew Sanger and Veitch to the rail, and indicated the *Lysander*. This, he told them, was to be their new hospital. Fifty new beds plus new blankets and bedding had been provided, and he suggested they begin transferring the most serious patients over to it as soon as possible. The *Ticonderoga*, he added, was no longer viable as a place for the sick.

Sanger thanked him, but pointed out that medical staff of any description were needed desperately. Ferguson did his best to recruit more from the able-bodied passengers, but even his powers of persuasion were barely adequate. He even flexed his authority to intercept one John Chambers and his wife Janet, who were simply catching a ride on board the *Lysander* to take up a position as assistant lighthouse keeper at Shortland's Bluff. Now, they were told, they were to be re-employed—at a rate of six shillings a day—as hospital attendants on board the *Lysander*, which was now a floating hospital.[8] This is in itself a testament to the depths of the emergency. Ferguson knew well that lighthouse keepers in the colony were regarded far more highly than nurses, and the step down the social ladder for the young couple—albeit a temporary one—would have been significant indeed. It is reported, however, that both served admirably on board the *Lysander*, without complaint, for the entire period of its quarantine.

Next, Ferguson turned his attention to the *Ticonderoga* herself. Dr Taylor had made his preliminary examination of the ship, and was visibly shaken by what he had seen. The lower decks were appalling, he said—virtually indescribable. People were so ill as to be crawling on hands and knees. How anyone could have endured a day down there, let alone three months, was utterly unfathomable. Believing—as virtually everyone at the time did—that diseases such as typhus were borne through the air by 'foul miasma', his immediate assessment was that it was poor ventilation that had been the root cause of the catastrophe. As Ferguson later stated, 'Doctor Taylor will report fully as soon as he has made himself acquainted with matters on board. Want of ventilation and cleanliness appear to me to have much to do with it . . .'[9]

Fresh provisions would be needed, and quickly. Ferguson had already arranged to draw upon his contacts in the upper echelons of Victorian colonial society, and fortunately Mr John Barker, Clerk of the Victorian Legislative Assembly and prominent landholder in the Westernport area, agreed to supply beef from his Boneo and Cape Shanck properties for five pence a pound. The lime-burner families, too, would be engaged to regularly supply eggs and fresh milk.

Turning to Boyle, Ferguson enquired how often his ship needed pumping. Mustering a little pride, Boyle stated that the *Ticonderoga* was tight as a drum, one of the finest ships he had sailed, and that her pumps rarely required anything beyond normal use. After some thought, Ferguson surprised the captain by instructing him to fill the holds of his ship with seawater, then have the pumps manned continually, day and night until the water, as well as the foul air, was drawn out. However, he added in his report, 'it was evident that to check the further spread of this disease, the people should all be landed out of the ship'.[10] Everyone, declared Ferguson—the sick as well as the healthy—as well as their belongings, were getting off the ship as soon as possible. Boyle announced that he had a number of large tents on board each capable of housing ten men. Ferguson bought the lot. He reported:

> As it was evident that to check the further spread of this disease, the people should all be landed out of the ship, I urged the immediate erection of large tents on shore, and Captain Boyle having twelve for sale, each capable of holding ten men, I purchased them on account of the Government for Seven pounds each, and ordered them to be at once erected and occupied.[11]

Then, he continued, the *Ticonderoga* would be thoroughly cleaned from top to bottom. Every bench, every locker, every inch of floor and deck would be swept, washed and disinfected with chloride of lime, then several coats of whitewash. Every remaining piece of bedding, every sheet or cloth, as well as the beds, benches and tables where the *Ticonderoga*'s passengers slept, ate, lived and died, would then be ripped from her insides and burned on a great and cathartic pyre or else thrown into the sea. In the end, no trace would remain of the *Ticonderoga*'s passengers, or the terrible disease that had literally decimated their numbers.

The disembarkation happened agonisingly slowly, but soon the little cove began to resemble a camp city. Boxes and trunks soon littered the sand and foreshore as people re-established themselves at the cove. People in their dozens, in various stages of illness from near death to experiencing the first symptoms, were deposited wherever there was something to lie on. However, some had already circumvented Ferguson's intentions to purge the ship and had taken their blankets and bedding from the ship, lice-ridden as they probably were, further risking the spread of the disease.

The first to come off the *Ticonderoga* were the dead—two at a time, in the rowboats—but even from among the fit passengers, few could be found to bury them, terrified as they were of themselves becoming victims of the contagion. A burial area had been set aside a little way from the shore, but with no coffins, and hardly anything left that could be used as even a shroud, the dead were buried, usually by their own family members, fully clothed along with their few meagre possessions. Even sadder perhaps, is that these humble burial plots were not to last, as the ground had been sited too close to the water's edge. In just a few years, therefore, the *Ticonderoga*'s victims, as well as their resting places, would be lost forever to erosion and the sea.

Nor, it transpired, was Point Nepean's sandy soil, with its meagre 10-foot water table, suitable for the digging of graves in any case. This too proposed a problem for the disposing of animal offal and carcasses, as well as the hastily dug toilets, all of which were liable to spreading more filth and illness with one decent rain.

The several hundred healthy passengers who had travelled on board the *Ticonderoga* likewise came to regard themselves as victims of the disease—albeit by default—being equally subject to the restrictions imposed by Dr Hunt and harbourmaster Ferguson. It was not long before some began to resent the confinement of this desolate place. Many who had lost loved ones wanted to pick up the pieces of their broken lives and start again in this new country; others wanted to put it all behind them and move on. For the time being, however, none would be allowed to do so. In front of them was a bay, behind them an ocean and standing in between them and the town of Melbourne was roughly 100 kilometres of scrub and bush, making it as unreachable as the moon.

Ferguson was aware of the potential for trouble rising out of a large number of discontented passengers. In his report to La Trobe, he added:

> As there is such a large body of people landed, I beg to recommend that a Sergeant and a small body of police be sent down overland and stationed at the Eastern boundary of the quarantine ground to maintain order, and check the insubordination which was beginning to show itself amongst the seamen and Emigrants before I left.

Soon, a contingent of around half a dozen sergeants accompanied by six mounted constables was beating its way overland on horseback through bush to set up camp, ostensibly to protect the borders of the quarantine station, but also to prevent those who might attempt to leave it, and be ready to react to any unrest.

On Sunday, 6 November, Ferguson returned from Point Nepean to Melbourne on board the *Empire*, feeling that he had aged an entire year in the few days he had spent there. He reported to an anxious Lieutenant-Governor La Trobe that the final 150 sick and 250 fit passengers had all been removed from the *Ticonderoga*, with some being accommodated in the requisitioned lime-burners' cottages, while others were living in primitive and makeshift conditions on the shore. The worst cases had been transferred to the hospital ship *Lysander*. The epidemic was far from over, though. People were still dying daily, although the numbers were gradually starting to decline. Dr Taylor was in charge, but Ferguson privately doubted whether he was up to the task. The *Ticonderoga*'s principal surgeon, Joseph Sanger, was recovering and now able to resume some work, and was once again being assisted on board the *Lysander* by Dr Veitch, although Ferguson described both of them as being 'in an extremely debilitated state'.[12] He meanwhile approached another physician, a William Farman, surgeon superintendent of the *Mobile,* to quietly take over some of Taylor's duties. Taylor, he decided, would now oversee the camp on shore, while Farman would undertake the cleaning of the *Ticonderoga* and work with Sanger and Veitch on board the *Lysander*. Supplies would still be needed—particularly tent material, blankets, bedding and mattresses, as well as the usual demands for wine and porter.

La Trobe and Ferguson realised, however, that the tragedy unfolding at Point Nepean could not be kept quiet for long, and both men readied themselves for the storm both had seen coming long before the arrival of the *Ticonderoga*.

25

Quarantine and outrage

To the people on the streets of Melbourne who gathered in huddles on that November Friday morning to hear the grizzly details of the *Ticonderoga* laid out by *The Argus*'s reporter under the memorable headline, 'Terrible State of Affairs on board an Emigrant Ship at the Port Phillip Heads', the notion of an overcrowded vessel struck down with disease was nothing new. During the latter half of 1852, the Colonial Land and Emigration Commission's four big double-deck ships had each arrived with varying amounts of sickness on board. The first of these had been the very large German ship, *Borneuf*, which had arrived in March with 83 of her passengers having died at sea, almost all of those being children and infants. This, though regrettable, was not seen as the catastrophe such an event would be deemed in later times. Children died frequently in the nineteenth century, particularly at sea, and in the case of the *Borneuf*, much of the blame was laid at the feet of the parents. In a report into the voyage, the Board concluded that 'the high mortality rate was largely attributed to the insurmountable objection of Irish and Scots parents to seeking medical attention for their children'.[1] The drinking water also failed on board this ship, with the inadequate storage facilities turning it putrid, green and undrinkable. Even so, only a handful of adults perished on board the *Borneuf*—a figure quite within acceptable limits—and the voyage was regarded as a success.

The *Wanata* was next. She was a ship of just over 1100 tons, arriving soon after the *Borneuf*. A total of 39 of her passengers had not survived the journey, but once again all but ten of those were children. Scarlatina, measles and 'fever' were cited as the chief complaints, and the *Wanata* was sent to the Red Bluff sanitary station for a period of quarantine.

Then, on 20 September, it was the turn of the mighty *Marco Polo* to make its grand arrival into Port Phillip, under the command of a man who was already a global celebrity of the high seas, 'Bully' Forbes. At first the newspapers were so enraptured by the time he had set—a record 68 days from Liverpool to Melbourne—that their triumphant headlines ignored the fact that 51 children and two adults had died under his care.

Slowly, however, people both in England and in the Australian colonies began to question the wisdom of crowding so many people into these Goliaths of the sea, simply to alleviate the logistical problems in which the Colonial Land and Emigration Commission had found itself. Letters to the Editor of prominent newspapers in both England and Australia began to reflect public concern, one of the earliest being from an anonymous writer in *The Argus* on 24 September:

Attention should be urgently directed to the injudicious and cruel system of sending out overcrowded vessels which seems to be gaining ground just now. Within the month three striking cases have occurred. The *Borneuf*, *Wanata* and *Marco Polo* have arrived from Liverpool with about 800 passengers each. The consequences of such overcrowding are sure to be fatal, and accordingly, the deaths were 83, 39 and 53 respectively during the voyages. The vessels were of the largest size, it is true, but it is perfectly obvious that no vessel, whatever its size, can safely carry such large numbers of passengers on a three months' voyage.

In England, too, many who had a chance to inspect these large ships before they set sail were likewise shocked at what they encountered, as this long but pointed piece to a London daily on 27 September 1852 indicates:

The overcrowding of emigrant ships

When a body of men take it in hand to do a thing, and do not do it so much from a conviction of its being the best thing in the world they can do, but rather as a compulsory matter, they do not do it well. The *juste milieu* is one of those rocks ahead against which they run doggedly, and so break their pates. Now they overdo the business, as if, in a splenetic fit, they said—'There! Take your ship; cram her full, and be off.' Mr Osborne, the indefatigable and the zealous, gives us instance of this. He went the other day on board an emigrant ship which was just setting sail, and found that, though she was a noble vessel of her class, and that two decks (blessed are the humble in the lower deck, certainly)—were set apart for the passengers, the berths being of the proper authorized dimensions, and, as excellent arrangements were made for ventilation and other indispensable necessities as possible—still this ship (considerably under a thousand tons burthen) carried not less than eight hundred emigrants and a crew of sixty men! In addition to this, there was the stately complement of two surgeons to do battle with seasickness, fever, human miasmatic exudations. This was not a trip to Gravesend or the Naze where the heroic endurance of a few half hours of agony would be compensated for by a participation 'in old English sports', a polka up on the 'gothic hill', and a promenade 'a la Musard' between avenues of shrubs and ham sandwiches. It was a certain life and death affair that was to last for months—from four to eight perhaps, more or less; and here are a greater part of a thousand souls under a care of two surgeons, and a medicine chest upon the same scale as we may infer sent by the Government on such a voyage. If this be not care-lessness for human life, we do not know what else to call it. We do not always know in what condition the decimated scarecrows land, but those who have voyaged across the tropics, in a crowded ship have some appreciation of the unutterable horrors men, women and children go through, or rather don't go through. Fever and dysen-tery play a leading part in the ghastly drama. Want of water in calm latitudes, or under the torrid zone may be 'better imagined than described'. Has anyone ever imagined the awful Golgotha which a plague ship becomes! If our kinsmen and our friends leave us forever to seek in a foreign land what they have failed to obtain in this, they ought not to be sent forth like felons in the hold of a convict ship or packed like the cargo of a slave vessel.

In Australia, meanwhile, one of those starting to add his doubt to the wisdom of commissioning very large vessels was Lieutenant-Governor La Trobe himself. Starting to sense the public mood, La Trobe, on 21 October when the *Ticonderoga* was still at sea, issued Dispatch Number 142 to his superior in London, Sir John Pakington, Secretary of State for the Colonies. In it he begged to direct 'the serious attention of Her Majesty's Government to the evils of disadvantages attendant upon the chartering of vessels of heavy burthen for the conveyance of large numbers of Emigrants to the colony'.[2] The full text of that exchange has been lost, but if La Trobe's fears were raised in this way in October, the November arrival of the *Ticonderoga* saw them horribly realised. In a dispatch of 9 November, he states:

I regret to be under the necessity of furnishing another example in proof of the propriety of the question being raised. On the 4th Inst. I received intimation through the Health Officer of the arrival of the Emigrant Ship 'Ticonderoga' from Liverpool, with 800 Government Immigrants, at the Port Phillip Heads, having lost 102 by death during her voyage from typhus and scarlet fever; and having an equal number of sick on board of the same disease; the Surgeon Superintendent also sick and the vessel in want of medicines and Medical comforts . . . I have appointed another Medical gentle-man provided with every necessary in the way of medicines and medical comforts. Every effort will at once be made to cleanse the Ticonderoga.[3]

News of the plague ship spread fast. The same dramatic article announcing the Ticonderoga's dreadful arrival in the Friday Argus was deemed important enough to be reprinted in the Geelong Advertiser the following day. With equal concern, the readers in the busy port town read of the drama unfolding even closer to their doorstep:

the authorities in Williamstown immediately furnished the govern-ment schooner Empire with the necessary supplies of live stock, beef, mutton, mild, vegetables, porter, wine spirits, and a medicine chest, and Dr Taylor, of the Ottillia, a gentleman of much practical experience, went down in her to the Ticonderoga, yesterday, to take charge, accompanied by Captain Ferguson, the Harbour Master. The Lysander ship, has also been taken up by the Government as a Quarantine Hulk, and proceeds to her destination at the Heads this day, having on board stores sufficient for all hands for three months, when further arrangements will be made which, we trust, will ame-liorate the fearful state of things on board . . .

As dire as the situation was at Point Nepean, La Trobe was at least thankful that a full-blown crisis in busy Port Phillip had been averted due to the quick thinking of the pilot, Henry Draper, whose action to divert the Ticonderoga to the nascent sanitary station he later described as having been 'judiciously made'.[4] Captain Boyle too, for-tunately, had had the wherewithal to begin offloading his passengers under his own volition without waiting for instruction. Had he made it to Melbourne, the outcry resulting from a full-blown typhus epidemic being unleashed on the under-policed and under-resourced colony in the grip of gold madness could scarcely be imagined. La Trobe could not, however, continue to count on the quick thinking of others, particularly as the newspapers were beginning to give full voice to the concerns of the public. Newspaper reporters now began to fall upon every scrap of news of the hapless vessel that they could find. On Tuesday, 9 November, *The Argus* published:

We have been kindly furnished with the following particulars relative to this unfortunate vessel by Charles Ferguson Esq., the Harbour Master at Williamstown, who has been down to the Heads in the *Empire* schooner, and returned on Sunday. It appears there were, on Friday about 714 emigrants on board; 100 deaths and nineteen births had occurred on the passage, seven of the former since the ship anchored at the Heads. There are at present 300 cases of sickness . . . tents have been erected with sails, spas, &c. of the ship on Point Nepean where a quarantine ground has been marked out . . . the *Lysander* ship, too, now at the Heads, will be fitted up as a hospital for the worst cases . . . both the surgeon and the assistant, belonging to the *Ticonderoga*, being in an extremely debilitated state. It is to be hoped the liberal measures being taken by the authorities in this case will counteract the further spread of the disease, which it is but natural to expect, when fresh air, exercise and liberal diet, are brought into operation.

Soon, however, the papers began to add their own thundering editorials to the narrative. On Monday, 15 November, *The Argus* editorial declared:

We must again advert to the evils arising from the sending out of large numbers of passengers in single ships. We lately alluded to several cases in which the mortality during the voyage had arrived at a very frightful extent. Since then, large English vessels have arrived also furnishing a sad list of deaths. Several vessels are now in quarantine, among them the *Ticonderoga*, which recently arrived with the terrible loss of 104 lives. When she anchored in our port, many scores of passengers were still ill, the doctor and his assistant were both laid up, and the medical stores were all consumed. From the result of such experience, it seems improper that any ship however large, however splendid her accommodation should endeavour to bring many hundred passengers for so long a voyage. Those vessels which have conveyed 200 or 300 passengers each have usually arrived without any serious loss of life; but those conveying 600 or 700 and upwards have frequently furnished such a list of casualties, as to lead us to strongly recommend to ship-owners to abstain from sending them, and passengers to avoid coming by them.

Word of the plague ship began to spread beyond the borders of the new colony, and soon a blistering article appeared in the combative but influential fortnightly *Australian and New Zealand Gazette*. In it, not only were the foretold consequences of employing large vessels laid bare, but the very practices of the Colonial Land and Emigration Commission, as well as assisted emigration in general, were brought into question:

In our last number we alluded to the fearful mortality which had taken place on board some ships from Liverpool to Australia, in consequence of over-crowding. Liverpool, or, rather, American ships, sailing from that port to the United States, have established an unenviable reputation for this system of packing live cargo, as Irish emigrants to America are evidently considered. Our impression was, that in Australian emigration a different course had been pursued by Liverpool shipowners with regard to Australian ships. And on inquiry we find that it is so; private ships sailing from Liverpool being in quite as good condition, both as regards comforts and provisions, as any out of London.

Our readers will be surprised that the floating pest-houses, in which two hundred and seventy-nine souls have been lost to their families and the colonies, are the property of, for the time being, and were shipped out under the eye of her Majesty's Emigration Commissioners, who have thus wasted the above enormous quantity of human life, and with it upwards of £5000 of the Victoria colonists' money. In the name of humanity, we trust the colonists will, as they have intimated, stop the remission of any further land funds, if this is to be the use made of it. But let us recount the mortality on board these sea-shambles *Borneuf*, 83 dead; *Wanata*, 39 dead; *Marco Polo*, 53 dead; and *Ticonderoga*, a hundred and four dead! Total, 279 persons, starting from England less than six months ago, full of life and spirits at the cheering prospects before them. These have been hurried into eternity from having put confidence in her Majesty's Emigration Commissioners, whose latest discovery it appears to have been that the best way of promoting the health and safety of 800 souls on board each ship was to stow them away in the space which private shipowners would have allotted to 700. But on this point we will let Mr Rankin, the chairman of the Liverpool Shipowners' Association, speak—The doctor is dead, and almost all the survivors are down with fever. The last case is the most striking, because the voyage, of 68 days only, must have been performed with winds invariably favourable. What, then, was the cause of this unusual and frightful mortality? The system of packing, which sends 800 in a space not more than enough for 700, and which stows passengers in lower deck berths without any better means of ventilation than a canvas windsail, which cannot be used in storms, when most needed.

As Chairman of the Liverpool Shipowners' Association, I deem it my duty to state that not one of the above vessels was sent out by private individuals, but all of them were taken up and sent out by the Commissioners of Emigration. Every emigration ship is inspected by the Government officer, and no more passengers are allowed than the act of Parliament authorizes. So that private ships are compelled to take no more passengers than they can carry in health and safety. But her Majesty's Emigration Commissioners have the power of experimentalizing as to how many out of eight hundred souls can be safely landed from one ship.

Our wonder is that they did not go the full length of the experiment, and stow away the whole of the live lumber in casks, with holes bored at the bottom. But happily, amidst this horrible slaughter, the weather was fine and the winds favourable, or few indeed would have reached their destination. In March last year, the Liverpool Shipowners' Association urged on the Government the fact that no ship, whatever might be her size, could carry more than 600 persons in safety. The *Great Britain*, the largest ship afloat, took out this number, and lost one. In the very teeth of the Liverpool Shipowners' Association, and in their own port, the emigration commissioners put on board 800, though the ships were not of the largest size! Had one of these ships only been thus fearfully visited, a pestilence, silent and uncontrollable, would have accounted for the slaughter. But here four ships sailing at different periods, though all under favourable circumstances on the voyage, similarly visited.

Till an investigation has taken place, let no man in his senses trust himself on board a Government emigrant ship. He may easily calculate his chance of getting to the end of the voyage. Here it is. The *Ticonderoga* had 800 souls on board at starting, and lost 104, including the doctor [*sic*]. The chance of being flung to the sharks is, therefore, just one in eight. People have usually been in the habit of considering themselves at least as well off in a Government emigrant ship as in a private one, but this is a delusion. We consider even Mr Rankin's estimate of 600 persons in a ship as much too high. We should very much like some financial member of the House of Commons, to ask what sum was paid to the owners of this *Ticonderoga*. We are curious to know the particulars of this Government floating hospital, if only for the information of the colonists who send their money to be thus lamentably spent. If we recollect rightly, the *Ticonderoga* is not a British-built ship, but an old American liner; the receptacle of many a former cargo of Irish emigrants. We will not be positive on this point, but we do not expect to see the assertion contradicted. If the colonial legislatures, when they get the power of doing as they please with their own money, will aid societies like this, they will expend their money to some purpose, and we have no doubt that they will do so, as soon as the Emigration Commission has ceased to drain their exchequers.

* * * *

Back at Point Nepean, Dr Taylor, as Ferguson had suspected, was not coping. Although an experienced surgeon superintendent, having only recently in fact completed a relatively trouble-free run from England on the *Ottillia,* nothing in his experience could have prepared him—or anyone else—for the deluge of woe that awaited him at Point Nepean.

Conditions continued to be primitive in the extreme. Some people were lucky enough to be housed in the requisitioned cottages and tents, but most were confined to the hastily constructed canvas lean-tos that had been put together by the *Ticonderoga*'s crew and able passengers. Some, remembered a Mrs Cain, daughter of the first permanent resident of Portsea, were confined to bark shelters, living like Aboriginal people, while their attendants and family 'waved branches over them to keep off the flies'.[5] Donald McDonald, in a description for a newspaper written decades later, recalls that at night his mother would have to shake the frost from the blankets covering their small beach lean-to made from timbers and ti-tree branches.

With a huge workload, little help and not much he could practically do to help his patients in any case, Dr Taylor began to feel the stress of his position acutely. A few days into the posting, his wife and his two eldest sons arrived, his wife to assist him on board the *Lysander,* making up tinctures and prescriptions, and his sons to help with the distribution of the stores. It would all end badly for Dr Taylor. A year later, he recounted his take on the whole sorry experience at Point Nepean in a long and somewhat wounded letter to Lieutenant-Governor La Trobe, in which he recounts a litany of injustices, particularly at the hands of Thomas Hunt, the man who had given him the job in the first place, but with whom he soon seriously fell out. Judging by the tone of his account, however, Taylor seems to have clashed with everybody—particularly the two men who were ostensibly there to assist him, Drs Sanger and Veitch:

> The first surgeon of the ship, complained Taylor, was himself all of fever and altogether unable to render any assistance, while the junior surgeon, a young man without experience and of intractable temperament, was comparatively useless.[6]

Taylor's is the splenetic rant of a man taxed beyond his capacities by a still desperate situation. In describing the entire set-up of the station as chaotic, he was undoubtedly correct. At one stage, he even had to shoot a stray bullock that had wandered into the station, then organise the cow-proof fence to prevent further bovine incursions. Overwhelmed, he could barely sleep, and was deprived of even some of the most basic necessities to make his tenure bearable:

> Such excessive labour and mental anxiety, together with the want of sleep for many nights in succession, soon began to exhibit their depressing effects on the system. My legs swelled more and more, my appetite failed and at last when in the nighttime, after writing out my Report for the day, on the ground having neither chairs nor tables. I could find time for an hour's rest that rest was denied me by the violent cramps which attacked my legs the moment I had fallen asleep.[7]

Aside from this, Taylor suffered acute diarrhoea, as well as the ignominy of the theft of his personal property, including his bed, forcing him to sleep on the ground, followed by his personal trunk being ransacked, with persons unknown making off with some of his clothes.

It appears that when Dr Hunt travelled down to Point Nepean on or about 9 November, he formed the opinion that Taylor was not the right person for the job and began moves to terminate his position once a replacement could be found. Lieutenant-Governor La Trobe, however, seems to have been left out of this particular intrigue, and was apparently put in the embarrassing position of calling upon Taylor on his one visit to the station in December, dining with him and renewing his appointment, only to have him summarily dismissed by Dr Hunt a few days later. When informed of his sacking, in person by Dr Hunt, a flabbergasted Taylor challenged Hunt's authority to dismiss him from an appointment ordained by the Lieutenant-Governor himself. According to Taylor, Hunt's response was to threaten to pull the poor man's tent down if he failed to vacate the area within two days.

In a letter informing La Trobe of his actions, Hunt stated: 'I have this day dismissed Mr Joseph Taylor from the office of Resident Surgeon and Store keeper at the Sanitary Station Ticonderoga . . . I find him a very inefficient officer, much more given to talk than act.'[8]

Then, piling woe upon woe, Taylor contracted typhus, which had him in its grip until well into the new year, 'from that time up until the middle of April, all is lost history to me, remembering nothing except some dreamy wanderings of my brain'.[9]

* * * *

Only very slowly did the death rate begin to decrease once the *Ticonderoga*'s passengers reached quarantine. On 20 November, *The Argus*, eager to keep its fixated readers up to date with the latest lurid details from Point Nepean, reported:

> Frequent deaths are still taking place amongst the unfortunate emigrants of the *Ticonderoga*, five having occurred the other day; two more surgeons have been sent down and Dr Hunt, the Health Officer at Williams Town [*sic*] proceeded to Point Nepean yesterday to see if any further measures could be adopted for the improvement of the Quarantine Station at that place.

On 16 November, John Hando, 49, whose sixteen-year-old daughter Anna Maria had been one of the *Ticonderoga*'s first victims on 23 August, also died. A broken heart could well have hastened his demise. In October, he had also lost his wife, Maria, and just four days earlier, his remaining daughter, Emma, also perished. Only eighteen-year-old Charles and his two brothers, aged seven and ten, were left of the family of seven that had boarded the ship thirteen weeks earlier.

Another of the English passengers, Mary Ann Cheeney, 33, died on 16 October, leaving her husband alone to raise their children, William and Mary, both under ten; Elizabeth Taylor, one, became the sole victim of her family the following day, and Janet Mattheson, twenty, died just one day before her infant son, George.

Perhaps one of the most poignant stories was that of one of the few childless couples on board the *Ticonderoga*, Andrew and Margaret Rutherford, aged 27 and 28 respectively, and about whom little else is known. Margaret had died on one of the ship's last days at sea, possibly even within sight of land, on 31 October, while her husband passed away in quarantine twenty days later, on 20 November. Unlike most of the ship's other victims, whose families were able, despite the tragedy of losing loved ones, to go on to establish family roots in Australia, nothing whatever remained of Andrew and Margaret's bold endeavour to come to Australia on the ship that would cost them their lives.

26

A Christmas escape

A few days before Christmas Day 1852, the Scots McIvor family were preparing for the Yuletide in their home in Coburg, a suburb to Melbourne's north, just a little off the track that would, after an extremely arduous journey of several weeks, eventually lead to Sydney. Not that the McIvors had ever taken that journey themselves, and nor were they likely to. Having migrated from Scotland a decade earlier, they had done all the travelling they ever intended to do. Nevertheless, many of their traditions had been brought with them, and one of those was the celebration of a very Scottish Christmas. Being Presbyterians, there was little in the way of showiness, but one or two hymns, a shortbread and a haggis could always be counted upon. This year, however, a sense of unease was running through the family, as it was for many of the Scots of Melbourne. Certainly, every Christmas in this new country was somewhat odd, occurring as it did in the midst of a summer that, before leaving the frigid climate of Inverness, they scarcely believed was possible.

The talk among the Melbourne Scots this Christmas was of the ship that had arrived at the Heads some weeks back, and was still confined to quarantine. A thousand Highlanders were said to be aboard her, and the loss of life had already been terrible. However, no passenger list was as yet available, so no one could have any idea who was on board. McIvor, in his sixties and very much the patriarch of the family, tried not to listen to the rumours, but as time went on, they became virtually unavoidable. The papers—his friends were telling him—were starting to talk about this 'fever ship', this 'plague ship' and her sorry passengers, stranded and sick, so close yet so far from their destination of Melbourne. 'The unfortunate new arrivals,' penned McIvor's grandson John Andrew McIvor many years later, in an article that appeared in *The Argus* in August 1934, 'were as remote as though on a distant island.' Old McIvor had been lucky, he knew. The ship on which he and his family had made the voyage had been a small one, and illness had hardly gained a foothold, despite the journey having taken much longer than that of the *Ticonderoga*.

A doctor, he had heard this very morning on one of his regular leisurely visits to Haymarket in Melbourne to meet friends and read the newspapers, had just returned from the quarantine station itself. Two or three people were still dying every day, he had said. Some said the disease was yellow fever, others that it was the dreaded scarlet fever. Others still said it was yellow jack, a terrifying sickness usually found in the American south, but since the ship had come from that part of the world in the first place and traded there regularly, that's what some had convinced themselves it was. McIvor listened solemnly but said nothing.

Then, late one evening on the day before Christmas Eve, while McIvor's wife—known to all simply as Granny—was making the shortbread with the imprint of the Scots thistle, a knock was heard at the door. Visitors at this hour were not usual, and when McIvor answered the door, he nearly fell back in the stoop with shock. Standing before him was a young man, barely older than a boy. He was filthy, thin and exhausted, but in the unmistakable accent of his homeland, uttered the words he had for days repeated over in his head,

Your cousin, the wife of Malcolm McRae, came in the ship *Ticonderoga*. I am her son, but my sister Janet and my two younger brothers died of the fever since we were landed at Point Nepean, and I have walked from that place with another young man and we followed the beach till we came to Melbourne.[1]

With that, the young man, seventeen-year-old Christopher McRae, collapsed in the doorway.

McIvor shouted to his wife, and as both of them brought the boy inside, she exclaimed loudly in Gaelic. Here was young Christopher, the son of her dear cousin Helen, having come all that way from Inverness—can you believe it?—and on that terrible ship everyone was talking about. They sat him down and he devoured the fresh scones that had been prepared, as well as the tea.

* * * *

A few weeks earlier, Christopher McRae had watched his father approach Captain Boyle on the deck of the *Ticonderoga* to seek permission to go ashore and bury his sister, ten-year-old Janet. The kind man had assented and Christopher helped to bring his sister's body up from where she lay in the female hospital. Then, in a small rowboat, they had been taken to the shore of the little beach where, guided by one of the seamen, they had been shown the freshly marked-up burial ground and prepared the little girl's grave. Upon returning to the ship, it transpired that his baby brother, Malcolm, his mother's joy, had died too. Then, a short time later, it was the turn of another brother, Farquhar, just six. As he told the story to his ageing cousins, Granny McRae let out a terrible cry, and an ancient Gaelic lamentation filled the room. She clutched her husband's hand; he could only shake his head and stare at the floor in silence.

Christopher had been able to bear the grief of the beach no longer. Besides, he sensed his turn too would surely come if he stayed there amid the death of the quarantine station. With another young man whose name has now been forgotten, one evening he simply decided to take a walk along the beach away from the station and not return. They had told his father, who was in no position to object. He was too busy looking after his wife, Christopher's mother Helen, but gave them the address of her cousins in Melbourne and told them to find them and tell them what had happened. Christopher and the unknown young man set out on their trek along the beach, neither knowing nor caring where it was leading, nor how they were going to get there. All they knew was that the settlement of Port Phillip was somewhere to the north, at the end of this beach. Exactly how far that was, they had no idea.

For two weeks they had walked, hugging the shore where they could, or scrambling over cliffs. They drank from puddles in the rocks, and their only sustenance came courtesy of the Aboriginal people who ate the shellfish on the shore, and a couple of surprised but kindly squatters or leaseholders who took pity on the lads and their story, furnishing them with an occasional meal.

They crossed rivers and creeks, sleeping where they could and travelling when they were able. Eventually, they came across a few outlying dwellings, which then became more frequent before passing, without them realising, the former quarantine station at Little Red Bluff, now abandoned. It was hard going and exhausting, but eventually they arrived in Melbourne, worn out after an overland journey of nearly 60 miles. At no time, despite the hardship, had they for an instant been tempted to return to the camp at the beach. Exactly how Christopher McRae managed to find his way to the address in Coburg has endured in the family as a minor miracle.

The tragedy of the McRae family was not yet finished. Three days into the new year, 1853, having lost four of her seven children, Helen McRae became one of the *Ticonderoga*'s final victims and also died, to be buried alongside her children: Janet, Farquhar, John and Malcolm. Having travelled so far from Scotland, she never did manage to again meet with her cousin Granny McRae in Coburg.

27

A visit from the Governor

The Australian summer began, and the people of the quarantine station were jolted into the realities of a climate that was entirely alien to them. Fair Celtic complexions that had never known harsh sunlight were now seared, first red then, eventually, a deep nut brown. Even the light had been a revelation, with the glare of the Australian sky forcing eyes to squint constantly in ways they had never had to do except at the very height of northern hemisphere summer—and even then only on a handful of days. Then there were the flies, which seemed to balloon exponentially in great black crawling clouds as the quarantine camp became established, feeding and breeding in the waste and remains of butchered animals, poorly disposed of in shallow pits. Little more than waving branches and smoke from fires could keep them at bay.

Cooking facilities remained basic, as did the water supply, which came exclusively from wells sunk into the sand and, thankfully, did not run dry and the food was plentiful and nutritious, being regularly supplied from the nearby cattle estates of Mr Barker and others. Some of the lime-burners whose leases remained intact—there were six issued on that part of the peninsula in all—were also able to make money selling eggs, milk and a range of other supplies from their smallholdings outside the boundaries of the camp.

Slowly, as the weeks went by, the health of most of the 300–400 patients (the precise figure is difficult to pin down) began to improve. Time passed slowly for both the healthy and the healing passengers, spent in long walks along the beach and the surrounding dunes, and among the twisted and alien trunks of the ti-trees, unlike any vegetation the passengers had ever seen in the glens or on the western isles of their old home of Scotland.

The sea, now that they were not actually on it, seemed beautiful and ever-changing, with the calmness of the bay in front of them contrasting with the drama of the open ocean just the other side of their little peninsula, in places only a few hundred yards to their rear. The infestation of typhus-carrying lice, so compounded in the sardine-like confines of the ship, here began to lessen as people were at last able to spread out. While there is no anecdotal evidence of sea bathing having taken place, it would be safe to assume at least some did occur, in which case the cleansing effect of washing away lice from the body would have been profound.

For many, simply the rest, walking along the shore and observing the changing moods and colours of the ocean and rocks were enough to begin the process of emotionally healing from the terrors of the voyage and its aftermath. The most serious cases remained on board the *Lysander,* and many of those would make up the 70 or so people who would die at the station between the arrival of the *Ticonderoga* in early November and the first days of 1853. Drs Veitch and Sanger were as busy as they had ever been during this period; however, with fresh food and medical supplies now available, their tasks became easier, as they saw by the numbers of deaths gradually declining and the recovery rate among patients gradually increasing.

Annie Morrison remained steadfast to the task she had undertaken since the early days of the epidemic, continuing to assist in the care, and now recovery, of the sick. In the many weeks since Dr Veitch's desperate call for volunteers, Annie had long since exceeded all expectations. As she grew from the role of assistant to something far more important, he had come increasingly to appreciate her knowledge of each patient and their continually changing condition. Steadily, he came to rely not only on her tireless dedication but on her quietly soothing presence.

The recovering passengers were not quite as alone as they had first supposed. From the beach, excellent views were to be had of the many ships that daily passed back and forth, heading either out of the Rip or entering the bay and travelling up to Melbourne, a city still being inundated with people in search of gold. The passengers watched the busy pilots—the same ones who had guided them over to the cove—going about their daily business of leading bigger ships, full of cargo and hopeful passengers, through the difficult Heads and into the lanes. As the weeks of incarceration went by, many wished they too could be on board one of those ships and escape the monotony of their closed beach settlement, but close as they were in yards, they may as well have been a thousand miles distant.

Nor was the newly opened—albeit still rudimentary—quarantine station the exclusive preserve of those from the *Ticonderoga*. Although it would not be officially gazetted until the following year, nor fully completed with permanent buildings until 1855, Point Nepean was now very much in use, and other ships flying the yellow flag also began to drop anchor in the cove. None, however, presented a case as serious as the *Ticonderoga*, and most lingered only a few days or a week, their passengers strictly confined to their ship, before once again departing.

In the second week of December, Thomas Hunt returned to take up residence on the *Lysander*. From here, he could direct the progress of the construction of the station proper, which was slowly getting under way, as well as inspect the state of the *Ticonderoga*'s passengers. It is presumed, too, that he had quietly lost faith in his appointee, Dr Taylor, and wished to keep a closer eye on him before his replacement could be organised.

A few days later, on 12 December, the camp became abuzz with the news that Governor La Trobe himself would be making a personal visit, and staying overnight in one of the staterooms of the *Lysander*—presumably situated a safe distance from the suffering and dying typhus patients in the ship's hospital ward. Late that afternoon, the government schooner, HM *Boomerang*, glided into view and tied up alongside the great hulk of the *Lysander*. At a time when such persons were the true celebrities of the day, from the beach the passengers strained to secure as best a view as they could of His Excellency, some catching a glimpse of his slim blue uniformed figure as it made its way from the smaller vessel to the larger one.

It was at dinner on board the *Lysander* that evening that La Trobe, perhaps a little too carried away in the moment, and without consulting his own Chief Health Officer, Dr Hunt, made the offer to Dr Taylor of continuing to run the quarantine station a permanent one, in front of a no doubt astonished and possibly furious Hunt, who rescinded the appointment soon afterwards in any case. To Taylor's deep and justified dismay, His Excellency, it seems, was happy to let the contradiction of his directive stand.

Christopher McRae and his friend were probably not the only ones to escape the beach camp, evade the guarding constables on the boundary line and make their own way north, but details are sketchy. Donald McDonald recalled, in a January 1917 edition of *The Argus*, that some restless passengers, 'hearing the continued call of the siren of Bendigo and Fiery Creek, bolted like Buckley of an earlier time, and made the toilsome circuit of the eastern shore'.

It is from McDonald also that we learn that some may have even found some romance to pass the time. The lime-burners, evicted to the boundaries of the station, were nevertheless suddenly in the proximity of a large amount of single females, and those who were healthy had a good deal of time on their hands. As McDonald somewhat eloquently put it in his article:

These gallants of the lime pits saw few women, and amongst the 'souls' of the *Ticonderoga* were spinsters still comely, others hardy, if not handsome. So the lime-burners broke bounds upon one side, and the maidens upon the other. Once again, love laughed at locksmiths and quarantine became a name.

Some, at least, made the attempt to engage in more cerebral pastimes, such as Charles McKay, who had travelled with his wife Margaret and their five children to take up a role as head of the prestigious Scotch College, and who had performed the role of schoolmaster on board the *Ticonderoga*. It appears that he made attempts to establish something similar on shore, seeking the help of the person who had performed the same role in the women's quarters, Isabella Renshaw. It seems to have not been a success, however, mainly due to Miss Renshaw herself becoming sick with fever during her time in quarantine.

As McKay would have realised, many of the faces to whom he had taught a few of the basics of reading and writing on the ship in the earlier stages of the voyage—as well as empowering some of them to sign their name for the first time—were now gone. He was aware, too, of his good fortune in that none of his family had caught the awful fever, and perhaps was civic-minded enough to wish to continue to give back to the small, deeply scarred community of which he was now a part. For his tireless efforts, both on the ship and on shore, McKay was eventually awarded the princely sum of £5.

Miss Renshaw was not nearly so lucky. Having been voted by the single girls with whom she travelled to be their matron and guardian, then having watched over them as they mixed with the other passengers on those risqué evenings spent on the warm deck as they passed over the equator, delighting all with their sweet voices singing the beautiful songs of the Highlands and feet moving swiftly in country dancing, and then having seen them fall, one by one, to the dreaded and unstoppable disease, cooling their brows and soothing them with words, Isabella Renshaw, 38, herself died at the quarantine station on 18 November.

In front of them, still anchored where she had disgorged her human cargo weeks before, lay the *Ticonderoga*, still a beautiful ship, now emptied of her passengers and thoroughly cleaned inside and out with limewater and whitewash. She would not stay empty for long.

28

The last journey

On 19 December, Dr Hunt, who had spent the last few days satisfying himself that the crisis was abating, gave the all-clear for the *Ticonderoga* to leave and complete the final stage of her long journey from Birkenhead to Port Phillip. Some passengers, though, now employed by the government in quarantine, were more than happy with their lot and elected to stay on at the cove, which would become known as Ticonderoga Bay as the station became established.

In her extensive research, Mary Kruithof has discovered the identities of those who remained behind as their fellow passengers departed.[1] James Swan, having travelled from Ayrshire with his wife Margaret and four-year-old son, and who was employed as one of the first of the station cooks, felt he had landed himself an excellent position. Some of the stonemasons—Robert Taylor, Alexander Gardiner and Henry Goodrich—likewise thought the terms of 6 shillings a day offered by Captain Ferguson to start building the station's first structures agreeable, and decided to remain there.

As more passengers recovered and more were released from the *Lysander*, the employed hospital attendants were also let go. This was not so for the Fanning family, who chose to stay on the *Lysander*, which for the time being would be a permanent part of the station, continuing to serve as a floating hospital. Having set the most sterling example in being among the first of the few at sea to answer the captain's and the doctors' calls for volunteer nurses, they continued to do so at the station, Mary as a nurse and John as a cook.

For the majority of those still on the beach, however, the time was approaching to leave it behind. Early on the morning of 22 December, Dr Hunt gave the final signal to depart and, once again, the *Ticonderoga*'s passengers began the difficult process of embarkation. Unlike at Birkenhead, however, there was no dock on which to line up, and certainly no brass band playing them off on their way. It was nevertheless another tediously slow process, with the ship's rowboats being the only means of ferrying people and their luggage to the ship.

None had been in greater need of the weeks of enforced rest than Captain Boyle, who had not only exhausted himself in the course of the terrible voyage, but had lost his own brother on the day they landed. Some of the passengers had not even realised that Boyle was still among them on the beach camp, but now he was quite literally back at the helm, directing the little flotilla of boats and again issuing commands to the crew in preparation to sail.

It took many hours for the hundreds of passengers, as well as their luggage, to be reloaded onto the ship. Many had dreaded the idea of ever setting foot on her again, and would have preferred the trials of any kind of overland route to Melbourne if one could have been arranged. For the many passengers who had lost family members while at sea, it was a particularly unwelcome reunion with the vessel, associating it as they did with nothing but death, filth and suffering. A handful of patients, still gravely ill, remained on the *Lysander* with their supporting families—some to recover, others to be numbered among the *Ticonderoga*'s final dead. For those who had the capacity to comprehend it, however, the imminent departure of the *Ticonderoga* while they remained in hospital must have seemed a death sentence in itself.

As soon as people stepped foot on board the *Ticonderoga*, they immediately felt they could have been on a different vessel entirely. The ship they had remembered from the voyage was now almost unrecognisable.

The first thing they noticed was the smell—or rather, the lack of it. The revolting typhus stench of hundreds of dead and dying people, which had seemed to pervade the very beings of those subjected to its stink, was now gone, replaced by the strong, acrid waft of the limewater that the crew had applied to every surface. The deck was tidy, ropes were properly coiled and a sense of order prevailed. That section where, several weeks earlier, corpses awaiting burial had been piled horribly under a rough piece of canvas was now just another part of the foredeck.

Down below, the difference was even more stark. Several fresh coats of whitewash had transformed the filth and gloom of the voyage's terrible denouement into a clean and orderly internal area that, on account of all the bunks having been disposed of, was also now remarkably more spacious. This, ironically, left precious few places to sit, and passengers now had to squeeze themselves and their trunks into any nook they could secure for the several hours' journey up to Hobson's Bay.

Before their departure, all those on deck, having once again picked out some of their better clothes for their belated arrival into Melbourne, stood transfixed as the last of the rowboats returned to the ship, laden not with people, but with some of the large pile of luggage that had, for all the weeks of quarantine, been kept out of the weather at a quiet corner of the beach. This colourful collection of trunks and boxes was the luggage of the dead, being brought solemnly back to the ship, the names of their deceased owners still clearly marked on the sides. The passengers watched the melancholy progress of the little boats quietly, as if observing a funeral procession. Then their eyes turned back to the shore, to the cemetery that had started as a patch of green but that now held nearly 70 of those who would never complete their journey. Even from the deck, some of the graves could be made out, marked by raw blocks of sandstone pulled up from the beach or some bits of timber purloined from the ship. Other graves were more pathetic, and perhaps even more poignant, indicated by nothing more than a couple of sticks nailed into a little cross. Many other passengers were simply buried in unmarked graves, decorated with little scatterings of seashells, pebbles and some of the more colourful wildflowers that abound on the peninsula in spring.

Weighing anchor at last, the *Ticonderoga* caught some of the warm wind blowing from the west and, again under the command of Thomas Boyle, turned away from the little beach forever.

29

The *Maitland*

The sight that greeted the people on board the *Ticonderoga* as she approached Melbourne's port in Hobson's Bay was an astonishing one. Even in ports much larger than this, Captain Boyle noted, it would be rare to find such a forest of masts. Dozens and dozens of ships of all sizes lay before them in the bay, and all with their sails reefed and their decks utterly empty—abandoned in a ghost town of sail. This was a picture of a city drained by a gold rush. For some time now, ships' masters had been reluctant to even tie up at the Hobson's Bay wharf, as their crews would immediately descend the rails and bolt off, seeking the quickest way to the goldfields. Standing off in deeper water, however, had done little to slow the practice, as smaller boats—keen to charge seamen a premium for quickly spiriting them away under the noses of their captains—had probably made more money than they could ever have hoped to at the Ballarat diggings.

A large ship like the *Ticonderoga* could likewise be guaranteed to be surrounded by a small flotilla eager to begin disembarking her passengers. Captain Boyle brought his big ship within sight of the large jetty at Hobson's Bay. There he dropped anchor and waited. Not a boat came near them. Some of the passengers, bewildered, waved handkerchiefs and called, but to no avail. Some of the craft in fact had set off in the opposite direction as soon as the *Ticonderoga* came to rest. Captain Boyle cursed bitterly to himself. He had suspected exactly this scenario might well occur, despite the many assurances ha had been given that any number of boats would be eager to disembark his passengers.

The *Ticonderoga*'s reputation had preceded her arrival into Melbourne. Ever since that first sensational headline appeared in early November, readers of *The Argus* had been lapping up every morbid detail of this 'plague ship'. Now nobody wanted to go near her. Even the hardened men of the small taxiing boats were wary of this big black beauty, allegedly riddled with disease. The papers had reported both yellow fever and scarlatina, but the rumour mill amplified this to include every ailment known to man. Hundreds had perished horribly within her wooden walls. Worse, she was not even British, but an American vessel—a Hell Ship—having journeyed through God knows what pestilential waters, picking up the dreaded yellow jack of the American south. One boat, at last, stood off from the *Ticonderoga* and answered the appeals of her passengers and crew. It was to no avail. The sailor apologised, but said they would simply have to wait there on board—wait for what exactly he did not say before once again disappearing.

And so they did wait, the rest of that day, then all night, then all the following day and then yet another night. This had not been planned for. The ship's bunks and bedding were long gone, and there was virtually nowhere to sleep. The galleys had not been prepared for use and food was limited to what remained of the old store of ship's biscuits. To many, the *Ticonderoga* once again began to feel like the prison of old.

Finally, on Christmas Eve, after some deft negotiating by Captain Boyle, a solution of sorts began to take shape. The weather was hot and windy, with an ominous bank of thick grey cloud building up in the western sky. With this dramatic backdrop, Boyle announced that a solution had been found. What he did not know was that it involved one of the most unfortunate vessels in the colony, the paddle-steamer *Maitland*.

She was old, a smallish vessel of just over 100 tons, built as a transport to run coal between Newcastle and Sydney. In 1851, the *Maitland* was bought as an investment by the colourful entrepreneur Captain George Ward 'Old King' Cole, who must immediately have regretted the decision. Cole had made a fortune around the colonies in such dubious trades as sandalwood and opium, had built the city's first private wharf on his property on the Yarra River, as well as the first screw steamer in the southern hemisphere, and was one of the young town's social celebrities. He counted Lieutenant-Governor La Trobe among his wealthy and influential friends, and was famous for his lavish outdoor parties, attended by hundreds of the well-to-do, with no expense spared. He had had recent success running passenger services across Bass Strait to Tasmania, but saw an opening in the market for providing a similar service between Melbourne and Geelong. Besides, he needed a cash flow to compensate for the recent decision of the government to close his private wharf due to the phenomenon of absconding ships' crews. Deciding to buy and refit the old *Maitland* as a passenger vessel, he put her under the command of one Robert Dyson. When nearly ready to begin operating, however, Dyson almost drowned in his cabin when, for no apparent reason, the *Maitland* started to sink around him while tied up at Queen's Wharf.

The reason for her sinking was never discovered, but Cole decided to fork out for the old tub to be re-floated and repaired nonetheless. But the *Maitland*'s ill luck continued, however, when in October 1852, the hapless Captain Dyson was at fault in a collision with another vessel, which he damaged severely, and which just happened to be the official boat of Governor La Trobe's Chief Health Officer, Dr Thomas Hunt—who, as we have seen in his dealings with Dr Taylor, was not a man to suffer fools or incompetence lightly.

Following the accident, a furious Hunt was forced to borrow a Customs boat to carry out his work, and promptly laid a charge against Captain Dyson and Cole, her owner, who he disliked in any case, eminent social status notwithstanding. Sensing that there was no future in the *Maitland* as a passenger ship, Cole decided to use her simply as a tug. Few people, however, wanted to use her, and Cole started to realise he had been saddled with a lemon. Thus when the big black clipper said to be a plague ship arrived and dropped anchor in the bay, only to be summarily ignored by all, Dyson saw an opportunity for the *Maitland* to at last turn a profit.

Being the only vessel to have approached her, Dyson and Boyle needed only a brief conversation. Yes, Dyson would take his passengers off and deposit them up the Yarra River at Queen's Wharf, but he would charge them handsomely for the privilege. For the passengers, there was no choice in the matter. Boyle, however, insisted that it would be done in an orderly fashion, with people being required to stay below decks until they were called up to embark on the *Maitland*.

As the preparations were beginning for the first of the passengers, the thunderstorm that had been threatening all morning broke suddenly and violently over the bay and a squall sprang up, rocking the ship dramatically. Then, at its height, a bolt of lightning struck one of the yardarms, setting it on fire. The accompanying thunderclap was startling enough for the people below, but with the accompanying shouts of 'Fire!' heard from above, pandemonium broke out below. Believing the *Ticonderoga* to be ablaze, passengers made a rush for the hatches, but Boyle quickly ordered them battened down to avoid a deadly panic. The flames were quickly extinguished by the crew, and Boyle managed to convince his people that they were in not, in fact, in danger, but he could see that all of them were frazzled and at the end of their wits.

The first group of passengers resumed their embarkation onto the *Maitland* without further incident—not that the welcome from

Captain Dyson was a warm one. Neither he nor his small crew would come anywhere near these ragged people, fearing they would be instantly struck down with whatever ghastly disease they happened to have. He angrily barked at them to load on, at one stage not even waiting for a husband to gather his wife and seven-week-old infant, who were left on the ship until the next run.[1] After what they had been through, for the passengers of the *Ticonderoga*, this was the final ignominy.

Back and forth the *Maitland* putted all day of that Christmas Eve, making the 12-kilometre run from the ship to Queen's Wharf on the Yarra River, observed by a growing crowd of onlookers. When word got around that they were from the dreaded plague ship stranded out in the bay, some quietly shuffled away, while still others gathered to gape. It was a world away from how the passengers had once envisaged their entry into Melbourne, but at least they had arrived, and could finally begin to think about the next stage of their journey and their lives.

One of the onlookers that day, despite the reputation accompanying the ship and her passengers, allowed his curiosity to prevail, and approached Captain Dyson as he was preparing to return to the ship for another load. He would like to go out and see this so-called plague ship for himself, he said, and requested a passage. Dyson looked at the man as if he were deranged, but was happy enough to accept his money. Out in the bay, not content with simply viewing the *Ticonderoga* from the deck of the *Maitland*, the curious passenger even went aboard her for a half-hour inspection while another load of people was being prepared.

Two days later, on 31 December 1852, one of the most controversial missives of the entire saga appeared in the letters to the editor pages of *The Argus*. Signing himself simply 'Observer', the anonymous gentleman penned the following:

Sir—On Friday last I had occasion to visit the Bay on business, and while going round the shipping in the Maitland, we called alongside of the *Ticonderago* [*sic*], for the purpose of bringing the passengers up to town. Being a sea-faring man and curious to know the state of the vessel which had been the scene of such unparalleled disease I went on board, and very soon ceased to be surprised at anything which had taken place on board this ill-fated vessel. The miserable squalid appearance of the passengers at once attracted my attention, and on looking down the hatchway, the smell and appearance of the between decks was so disgusting, that though accustomed to see and be on board of slave vessels, I instinctively shrank from it. I have no hesitation in expressing it as my decided opinion that the disease in this ship was mainly caused by the carelessness and inattention to cleanliness on the part of the master and his officers, and the want of ventilation. Several people were lying about the decks, apparently in the last stage of disease, and the passengers were bundled over the side without any accommodation ladder or the least regard to decency and decorum. In fact, the captain and crew seemed to look upon them as perfect nuisances, to be got rid of on any terms. The invalid women were carried over the side on men's backs, and one poor creature was separated from his child of seven weeks old, another child of 5 years of age died on board the steamer before we reached the wharf, no arrangements were made at the wharf for the reception of the sick, and two women in a dying state, were taken away in common wharf drays.

Bad as this is, I am sorry to say it is but an every day occurrence at our wharfs, and while our government, on the principle of straining at gnats and swallowing camels, is ever ready to insist on ventilation of berths and limitations of passengers in Colonial crafts on short voyages, never scruples to tolerate Yankees, and others, and proffer facilities, when they are smart enough to secure the presence of our illustrious Governor and his sapient suite to Sunday dinners in their well provided cuddies, when of course it would display great want of taste to talk about, much less to examine, between deck berths or the miserable creatures who occupy them. What is the use of having Quarantine laws if they are not enforced and upon what principle do we for our own real or imaginary safety stop a vessel at the Heads for disease, without at the same time providing an hospital there for their cure as is done in every other civilized country—and why is this ship allowed to come and vomit her diseased and dying freight in the midst of an over-crowded city? Men despair of the Government ever doing anything effective in these matters, unless it is forced upon them by the voice of the people through our independent press.

Was there any truth to what this man reported having seen, or did he simply wish to re-stoke the smouldering fires of the *Ticonderoga*'s infamy in the press? The ship had most certainly been cleaned, but her passengers had been forced to spend another three unplanned-for nights on board the ship, and were undoubtedly famished and at the end of their tether.

There is also some evidence to suggest that at least some passengers were still suffering from illness, but this was unlikely to have been typhus. Dr Sanger remained convinced that no typhus cases left the quarantine station—both he and Dr Veitch had rigorously inspected everyone before embarkation and found no evidence of the dread disease.

From Queen's Wharf in Melbourne's centre, the *Ticonderoga*'s passengers, hot, exhausted and demoralised, made their way slowly up through the dusty streets of the city three blocks away to the Immigration Barracks and labour exchange at the corner of Spencer and Collins Streets. It was an austere building that was only two years old, but a vast improvement on the appalling 2000-strong tent city on the south side of the Yarra that had greeted all assisted immigrants up until 1848. The colonial government in no way wanted to encourage the notion of dependence on charity, and the Barracks, it was made clear, was only available for a short stay, despite the traumas undergone by its inmates.

Finally, the bedraggled survivors of the *Ticonderoga* lined up in front of the reception desks to become simply another intake of new arrivals from Britain, like thousands who had come before and even more who would follow, stating their name, occupation, religion and marital status. For this last category, many found themselves having to describe themselves, for the first time, as 'widow' or 'widower'.

As the new arrivals shuffled in—some had managed, as reported by the 'Observer', to find a lift up from the wharf on bullock drays—they were watched with great interest by the man representing the Board in Victoria, Immigration Agent Edward Grimes. He was only too well aware of the sorry saga of the *Ticonderoga*, not least the damage it had done to his organisation's reputation and the notion of assisted emigration generally. To his horror, he would discover a number of cases of what he believed to be typhus still prevailing among these new arrivals, and would start another round in the to-ing and fro-ing of recriminations and blame. In a furious letter to the Colonial Secretary, Lonsdale, he charged that Dr Hunt had been negligent in his duty by allowing several still-sick passengers to leave the quarantine station early, essentially backing up the opinions expressed by the 'Observer'. Hunt would have none of it, and insisted that all those who had left Point Nepean were typhus-free, later noting that no further outbreak of typhus that could in any way be associated with the arriving passengers was reported.

Whatever their condition, most of those from the *Ticonderoga* would not have to reside long at the Barracks. The single women were the first to be snapped up. On a daily basis, representatives of the families of the wealthy, desperate for domestic labour, would scour the faces of the new arrivals and make the brightest looking girls a handsome offer—usually far in excess of what they could have expected at home—to be maids, cooks or nannies. So denuded of ordinary labourers had the gold rush made Melbourne that the men also could suddenly find themselves in positions paying as much as £70 a year with lodging for them and their families provided. This was a fortune compared with what they had earned at home.

By mid-February, however, Edward Grimes was obliged to put in a bill to the government for having to continue to provide for the upkeep of no less than 30 widows, orphans and other families who could not find a placement. Some, it seemed—at least for the time being—were unable to adjust to their new life after the terrible shock of the journey.

30

Life goes on

A few days after the appearance of the letter penned by the so-called 'Observer', Dr Sanger had his right of reply in *The Argus*:

Sir—

A garbled and false representation respecting the state of the ship *Ticonderago* [*sic*] having appeared in *The Argus* of Friday last written by a person who signs himself 'Observer'. I beg you will allow me the space of a few lines to disabuse the public on that subject, more particularly as that statement unjustly reflects on the conduct of the Captain and Officers of the vessel. Those gentlemen having evinced the most hearty desire for the welfare of the emigrants throughout the whole of her disastrous voyage. So far from the generality of the people being in an emaciated condition, as 'Observer' seems to imply, the fact is, that out of nearly 600 only two were sent to the hospital; about a dozen were suffering more of less from diarrhoea or debility, none severely; the rest were in perfect health. The apparently unseemly haste with which the passengers were hurried over the side was caused by the impatience of the captain of the steamer, who would not wait a moment even to allow the husband of the mother of a seven-week's infant to join his wife with the child. When the people were re-embarked from the Sanitary Station on the Monday previous, the ship was perfectly clean; but it having been necessary to take down the berths, and destroy them for the purpose of thoroughly purifying the vessel, the passengers were obliged for a few days they remained on board to lie on the decks, thus causing an untidy appearance, and a difficulty of attending minutely to cleanliness. As regards the Government officials, I can testify that the greatest pains were taken to thoroughly eradicate the disease before granting the ship pratique, and not a single case of infectious disease existed at the time the vessel left Point Nepean. I am, Sir, Your most obt. Servt., J.C. SANGER, M.D., Surgeon Superintendent ship *Ticonderago* [*sic*]

It was one of the last public words on the whole affair, as gradually the interest of the public moved on.

Joseph Sanger would recover from the trials of the *Ticonderoga* and, unperturbed by what he had been through, would continue to serve at sea under the Colonial Land and Emigration Commission for many years. No drama he would subsequently encounter, however, would ever eclipse that of the *Ticonderoga*. He was highly praised for his role, and his gratuity was increased from £200 to £250.

The family lines established by the surviving passengers of the *Ticonderoga* spread into all aspects of Australian life, with many thousands claiming their place as descendants to this day. The last known *Ticonderoga* survivor, Mrs Isabel Hennessey of Mortlake in Victoria, lived until 1944, having arrived 92 years earlier, with her family as an infant.[1]

Christopher McRae, who had walked the 60 miles from the camp to his relatives in Coburg, lived to the age of 96, a resident of the Victorian agricultural town of Maffra. His mother's grave and those of his siblings were relocated to the quarantine station's new cemetery in 1952 with a new headstone that reads:

Sacred to the memory of Helen McRae the beloved wife of Malcolm McRae who departed this life January 3 1853 aged 41 years Her daughter Janet died November 1852 aged 11 years. Her son Malcolm died 6 November 1852 aged 2 years Her son Farquhar died 22 November 1852 aged 6 years Her son John died 22 January 1858 aged 16 years.

Charles McKay, the sexton and schoolmaster, survived; however, the effects of the voyage on his health were such that he declined to take up his position as headmaster of the prestigious Scotch College. Instead, he settled himself in Kilmore, about 40 kilometres north of Melbourne, running a tiny school for the local children, many of whom were of Highland descent. It was an area, say his family, that reminded him of his home in Sutherland. McKay died just fifteen years later, at the comparatively young age of 61.

Captain Thomas Boyle was praised effusively for his steadfast and humane command during the crisis, particularly by Lieutenant-Governor La Trobe who, 'in appreciation of his conduct throughout the voyage and its termination',[2] granted him a double gratuity of nearly £130 instead of the agreed £64. There were, however, a number of caveats and hidden clauses, which in the end caused Boyle to lose money on the saga.

After the last of his passengers had left the ship, he found he was still carrying the large amount of luggage from the deceased that had been so poignantly observed by the passengers as it was loaded back at Point Nepean. Now Boyle found he would be charged £60 for it to be transferred up to the Immigration Barracks. With the custom being to regard a ship's passengers as under the care of their captain until reaching port, Boyle was also forwarded the bill for the extra food supplied to them while in quarantine at Point Nepean, as it was regarded that, while they remained there, the contracted journey had not been completed. To add to the insult, he then discovered that, for this same reason, the second half of the payment per head of the passengers who had died, and which he had expected to be paid by the Colonial Land and Emigration Commission, would not be forthcoming. To perhaps soften the blow somewhat, Grimes agreed to sell off their belongings and give the proceeds to Boyle as compensation, but it is not known whether this ever transpired.

As a final blow, Boyle found that the small amount of cargo he had brought over from Britain with the intention to sell it would have to stay in the holds, as the Hobson's Bay stevedores refused to touch it, nor have anything whatever to do with the plague ship. Bitter and broke, Boyle set sail in his empty ship from Port Phillip on 15 January 1853. On his way out of the Heads, he passed for the final time the quarantine station on the little beach. He could see that the tents he had sold on the spot to Harbour Master Ferguson were still up, but the beach otherwise looked deserted. Somewhere behind them, on a patch of buffalo grass in the sun, lay the grave of his younger brother and third mate, William, who had, like nearly 170 others, fallen to illness on board the ship. He thought of the little memorial he had arranged to be placed there in his memory, and was pleased he was resting in such a pretty spot, but knew that he was unlikely ever to visit it again.

Passing out through the Heads, the *Ticonderoga* set course for Akyab in Burma, her next port of call, where Boyle felt he could pick up a decent cargo. Having left Australia, never to return, from this point on, Thomas Boyle's story is a mystery. Beyond his leaving Port Phillip for Akyab, no further record of his life and career can be found.

The *Ticonderoga*, however, sailed on. In July 1863, she was recorded as having been 'sold to foreigners', and the following year was registered in Calcutta,[3] from where she continued to ply the routes of the Empire's 'far east', being sold twice more, until eventually being wrecked off the southern coast of India in October, 1879. Even then, in the waning years of the Clipper age, she drew attention as one of the most beautiful ships to sail the seas.

31

The aftermath

Back in England, the relatives of those who had perished on the ship waited in vain for news of their safe arrival. Yet, despite several entreaties from increasingly worried families, the Board remained silent. Eventually, an unsigned letter appeared in the London *Times*, in April 1853:

Sir,

I beg to call your attention to the case of the *Ticonderoga*, the unfortunate emigrant vessel that sailed from Birkenhead last year with from 800 to 900 Government emigrants to Australia, and of whom no fewer than about 180 died on the passage and in quarantine. Nearly three months have now elapsed since advice was received in this country of the arrival of the vessel, and of the state of the passengers, and of course great anxiety must have been felt to learn the particulars; but your readers will scarcely credit the statement, that till the arrival of the *Great Britain*, a few days ago, no official advices had been received by the Board of Emigrant Commissioners of the arrival of the vessel, and that up to this hour no list of the passengers who died has yet been received. Thus, though about a fourth part of the number of passengers have been cut off by death, the thousands of anxious relatives are still kept in suspense as to the fate of their friends. I am at all times desirous to exercise leniency in judging of the operations of Government establishments and officials, but I can scarcely conceive a more harrowing case of painful solicitude than must be felt by the sorrowing relatives of this large body of emigrants; neither can we suppose other than great remissness of duty somewhere in connexion with this lamentable case. I may add that the agents of the vessel having had no charge of the shipment of the passengers, and the owners being resident in America, there is no other source open for the desired information than the Board of Emigrant Commissioners.[1]

Their sole consolation was that after the *Ticonderoga*, no more vessels of such large burden would be hired by the Board to transport assisted passengers.

A Commission of Inquiry was undertaken in the new year, which resulted in a large amount of opinions and paper being sent around the offices of the Victorian Colonial government, and back and forth to London; yet, no one from the actual ship seems to have been consulted.

One alarming revelation from the inquiry was the practice of ship owners to quietly circumvent the government's withholding—in the case of death—of the second half of the passenger payment by taking out insurance on their human cargo. This way, whether delivered alive at their destination or not, the owners would still receive their money in full. An appalled parliament quickly outlawed the practice.

Health Officer Dr Hunt's lengthy report, delivered well into the next year, left nothing to the imagination in its lurid descriptions of the state of the vessel:

The ship, especially the lower part was in a most filthy state, and did not appear to have been cleaned for weeks, the stench was overpowering, the lockers so thoughtlessly provided for the Immigrants use were full of dirt, mouldy bread, and suet full of maggots, beneath the bottom boards of nearly every berth upon the lower deck were discovered soup and bouille cans and other receptacles full of putrid ordure, and porter bottles etc, filled with stale urine, while maggots were seen crawling underneath the berths . . . The great mortality seems to have been occasioned by the crowded state of her decks and want of proper ventilation, particularly through the lower deck; this caused debility and sickness among her passengers to such an extent that a sufficient number could not be found to keep them clean; dirt and filth of the most loathsome description accumulated, tainting the atmosphere and affecting everyone who came within its influence, as with a poison.

Governor La Trobe was also kept busy expending a good deal of ink over the matter in the first few months of 1853, but eventually chose, like any good politician, to deflect much of the blame onto the victims themselves, concluding in a dispatch to his boss, Sir John Pakington, that:

Looking to its general structure, and capacity, no vessel (i.e. *Ticonderoga*) could have been better suited to the purpose and there can be no doubt that under circumstances securing the unbroken maintenance of order, cleanliness, and general discipline, a yet larger number of persons might have been conveyed in safety to the Colony. In the case of troops there would have been no difficulty whatever, but with an unorganised body of emigrants of the classes selected for the *Ticonderoga*, little surprise can be felt that nor ordinary exertion and abilities could suffice to introduce at one system and order and overcome that repugnance to cleanliness and fresh air which distinguishes certain classes of the labouring populations of Europe; and dirt and disease having once taken hold of the vessel, no efforts of the officers in charge would be effective in stemming its progress.[2]

* * * *

Dr James William Henry Veitch, my great-great-grandfather, never stepped foot on a ship again—and certainly never returned to the sea. Following the example of his superior, Dr Sanger, he too applied for an increase in his remuneration for the extra duties he had undertaken when Sanger became ill, as well as the extra time he had spent working at the quarantine station, both at the camp and on board the *Lysander*. His efforts were unsuccessful. It was pointed out that, according to the letter of his contract, his payment would be due only upon completion of the voyage, and while the ship was still in quarantine, it was deemed that the voyage had yet to be completed. The matter went all the way to La Trobe, who—as usual—deferred the decision to another official, who refused it a second time, and there the matter rested. He was, however, offered a certificate enabling him to claim his passage money back to England. He never used it.

Having hailed from a long line of respected marine and naval surgeons, James Veitch halted the tradition there and then, choosing instead to head inland from Queen's Wharf to join the countless others trying their luck on the goldfields around Eaglehawk near Bendigo. In this, not surprisingly, he was wholly unsuccessful. The family believes he then alternated between practising as a country doctor, then a farmer and a storekeeper, before in 1874 successfully applying for the position of District Health Officer for the Shire of Strathfieldsaye in Central Victoria. His letter putting himself forward for the position is the only known example of his handwriting. In it, he briefly states his qualifications from the London Society of Apothecaries as well as his membership of the Victorian Medical Board. No mention is made of either the *Ticonderoga* or his time on her at sea or in quarantine.

Eventually, James William Henry Veitch became a long-standing member of his local council, where among his achievements was the establishment of a number of schools in his local area, including one near his own modest property near the tiny settlement of Mandurang. After nearly two decades of service, he offered his resignation, which according to the newspaper article reporting the news, was only most reluctantly accepted by his fellow councillors, who gave him a rousing send-off with many speeches and deposited in his hand a purse full of gold sovereigns. Again, despite a handsome summary of his life and career, the article fails to mention the *Ticonderoga*, or the part he played in her story.

In his 1892 obituary in the *Bendigo Evening News*, Veitch's 'portly form and kindly face' are remembered, as is his early life in England and his work for many steadfast years in the local shire. Once more, although he is described as a surgeon, no mention is made of the *Ticonderoga* or the disaster of 40 years earlier.

* * * *

James did not leave for central Victoria alone. After departing the ship for the last time, he had a particularly important matter to attend to: marrying the woman with the dark eyes and the soft Highland accent who had travelled all the way from far-away Tobermory on the Isle of Mull in Scotland's Western Isles. Annie Morrison, having supported the desperate doctor in the darkest hours of the *Ticonderoga*'s journey, answering the call to assist the sick when few others were prepared to do so, now became Anne Veitch.

They were married at the Presbyterian church of St Peter's Eastern Hill in January 1853, the marriage certificate witnessed by a John and Alexandrina McLean of Merri Creek. They lived as respected members of their local community until Anne passed away in 1892 at the age of 64. Just eight months later, James William Henry himself followed her to the grave.

James and Anne bore no less than eight children. Their youngest, Henry, lived to the age of 92 and died the year I was born, 1962, having met—albeit briefly—my own father, John. Knowing this somehow seems to shrink the years, making the story of the Hell Ship and her voyage seem not that very long ago at all.

Epilogue

In April 1891, Donald McDonald visited the cemetery at the Point Nepean Quarantine Station for the first time since having been there with his family nearly 40 years earlier. Although still sited just back from the pretty foreshore of the cove, now named Ticonderoga Bay, he noted that the graves were in disrepair, many with indecipherable names, others just little mounds with no identifying marks at all. He sat for a long time, until the sun began to set, reflecting on those times and all that had happened in his life subsequently.

In 1917, he wrote of the experience in the venerable Melbourne newspaper *The Argus*. He recounted that, walking among the few headstones, he noted the sandstone blocks were even back then covered in moss and beginning to crumble back to sand. 'Half obliterated as the inscriptions were, the words "from the ship *Ticonderoga*" were readable on many', he wrote. Lingering until the autumn darkness fell, McDonald says that he became disoriented on his way back, and at one point had to strike a match to find the path leading him away. In the light of the match, amid the thick tea-tree scrub, a single headstone was briefly illuminated and the name became clearly visible. 'Margaret McDonald,' it read—it was the grave of his own mother, who he had buried at this very spot all those decades ago.

When, a few years later, McDonald again visited the little graveyard, his mother's headstone was gone. Looking back at the incident and on the *Ticonderoga* herself, McDonald reflected:

In such a swelter of humanity, typhus was king, and his sceptre a busy scythe . . . but with all its suffering and death, there was some soul of goodness in the things evil of those good old ghastly times.

Acknowledgements

I am enormously grateful to my cousin, Pat Hocking, who in stellar fashion has performed the role of unofficial Veitch family historian for many years, and whose impressive archive of letters and documents pertaining to James William Henry Veitch she made available to me. I have never learned so much about my family in such a short time.

Thank you to my brother Simon for sourcing and restoring some of the images used, particularly tracking down the original portrait of our ancestors James and Annie Veitch. Thanks also to my sister Kate for her encouragement and editorial support.

Likewise, thanks to the small but dedicated team at the Point Nepean Historical Society in Sorrento, just a stone's throw from the old quarantine station itself. Thank you especially to Janet South, who prepared several large folders of wonderful information regarding the *Ticonderoga*, her passenger list, and an extensive history of the station, where a great deal of the drama of the story took place.

Thanks particularly to Mary Kruithof, whose pioneering interest and research in her 2002 book *Fever Beach* brought the story of the *Ticonderoga* to public light for the first time in 150 years.

And finally, and most importantly, profound thanks to my wonderful partner, Brook, who from the very beginning has been, and continues to be, an indispensable source of support and encouragement.

A note on sources

Only one book has ever previously been written telling the story of the *Ticonderoga*, namely *Fever Beach* by Mary Kruithof, a fellow *Ticonderoga* descendant. Mary's ancestors were the Fanning family who travelled to Melbourne from Londonderry, Ireland, and she tells me she wrote the book as a purely private venture after being encouraged by friends and family to commemorate the 150th anniversary, in 2002, of the *Ticonderoga*'s arrival. Although privately published, Mary has had to write a second edition, and frequently orders more and more copies as the popularity of *Fever Beach* continues to outstrip her initial expectations, and deservedly so. It is a wonderful book, brilliantly researched, and provided my main secondary source in writing my own account of the *Ticonderoga*.

A significant speech delivered in November 1992 at the old Point Nepean quarantine station by historian Florence Chuk was the first many people learned of the *Ticonderoga* story, and, along with her notes which she so generously lent to me, also provided me with many quotes and pieces of information. Her book *The Somerset Years* gave me a good deal of background on some of the *Ticonderoga*'s passengers, who would otherwise just have been names on a list.

A handful of other works mention *Ticonderoga*'s voyage, including *Doctors at Sea* by Robin Haines and Rob Mundle's *Under Full Sail*. *Doctors at Sea* provided me with a most detailed picture of the role of surgeons at sea in the nineteenth century, their importance to the passengers, and the problems they faced. Rob Mundle, a sailor himself, gives an excellent background to the clipper era and its importance in *Under Full Sail*, also bringing to life such characters as the great Bully Forbes, as well as brilliantly explaining the advent of the vital Great Circle route.

Author Don Charlwood had a life-long passion for the story of the emigrants under sail, and his book *The Long Farewell* is a superb collection of first-hand accounts of those who made the journey from Britain.

A history of life within Britain's emigration depots, particularly at Birkenhead, is captured with wonderful colour by Keith Pescod in his work *Good Food, Bright Fires & Civility*.

Unfortunately, the diary or detailed first-hand account by a *Ticonderoga* passenger is yet to be found, but many anecdotes and letters exist. Only in later life did passengers like Christopher McRae, James Dundas and Donald McDonald first pen their thoughts, and then only in a handful of feature stories for various newspapers. McDonald's brief account of the voyage and of revisiting his mother's grave at the quarantine station only appeared in *The Argus* in 1917. The story of the young McRae's remarkable 60-mile trek from the quarantine station to the door of his relative in Coburg came to light in a Saturday afternoon edition of *The Argus* on 4 August 1934, in an article written by his distant relative, John Andrew McIvor. In this he also quotes another unnamed *Ticonderoga* survivor as having told him, in 1909, that, 'Whole families were wiped out: in some cases both parents died, leaving young children. Of 15 families from St Kilda—that ultima thule of the Scottish Isles flung out towards Iceland—only 15 individuals survived'.

As I detail in the book, my own forays into the bowels of the Public Record Office in London yielded such gems as the original correspondence of Lieutenant-Governor La Trobe to the *Ticonderoga* disaster and its aftermath, including the decision to deny my great-great-grandfather's request for increased remuneration due to the extra duties he undertook after the *Ticonderoga*'s principal surgeon, Sanger, became ill.

I am particularly gratified to know that in 1952, on the centenary of the landing of the 'Hell Ship', the Point Nepean site where my ancestors first stepped foot onto Australian soil was officially renamed 'Ticonderoga Bay'.

Notes

1 A LONELY BEACH

1 R. Mundle, 2016, *Under Full Sail*, Sydney: HarperCollins, p. 5

2 BIRKENHEAD

1 K. Pescod, 2001, *Good Food, Bright Fires & Civility: Emigrant Depots of the Nineteenth Century*, Melbourne: Australian Scholarly Publishing, p. 40

2 A. Jarvis, 1991, *Liverpool Central Docks 1799–1905: An Illustrated History*, Stroud: Sutton, p. 43

3 D. Charlwood, 1981, *The Long Farewell: Settlers Under Sail*, London: Allen Lane, p. 76

4 Jarvis, 1991, p. 77

3 WAKEFIELD AND 'THE BOARD'

1 P. Adams, 2013, *Fatal Necessity: British Intervention in New Zealand, 1830–1847*, Wellington: Bridget Williams Books, p. 392

2 Pescod, 2001, p. 7

3 M. Kruithof, 2002, *Fever Beach: The Story of the Migrant Clipper Ticonderoga, Its IllFated Voyage and Its Historic Impact*, Mt Waverley, Vic: QI Publishing, p. 7

4 Kruithof, 2002, p. xiii

5 Charlwood, 1981, p. 57

6 R. Haines, 2003, *Life and Death in the Age of Sail: The Passage to Australia*, Sydney: UNSW Press, p. 49

7 Charlwood, 1981, p. 55

4 AUSTRALIA 1851: GOLD VERSUS WOOL

1 Pescod, 2001, p. xv
2 S. B. Lunn, 2012, *The Divergence*, thewordverve (online), p. vi
3 Kruithof, 2002, p. 7

5 THE SCOTS

1 Prebble, 1963, p. 201
2 Victorian State Parliament, 1852, 'Emigration From the Highlands and Islands of Scotland', p. 3, available from: www.parliament.vic.gov.au/papers/govpub/VPARL1852-53Vol1p855-884.pdf
3 Prebble, 2003, p. 203
4 Kruithof, 2002, p. 9
5 Victorian Parliamentary Papers 1852/53O
6 Victorian State Parliament, 1852, 'Emigration From the Highlands and Islands of Scotland', p. 11
7 Kruithof, 2002, p. 11
8 Kruithof, 2002, p. 31
9 Pescod, 2001, p. 136

6 THE AGE OF THE CLIPPERS

1 H. La Grange and J. La Grange, 1936, *Clipper Ships of America and Great Britain 1833–1869*, London: G.P. Putnam's Sons, p. 29
2 A. H. Clark, 1912, *Early Clipper Ships, 1842–1848*, New York: GP Putnam's Sons, pp. 65–6
3 Mundle, 2016, p. 15
4 La Grange and La Grange, 1936, p. 36

7 THE TICONDEROGA

1 Knoblock, 2014, p. 342
2 Knoblock, 2014, p. 342

8 EMIGRANTS AND NUMBERS

1 Pescod, 2001, p. 193

2 British Public Record Office, List of Ships Chartered by the Land and Emigration Commission, CO 386/179, Folio 7

9 DEPARTURE

1 Haines, 2005, p. 171
2 Kruithof, 2002, p. 25
3 British Parliamentary Paper Relative to the Australian Colonies, no. 15, April 1, 1853
4 Charlwood, 1981, p. 87
5 Charlwood, 1981, p. 94
6 Kruithof, 2002, p. 40
7 Kruithof, 2002, p. 40
8 Letter recalling the event by passenger Christopher McCrae

10 CLEARANCES AND FAMINE: THE TRAGEDY OF THE HIGHLANDS

1 Prebble, 1963, p. 13
2 Prebble, 1963, p. 21
3 Prebble, 1963, p. 28
4 D. McLeod, 1841, *History of the Destitution in Sutherlandshire*, Edinburgh: self-published, p. 35
5 Prebble 1963, p. 125
6 Prebble, 1963, p. 201
7 Prebble, 1963, p. 205

11 LIFE AT SEA

1 Charlwood, 1981, p. 102
2 Kruithof, 2002, p. 46
3 Kruithof, 2002, p. 48
4 Letter written by Christopher McRae in 1917 addressed to Mr Kendall, Officer in Charge, Quarantine Station Point Nepean, held in the collection of the Point Nepean Historical Society, Sorrento, Victoria.
5 Personal notes of Frank McKay, care of Nepean Historical Society
6 Personal notes of Frank McKay, care of Nepean Historical Society
7 Personal notes of Frank McKay, care of Nepean Historical Society

8   Kruithof, 2002, p. 36

9   Kruithof, 2002, p. 36

10   Charlwood, 1981, p. 201

11   British Parliamentary Papers, Papers Relative to Emigration to the
     Australian Colonies, First Report from the Select Committee on Emigrant
     Ships with Minutes of Evidence, Explanation of deck plans by Kenneth N.
     Sutherland R.N., House of Commons, Sessional Papers 1852/53 vol. LXVIII

12   Haines, 2003, p. 190

12 DEATH AT SEA

1   Haines, 2005, p. 9

2   Letter from Christopher McRae to Mr Kendall, 1917

3   Welch 1969, p. 19

4   Kruithof, 2002, p. 46

13 A LONELY ENCOUNTER

1   Kruithof, 2002, p. 50

14 THE GREAT CIRCLE

1   Charlwood, 1981, p. 20

2   Charlwood, 1981, p. 21

3   Charlwood, 1981, p. 23

15 SURGEONS AT SEA

1   British Parliamentary Papers Relative to the Australian Colonies, no. 15,
     1 April 1853, *Objection to Chartering Vessels of Great Burthen for the
     Conveyance of Emigrants*

2   Haines, 2005, p. 57

3   Charlwood, 1981, p. 10

4   Charlwood, 1981, p. 191

5   'GOVERNMENT AND GENERAL ORDERS', *Sydney Gazette* Saturday
     30 July 1814

6   Haines, 2005, p. 8

7   Haines, 2005, p. 29

8   P. Stanley, 2003, *For Fear of Pain: British Surgery 1790–1850*, Amsterdam: Rodopi, p. 99

9   Veitch, 1818, p. 451

10   Report of the Metropolitan Commissioners in Lunacy to the Lord Chancellor, 1844, London, p. 234

11   Private letter in collection of Veitch family history of Pat Hocking

17 TYPHUS TAKES HOLD

1   Online Etymology Dictionary, *Typhus*, 2018, available from: www.etymonline.com/word/typhus

2   Kruithof, 2002, p. 53

18 THE BOX WITH THE DULL PINK RIBBON

1   British Parliamentary Papers, 1854, vol. XLVI, pp. 52, available from: www.mylore.net/files/Download/Parl%20Papers%201854.pdf

2   Letter from Governor La Trobe to Sir John Pakington, January 4, 1853, Public Record Office, CO 309/13

3   Letter from Dr Joseph Charles Sanger, November 4, 1852, Victorian Public Records, VPRS 1189/1112/8252

4   Letter from Dr Joseph Charles Sanger, November 4, 1852

19 THE SOUTHERN OCEAN

1   Kruithof, 2002, p. 39

2   B. Carroll, 1970, 'Fever Ship', *Parade*, August 1970, p. 25

3   William Turnbull, 1806, *The Naval Surgeon Comprising the Entire Duties of Professional Men at Sea*, London: Richard Phillips, p. 122

4   Turnbull, 1806, p. 122

5   Turnbull, 1806, p. 122

6   Charlwood, 1981, p. 287

7   Charlwood, 1981, p. 287

8   Charlwood, 1981, p. 287

9   Kruithof, 2002, p. 54

10   Journal of George Pollock Russell, voyage of 1854

11   Charlwood, 1981, p. 126

12   S. Jefferson, 2014, *Clipper Ships and the Golden Age of Sail: Races and Rivalries on the Nineteenth Century High Seas*, London: Bloomsbury, p. 60

13   Letter from Christopher McRae to Mr Kendall, 1917

14   J.H. Welch, 1969, *From Hell to Health: The History of Quarantine at Port Phillip Heads 1895–1966*, Penrith: Nepean Historical Society, p. 18

15   Kruithof, 2002, p. 51

20 HELL SHIP

1   Letter from Christopher McRae to Mr Kendall, 1917

2   Victorian Public Records Office, 2002, 'Register of Births and Deaths of Emigrants at Sea 1847-53', CO 386/170, Folios 85–90

3   *Philadelphia Medical and Physical Journal*, vol. 1, 1805

4   Kruithof, 2002, p. 56

5   Letter from Christopher McRae to Mr Kendall, 1917

21 ARRIVAL

1   H. Draper, 'The Narrative of Captain H.J.M. Draper, One Time Port Phillip Sea Pilot', reproduced in *The Log: Quarterly Journal of the Nautical Association of Australia Inc*, February 2002, vol. 35, no. 1, issue 47, p. 6

2   H. Draper, in *The Log*, 2002, p. 6

3   Kruithof, 2002, p. 64

4   H. Draper, in *The Log*, 2002, p. 6

22 PROTECTING THE COLONY

1   National Australian Museum, 2013, *Batmania: Who's Who*, available from: https://web.archive.org/web/20140303233422/http://www.nma.gov.au/engage-learn/schools/classroom-resources/multimedia/interactives/batmania_html_version/whos_who

2   Extract from the diary of Dr Barry Cotter, April 1840, available from: https://drbarrycotter.com/chapter-6/

3   Welch, 1969, p. 21

4   Welch, 1969, p. 22

5   Carroll, 1970, p. 26

6   Kruithof, 2002, p. 64

23 A COLONIAL CRISIS

1   Carroll, 1970, (page not visible)

24 THE LYSANDER

1   Letter from Dr Sanger, Victorian Public Records, VPRS 1189/112/52/8252

2   Letter from Dr Sanger, Victorian Public Records, VPRS 1189/112/52/8252

3   Welch, 1969, p. 23

4   Welch, 1969, p. 22

5   Welch, 1969, p. 23

6   Welch, 1969, p. 24

7   Welch, 1969, p. 25

8   Kruithof, 2002, p. 82

9   Welch, 1969, p. 29

10   Welch, 1969, p. 24

11   Welch, 1969, p. 32

12   Welch, 1969, p. 35

13   Welch, 1969, p. 23

25 QUARANTINE AND OUTRAGE

1   Kruithof, 2002, p. 99

2   Letter from Governor La Trobe to Sir John Pakington, 21 October 1952,
     Public Record Office

3   Letter from Governor La Trobe to Sir John Pakington, 9 November,
     Public Record Office

4   Kruithof, 2002, p. 83

5   Welch, 1969, p. 33

6   Letter from Dr Taylor to Governor La Trobe, 4 November 1853,
     Victorian Public Records, VPRS 1189/132 D 12053

7   Letter from Dr Taylor to Governor La Trobe, 4 November, 1853

8   Letter from Dr Hunt to Governor La Trobe, 6 January, 1853, VPRO 1189/131
9   Letter from Dr Taylor to Governor La Trobe, 4 November, 1853

28   THE LAST JOURNEY
1   Kruithof, 2002, p. 83

29   THE MAITLAND
1   Kruithof, 2002, p. 86

30   LIFE GOES ON
1   Welch, 1969, p. 36
2   Kruithof, 2002, p. 107
3   Carroll, 1970, p. 24

31   THE AFTERMATH
1   Welch, 1969, p. 28
2   Letter from Governor La Trobe to Sir John Pakington, 26 January 1853, Victorian Public Records Office, VPRS 1084

Bibliography

Adams, P. 2013, *Fatal Necessity: British Intervention in New Zealand, 1830–1847*, Wellington: Bridget Williams Books.

British Parliamentary Paper Relative to the Australian Colonies No 15. 1/4/1853.

Carroll, B. 1970, 'Fever Ship', *Parade*, August 1970, p. 25.

Charlwood, D. 1981, *The Long Farewell: Settlers Under Sail*, London: Allen Lane.

Chuck, F., 1987, *The Somerset Years: Government-Assisted Emigrants from Somerset and Bristol Who Arrived in Port Phillip/Victoria, 1839–1854*, Ballarat, VIC: Pennard Hill Publications.

Clark, A. H., 1912, *Early Clipper Ships, 1842–1848*, New York: GP Putnam's Sons.

Haines, R. 2003, *Life and Death in the Age of Sail: The Passage to Australia*, Sydney: UNSW Press.

——2005, *Doctors at Sea: Emigrant Voyages to Colonial Australia*, Melbourne: Palgrave Macmillan.

Jarvis, A. 1991, *Liverpool Central Docks 1799–1905: An Illustrated History*, Stroud: Sutton.

Jefferson, S., 2014, *Clipper Ships and the Golden Age of Sail: Races and Rivalries on the Nineteenth Century High Seas*, London: Bloomsbury.

Knoblock, G.A. 2014, *The American Clipper Ship, 1845–1920: A Comprehensive History, with a Listing of Builders and Their Ships*, Jefferson, NC: McFarland and Co.

Kruithof, M. 2002, *Fever Beach: The Story of the Migrant Clipper Ticonderoga, Its Ill-Fated Voyage and Its Historic Impact*, Mt Waverley, Vic: QI Publishing.

La Grange, H. and La Grange, J. 1936, *Clipper Ships of America and Great Britain 1833–1869*, London: G.P. Putnam's Sons.

London Medical Repository Monthly Journal and Review 1818, vol. X, p. 451.

Lunn, S.B. 2012, *The Divergence*, thewordverve (online).

Maury, M.F. 1847, *Wind and Current Chart of the North Atlantic*, Washington, DC: US Hydrographical Office.

Mundle, R. 2016, *Under Full Sail*, Sydney: HarperCollins.

National Australian Museum, 2013, *Batmania: Who's Who*, available from: https://web.archive.org/web/20140303233422/http://www.nma.gov.au/engage-learn/schools/classroom-resources/multimedia/interactives/batmania_html_version/whos_who

Pescod, K. 2001, *Good Food, Bright Fires & Civility: Emigrant Depots of the Nineteenth Century*, Melbourne: Australian Scholarly Publishing.

Philadelphia Medical and Physical Journal 1805, vol. 1.

Prebble, J. 1963, *The Highland Clearances*, Harmondsworth: Penguin.

Stanley, P. 2003, *For Fear of Pain: British Surgery 1790–1850*, Amsterdam: Rodopi.

The Log, Quarterly Journal of the Nautical Association of Australia Inc. February 2002, vol. 35, no. 1, issue 47.

Towson, J.T. 1847, *Tables to Facilitate the Practice of Great Circle Sailing*, London: British Admiralty.

Turnbull, W. 1806, *The Naval Surgeon Comprising the Entire Duties of Professional Men at Sea*, London: R. Philips.

Veitch, J. (Snr) 1818, 'Remarks on the necessity of attention to the surface of the body in the treatment and prevention of several complaints; with a recommendation of the more general employment of the vapour-bath', *London Medical Repository Monthly Journal and Review*, vol. X, p. 451.

——1824, *Observations on the Ligature of the Arteries, Secondary Hemorrhage, and Amputation at the Hip-joint*. London: V. Nicol.

Victorian Parliamentary Papers 1852/53O.

Watson, D. 1984, *Caledonia Australia: Scottish Highlanders on the Frontier of Australia*, London: William Collins.

Welch, J.H. 1969, *From Hell to Health: The History of Quarantine at Port Phillip Heads 1895–1966*, Penrith: Nepean Historical Society.